The Pragmatic Century

The Pragmatic Century

Conversations with Richard J. Bernstein

Edited by

Sheila Greeve Davaney
and
Warren G. Frisina

State University of New York Press

Published by
State University of New York Press, Albany

Printed in the United States of America

For information, address State University of New York Press,
194 Washington Avenue, Suite 305, Albany, NY 12210-2384

Production by Michael Haggett
Marketing by Anne M. Valentine

Library of Congress Cataloging-in-Publication Data

The pragmatic century : conversations with Richard J. Bernstein / edited by Sheila Greeve Davaney and Warren G. Frisina.
p. cm.
Includes bibliographical references and index.
ISBN 0-7914-6793-7 (hardcover : alk. paper) — ISBN 0-7914-6794-5 (pbk. : alk. paper) 1. Bernstein, Richard J. 2. Pragmatism—History—20th century. I. Davaney, Sheila Greeve. II. Frisina, Warren G., 1954–

B945.B4764P73 2006
191—dc22

ISBN-13: 978-0-7914-6793-0 (hardcover : alk. paper)
ISBN-13: 978-0-7914-6794-7 (pbk. : alk. paper)

2005024125

10 9 8 7 6 5 4 3 2 1

Contents

Preface

Few contemporary philosophers are as influential in so many different intellectual disciplines and discussions as Richard J. Bernstein. He is at home not only among American pragmatic philosophers with whom he is so closely identified but equally with Continental thinkers. Moreover, he has engaged a wide range of perspectives in other disciplines, including the work of social theorists, cognitive psychologists, and psychoanalysts. Bernstein is perhaps the premier thinker on the contemporary scene who has simultaneously been able to maintain disciplinary integrity while participating in and encouraging cross-disciplinary conversation and a more encompassing critical dialogue. Thus, in an age of extreme specialization, Bernstein's influence has far extended beyond the boundaries of philosophy.

Bernstein is able to engage so many different thinkers for several reasons. First, without ever losing his critical edge, he nonetheless assumes that different perspectives and various disciplines have something to offer each other. While unafraid to participate in rigorous debate, he has embodied a model of philosophy as dialogue, mutual conversation, and openness to multiple points of view. Precisely as a representative of pragmatism, Bernstein has argued for the importance of building visions of reality from the variety of disparate resources available to us at any given time. Where other contemporary thinkers have turned inward to more narrow conversations, Bernstein has been a leading exponent of more broad-based discussions in which mutual enhancement, not destruction, is the goal.

Second, Bernstein has played such a wide-ranging role in contemporary intellectual life because he has that rare capacity to weave a coherent vision out of the disparate strands of seemingly conflicting intellectual traditions. Bernstein has regularly showed us how to see past surface contradictions to the underlying problems we share and to the sometimes-common assumptions that animate contemporary sensibilities. With a unique genius, Bernstein has been able to balance the recognition of real differences while also acknowledging places of agreement or a shared problematic. The result has been that Bernstein has led his fellow intellectual explorers to whole new ways of viewing what seemed like intractable problems or mutually exclusive perspectives. In books such as *Praxis and Action, The Restructuring of Social and Political Theory, Beyond Objectivism and Relativism, The New Constellation: The Ethical-Political Horizons of Modernity/Postmodernity, Hannah Arendt and the Jewish Question,* and *Freud and the Vexed Legacy of Moses,* Bernstein has built intellectual bridges that link hermeneutics, pragmatism, critical theory, and psychotherapy into a powerful new vision.

Both Bernstein's open and dialogical approach to multiple perspectives and his own constructive positions have encouraged his inclusion in a wide range of debates and conversations. Significantly, in an age when religion is viewed as problematic by many philosophers or somewhat naively reappropriated by others, Bernstein has been a leading interlocutor with scholars of religion on the contemporary scene, especially those who share an interest in the pragmatic lineage of American thought. In these exchanges, Bernstein has thoroughly explored the ramifications of a historicized and fallibilistic interpretation of philosophical and religious efforts to come to terms with human existence while steadfastly affirming the possibility for a progressive democratic and pluralistic society to which philosophy and religious reflection might centrally contribute.

The chapters in this volume represent a collective attempt to develop a critical assessment of the significance of Richard J. Bernstein's intellectual contributions. Written by scholars who share a combined interest in both the American pragmatic tradition and contemporary reflection about religion, these chapters explore central themes in Bernstein's work. Embodying the dialogical commitments so evident theoretically in Bernstein's philosophy, the volume includes responses from Bernstein to each chapter, thus enhancing the level of critical engagement in a manner not typical of these collections. Moreover, Bernstein himself has included two new essays to begin and conclude the volume. The first,

"The Pragmatic Century," orients readers to Bernstein's understanding of the historical role pragmatism plays in contemporary intellectual life. Importantly, Bernstein argues for a shift in the assumed history of American pragmatism. Often that history has interpreted pragmatism as a singular American movement that enjoyed its ascendancy in the early part of the twentieth century, only to be eclipsed and marginalized by the rise of analytic philosophy. Over against this version of pragmatism's history, Bernstein offers an account in which pragmatic themes continued to animate the most exciting elements in twentieth-century intellectual life, including non-American developments. Hence, for him, the current resurgence of pragmatism is not the recovery of an abandoned form of American thought but the continuation of deeply ingrained concerns both in American and Continental intellectual development.

Bernstein's chapter "Democracy" concludes this volume. In it he offers an encomium to the continuing values of democratic ideals. In a contemporary world in which intellectuals, including Bernstein, are acutely aware of the complex relations of power, politics, and public life, Bernstein still maintains the possibility and importance of democratic participation in the public realm. He argues for a Deweyean renewal of commitment to enhancing and enlarging the democratic potential of our society. It is to such creative and critical public engagement that Bernstein's life and work have been dedicated.

The chapters in this volume are responses to these lifelong intellectual, political, and moral efforts of Richard J. Bernstein. They take seriously his import for the twentieth century and for the new century that now unfolds. They cover a variety of topics, from Bernstein's place as an interpreter of both American and Continental thought (Frankenberry and Colapietro), to the possibility of system building and analysis in an antimetaphysical age (Neville), to the potential for theological and ethical reinterpretation in contemporary society (Doak and Chopp). Bernstein's work on Jewish thinkers such as Freud and Arendt becomes the occasion to reflect on their importance both within Jewish thought and more broadly in the modern world (Schmidt). Importantly, Bernstein's pragmatism inspires not only reflection on the implications of pragmatism for our general historical moment but also encourages constructive exploration of what pragmatism, historicism, and naturalism suggest for contemporary Jewish self-understanding (Levinson). Hence, the chapters reflect both the broad reach of Bernstein's insights and their relevance for particular historical communities. In all of these writings, there is evidenced a profound appreciation for Bernstein's prodigious work. But they also, in a truly Bernsteinian manner, engage that work critically. Thus, while presenting a strong assessment of Bernstein's central claims, these chapters also challenge him on issues such as race (Hart) or take him to task for his critique of other pragmatists such as Richard Rorty (Frankenberry). But whether in appreciation or in critique, these chapters seek to embody that critical openness and profound willingness to engage others in a public and democratic fashion that have so characterized the work and life of Richard J. Bernstein. Thus, both substantively and stylistically, they contribute to the legacy that Richard J. Bernstein has bequeathed us all.

Acknowledgments

The editors wish to acknowledge the Highlands Institute for American Religious and Philosophical Thought (HIARPT), which held a conference focused upon the work of Richard Bernstein in 2000. Many of the writings in this volume were first presented in this context. The leadership of HIARPT, especially of Creighton Peden, has been supportive of this project from its inception. We are also appreciative of the work of Sheila Davaney's assistant, Maggi Mahan. Ms. Mahan has guided this volume to its successful completion, and we are grateful for all of her able assistance.

The Pragmatic Century

Richard J. Bernstein

There are many ways of telling the story of the vicissitudes of pragmatism in the United States. I want to begin with a brief account of what may be considered the standard story, because I intend to challenge it. The standard story goes something like this. Pragmatism was popularized primarily through the lecturing and writing of William James at the beginning of the twentieth century. We can even date the explicit introduction of the term "pragmatism" by James in his 1898 address, delivered at the University of California, Berkeley, "Philosophical Conceptions and Practical Results." In that address, James generously acknowledged his debt to Peirce, "one of the most original contemporary thinkers," and he refers to "the principle of practicalism—or pragmatism as he called it, when I first heard him enunciate it at Cambridge in the early 1970s." James initially gives a rather metaphorical description of "Peirce's principle": "the soul and meaning of thought, he says, can never be made to direct itself towards anything but the production of belief, belief being the demicadence which closes a musical phrase in the symphony of our intellectual life." Furthermore, "beliefs, in short are really rules of action; and the whole function of thinking is but one step in the production of habits of action" (James 1967: 348). In 1898, Peirce was barely known as a philosopher (except to a small group of admirers like James). As James's popular version of pragmatism spread, Peirce was so appalled and outraged that he renamed his own doctrine of meaning "'pragmaticism,' which is ugly enough to be safe from kidnappers" (Peirce 1931: 5.414). There is the famous quip that pragmatism is the movement that was founded on James's misunderstanding of Peirce. In the 1890s, the young John Dewey was in active communication with James and was working on his *Studies in Logical Theory*. Earlier, when Dewey was a graduate student at Johns Hopkins University, he studied logic with Peirce. At the time, Dewey was much more influenced by the Hegelian, G. S. Morris. Dewey originally characterized his own philosophic orientation as "instrumentalism" or "experimentalism," but as Dewey's reputation and renown grew during the early decades of the twentieth century, "pragmatism" is the name that took hold as the name identifying the style of thinking exemplified by Peirce, James, Dewey, and Dewey's close associate at Michigan and Chicago, George Herbert Mead. With the passing decades of the twentieth century, pragmatism began to fade from the philosophic scene. During the 1950s, a quiet but dramatic revolution was taking place in American philosophy departments. Positivism, logical empiricism, the philosophy of science, and the new logic inspired by the legacy of Frege and Russell captured the imagination of young philosophers. These currents, together with the varieties of conceptual analysis and ordinary language philosophy practiced at Oxford, reshaped most of the prestigious philosophy departments in the United States. It is from this period that we can date the infamous Anglo-American analytic/Continental split in philosophy with its ugly ideological resonances. Furthermore, the philosophies of Peirce, James, Dewey, and Mead were almost completely marginalized. To the extent that their contribution was even acknowledged (and this was rare indeed), a patronizing attitude was prevalent. The pragmatists might have had their hearts in the right place, but they lacked the rigor, clarity, and argumentative finesse required for "serious" philosophizing. Furthermore, the original pragmatic thinkers had not made the "linguistic turn." The sad truth is that, from that time until today, the overwhelming majority of PhDs in America have never really studied—and probably have never even read the classic American pragmatic thinkers. By the 1950s and 1960s interest in pragmatism reached an absolute nadir. The pragmatic movement seemed quite moribund—except for a few courageous persons who tried to keep the tradition alive.

It was primarily due to the provocative intervention of a single individual that the interest in pragmatism began to change. Richard Rorty, a philosopher from Princeton who made his reputation as a bright, analytic philosopher, began to question the foundations and pretensions of analytic philosophy. He shocked many of his colleagues when he declared that Wittgenstein, Heidegger, and Dewey were the three most important philosophers of the twentieth century. Analytic philosophers might concur with his judgment about Wittgenstein, just as Continental philosophers might endorse Rorty's judgment about the significance of Heidegger. But virtually no one (except a few dedicated followers) would have even dared to claim that Dewey was one of the most important philosophers of the twentieth century. Since the publication of *Philosophy and the Mirror of Nature* in 1979, Rorty has identified himself (and his controversial views) with the pragmatic tradition. There is now a virtual industry of scholarship showing how Rorty misunderstands, distorts, and betrays the pragmatic tradition. Nevertheless, many thinkers (who probably have never even read a word of the classic pragmatic thinkers) have come to identify pragmatism or neopragmatism with Rorty's idiosyncratic philosophic outlook. Although Rorty still remains a key player, today there are many thinkers from diverse disciplines—religious thinkers, political and social theorists, literary critics, and lawyers who think of themselves as pragmatists. It is becoming increasingly common to speak about the "resurgence" or the "revival" of pragmatism.

Now, although some variation of the aforementioned account is generally accepted as an accurate narrative, it is—so I want to argue—superficial and misleading. It misses what is most important, vital, and philosophically significant about the pragmatic tradition. If I may steal a phrase from Heidegger, it is correct (*richtig*), it just isn't true (*wahr*). The thesis I intend to sketch is that the classic American pragmatists introduced a number of interrelated themes that have been explored and elaborated in novel ways throughout the twentieth century. Sometimes this has happened because of direct influence, but more frequently we can detect independent lines of inquiry that exemplify a pragmatic way of thinking and reinforce pragmatic insights in novel ways. I fully endorse Hilary Putnam's claim that pragmatism is a "way of thinking" that involves "a certain group of theses, theses which can and indeed were argued very differently by different philosophers with different concerns." He summarizes some of these key theses as "(1) antiskepticism; pragmatists hold that doubt requires justification just as much as belief; (2) fallibilism: pragmatists hold that there is never a metaphysical guarantee to be had that such and such a belief will never need revision (that one can be fallibilistic and antiskeptical is perhaps the unique insight of American pragmatism); (3) the thesis that there is no fundamental dichotomy between "facts" and "values"; and the thesis that, in a certain sense, practice is primary in philosophy" (Putnam 1994: 152). I think this list might be supplemented with a few other closely related theses, although I do agree that the classical pragmatists would endorse Putnam's claims—even if they interpret them in divergent ways. It is only now at the end of the twentieth century that we can appreciate how much of the best philosophic thinking of our century can be understood as variations on pragmatic themes. This is my warrant for calling the twentieth century "The Pragmatic Century." Let me be explicit and blunt. I not only think that pragmatic themes have had a strong influence on the range of cultural and social disciplines, but that we can detect the centrality of pragmatic concerns in Continental philosophy. I sometimes like to speculate that future intellectual historians will look back on the so-called analytic-Continental split as a minor ideological ripple that holds little philosophic interest when compared with the common pragmatic themes of our time. But that is part of a larger narrative. Here I want to limit myself to *beginning* my counternarrative to the standard one.

Let me start by going back to what Rorty himself identified as the central chapter of *Philosophy and the Mirror of Nature*, "Privileged Representations." This is where Rorty deals with Quine's critique of the language-fact distinction and Sellars's critique of the "myth of the given." The reason Quine and Sellars are so important for Rorty's overall argument is that he claims that modern epistemology and analytic philosophy rest on the "Kantian picture of concepts and intuitions getting together to produce knowledge." For Rorty, this turns out to be the equivalent to "saying that if we do not have the distinction between what is 'given' and what is 'added by the mind' or between the contingent (because influenced by what is given) and the 'necessary' (because entirely 'within' the mind and under its control), then we will not know what would count as a 'rational reconstruction' of our knowledge" (Rorty 1979: 169). According to Rorty, Quine renounces the language-fact distinction (along with the conceptual-empirical and analytic-synthetic distinctions), while Sellars questions the given-postulated distinction.But without at least one of these Kantian distinctions, "analytic philosophy could not be written." It is by pressing (some would say distorting) Sellars's and Quine's critiques all the way that Rorty arrives at his own distinctive version of pragmatism—one that abandons both of these Kantian distinctions and repudiates epistemological foundationalism.

I want to return to the article of Sellars that so influenced Rorty, "Empiricism and the Philosophy of Mind." It is here that we find Sellars's famous critique of the myth of the given. What is so striking about this 1956 monograph is the way in which it reads like a commentary on a famous series of papers that Peirce published in 1868–1869 ("Questions Concerning Certain Faculties Claimed for Man," "Some Consequences of Four Incapacities," and "Grounds of Validity of the Laws of Logic: Further Consequences of Four Incapacities," collected in Peirce 1931: volume 5). I think that the real beginning of American pragmatism dates from the publication of these articles rather than the more popular articles that Peirce published a decade later. The language and concerns of Peirce and Sellars reflect the differences of their philosophic contexts, but there is a remarkable similarity of the arguments advanced. Sellars, like Perice, claims that the epistemological doctrine of immediacy or direct intuitive knowledge lies at the heart of much of modern (Cartesian) epistemology. I do not think that there is an argument presented by Sellars that is not anticipated by Peirce. Both reject the very idea of epistemological foundationalism, and both reject the idea of "self-authenticating epistemic episodes." Both also claim that we can give an adequate account of the intentionality of mental states and our privileged first-person access of our own thoughts without any appeal to immediate introspection. Profound similarities also exist in the alternative conception of language, knowledge, and inquiry that they develop. Sellars's linguistic turn is anticipated in Peirce's more comprehensive theory of signs. Both agree that there is an irreducible intersubjectivity or, more accurately, sociality involved in the acquisition of conceptual capacities and the mastery of language. Sellars is clearly drawing on the insights of the later Wittgenstein, especially in his characterization of what he calls the "logical space of reasons" embedded in normative discursive practices. But in doing so, he is calling attention to the pragmatic motifs that recur throughout the *Philosophical Investigations* (Wittgenstein 1978). Both Peirce and Sellars argue that an adequate account of concepts and language presupposes the acknowledgment of norms implicit in practices. Sellars gives an eloquent expression of Peirce's antiskeptical fallibilism when he asserts that "empirical knowledge, like its sophisticated extension science, is rational, not because it has a foundation, but because it is a self-correcting enterprise which can put any claim into jeopardy, though not all at once." This is a principle that all pragmatists would endorse.

It is not surprising that there should be so much agreement between Peirce and Sellars. I do not think that this is to be explained by direct influence (although Sellars is clearly familiar with Peirce's work.) Both of these philosophers came to their insights by way of a pragmatic reading of Kant. By this I mean that they both appreciate Kant's insights about the character of experience and empirical knowledge insofar as it already involves conceptual capacities but nevertheless voice a certain caution about Kant's transcendental machinery. Both are arguing for a more pragmatically open appropriation of Kant—one that also reflects some of the Hegelian criticisms of Kant—and is compatible with the fallibilistic spirit of modern science and the social character of linguistic practices.

Here Rorty (who I will not discuss here) has done a serious injustice to a robust understanding of the pragmatic tradition. Kant is Rorty's bête noire. Rorty frequently writes as if Kant is the source of everything that is misguided about modern epistemology, and that his "rigid" dichotomies are the basis for much of analytic philosophy. Indeed, in "Pragmatism, Relativism, and Irrationalism," Rorty's presidential address to the American Philosophical Association (APA), he virtually excludes Peirce from the pragmatic tradition because he "remained the most Kantian of thinkers." Rorty dismisses Peirce when he remarks that Peirce's contribution to pragmatism was merely to have given it a name, and to have stimulated James.

But we do a great injustice to the pragmatic legacy if we downplay the Kantian (and the Kantian-Hegelian) influence. It was a reflection on Kant's categories that led Peirce to his pragmatism. Even Dewey wrote his dissertation on Kant, although he was reading Kant through the spectacles of neo-Hegelianism. Futhermore, we can see both the continuity and the fertility of this legacy by turning to the recent work of Hilary Putnam, John McDowell, and Robert Brandom. Each of these thinkers illustrates my general thesis that the resurgence and development of pragmatism are not exclusively due to the influence of the classic American pragmatic thinkers but the result of the dialectical thinking through of issues that are at the cutting edge of philosophic discussion. From the time that I first started working on the classic pragmatic thinkers in the 1950s, I have always felt that contrary to the myth of the pragmatists being passé, they were actually ahead of their times. And it is only now at the end of the twentieth century that philosophy is catching up. This is what Hegel might have called the "cunning of Reason" (*List der Vernunft*).

Let me begin to show this by turning to the philosophic development of Hilary Putnam. Putnam received his graduate education at UCLA at a time when Hans Reichenbach taught there. The young Putnam was the very exemplar of the "tough-minded" analytic philosopher who possessed a sophisticated understanding of mathematical logic and recent developments in quantum physics. His early heroes were Reichenbach, Carnap, and Quine. He thought of himself as a philosopher of science working in the tradition of logical empiricism, even though he was critical of many aspects of this tradition. He moved in that inner circle of analytic philosophy—UCLA Princeton, MIT, Harvard. Many of the "positions" that he advocated, including "functionalism," "scientific realism," and "metaphysical realism," became the "hot" topics debated by analytic philosophers. This is not the occasion to follow in detail his philosophic development, but what is most manifest and exciting is the explicit pragmatic turn that his thinking has taken—especially during the past two decades. Putnam is extremely knowledgeable about Peirce, James, and Dewey, and he has made significant contributions to the scholarship of these three pragmatists. In the best tradition of pragmatism, he has not been hesitant to press his criticisms of them. But what I find most impressive is the way in which his distinctive philosophic orientation integrates Peircian, Jamesian, and Deweyean motifs. Temperamentally, and by training, Putnam is closest to Peirce, who also came to philosophy trained as a logician and a natural scientist. But Putnam argues that Peirce's "convergence thesis"—the thesis that at the ideal "end of inquiry" there will be a convergence of our knowledge of reality—is mistaken. It is a thesis that is no longer compatible, so Putnam argues, with a more contemporary scientific outlook. Indeed, Putnam argues that the convergence thesis betrays the deeper pragmatic insight about irreducible pluralism. One might think that James's graceful metaphorical style of philosophizing might offend the "tough-minded" proclivities of Putnam—as Peirce had been offended. But Putnam is a great fan of James and thinks that philosophers have failed to appreciate James's argumentative finesse. What Putnam finds especially attractive about James is his "direct realism"—what James called "natural realism"—the thesis that we have direct perceptual contact with a real world of common sense objects. Like James, Putnam rejects the idea that we are really only in an immediate contact with our own "sense data," which are then taken to "represent" external real objects. But Putnam's interest in this aspect of James's thought goes beyond a technical interest in a proper theory of perception. Rather, it is an essential aspect of his pragmatic vision of "realism with a human face." Like all of the classical pragmatists, Putnam takes the contributions of natural science seriously. But he rejects all versions of reductionism, eliminativism, and what John McDowell has called "bald naturalism." The everyday world in which we live our lives—our *Lebenswelt* (the word Putnam uses)—is just as real as what we learn from science. In this respect, Putnam now rejects all forms of scientific realism and metaphysical realism that do not do justice to the human position—the human world of everyday objects and persons that we confront as agents. Like Dewey, Putnam thinks that a good deal of traditional philosophy has been motivated by a "quest for certainty" or, to use his own term, a "craving for absolutes." Putnam even thinks that, despite claims to the contrary, much of analytic philosophy has been motivated by the same craving—a craving that needs to be exposed and exorcised. Putnam also appropriates Dewey's multifacted critique of the fact-value dichotomy. Without values, there would not even be a world of facts. Furthermore, values are objective and can be rationally debated.

Objectivity—including moral objectivity—is not incompatible with moral disagreement. In Dewey, Putnam finds a political ideal that he himself endorses—the ideal of human flourishing in a democratic community. He defends and endorses the Deweyean thesis that "democracy is not just a form of social life among other workable forms of social life; it is the precondition for the full application of intelligence to the solution of social problems" (Putnam 1991: 217).

Hilary Putnam started his philosophic career as the very model of a "tough-minded" analytic philosopher. Some of his "hard-core" analytic colleagues think that he has gone soft and fuzzy. But let me remind you that when William James sought to characterize the distinctive pragmatic esprit, he employed what I think is still one of the best philosophic distinctions ever invented—the distinction of the "tough-minded" and the "tender-minded." And he argued that pragmatism combines the virtues of both of these poles and avoids the vices of these extremes. This is Putnam's way of making a similar point.

> I would agree with Myles Burnyeat who once said that philosophy needs vision and argument. Burnyeat's point was that there is something disappointing about a philosophic work that contains arguments, however good, which are not inspired by some genuine vision, and something disappointing about a philosophic work that contains a vision, however inspiring, which is unsupported by arguments. . . . I take [vision] to mean vision as to how to live our lives, and how to order our societies. Philosophers have a double task: to integrate our various views of our world and ourselves . . . and to help us find a meaningful orientation. (Putnam 1999: 44)

Putnam cites Myles Burnyeat here, but he might have cited William James, who said much the same thing in *A Pluralistic Universe.* As Putnam has shown, James had a healthy respect for arguments and invented a number of ingenious arguments, but it was James who said "a man's vision is the great fact about him." He also declared, "where there is no vision the people perish." When philosophers have a genuine vision, then one can read them over and over again "and each time bring away a fresh sense of reality" (James 1977: 14–77). The philosophic humane pragmatic vision that has emerged in Putnam's development during the past half century beautifully illustrates the way in which pragmatic themes that we see in Peirce, James, and Dewey have been appropriated, criticized, refined, and transformed in novel ways.

In turning to John McDowell and Robert Brandom (sometimes referred to as "the Pittsburgh neo-Hegelians," or, as I prefer to say, "the Pittsburgh pragmatic neo-Hegelians," I must be much briefer, not because their thought deserves less attention but because of space constraints. McDowell's philosophic credentials as an analytic philosopher are impeccable. Trained at Oxford, he has been philosophically engaged with the works of the most important analytic philosophers of our time. He has a strong background in classical philosophy and has written illuminating articles on both Aristotle and Wittgenstein. There is little evidence that McDowell has more than a superficial acquaintance with the classical American pragmatists. But in his thought-provoking book, *Mind and World*, and his recent John Dewey lectures delivered at Columbia University he shows how deeply he has been influenced by the pragmatic reading of Kant, Hegel, Wittgenstein, and Sellars. One can begin to wonder what is happening to the analytic-Continental split when a philosopher with McDowell's background and analytic credentials announces in his preface "that one way that I would like to conceive this work is a prolegomenon to a reading of [Hegel's] *Phenomenology*" (McDowell 1996: ix). The pragmatic themes that I find in McDowell's work are due to his own appropriation of Sellars's critique of the myth of the given. McDowell is a good example of a philosopher who, following his own independent line of inquiry, has evolved an orientation that echoes (and reinforces) pragmatic themes. In *Mind and World*, McDowell seeks to show that there is a way of dismounting from the oscillating seesaw between the myth of the given and coherentism. This was also the basic project of the pragmatists and is especially evident in Peirce's work. Peirce declared that "the truth is that pragmaticism is closely allied to Hegelian absolute idealism, from which, however it is sundered by its vigorous denial that the third category . . . suffices to make the world, or is even so much as self-sufficient. Had Hegel, instead of regarding the first two stages with his smile of contempt, held on to them as independent or distinct elements of the triune Reality, pragmaticists might have looked upon him as the great vindicator of their truth" (Peirce 1931: 5.436) Peirce is here referring to his elaboration of the categories of Firstness, Secondness, and Thirdness. The point that Peirce emphasizes in distinguishing Secondness and Thirdness anticipates that crucial point that McDowell makes when he insists that there are "rational constraints on our thinking that come "from outside thinking, but not outside what is thinkable" (McDowell 1996: 28). Peirce would certainly agree with McDowell when he goes on to say, "When we trace justifications back, the last thing we come to is still a thinkable content; not something more ultimate than that, a bare pointing to a bit of the Given" (McDowell 1996: 28). Like Peirce, and the other pragmatists, McDowell doesn't think that spontaneity—the source of our conceptual capacities—can be naturalized, if "naturalized" is taken to mean reduced to a bald or disenchanted nature. Like the pragmatists, McDowell seeks to develop a richer and thicker conception of nature in which we can find a place for the second nature characteristic of human beings. McDowell appeals to Aristotle to justify his conception of nature. But he might have just as well appealed to John Dewey, who argued for the continuity of human experience and nature. It is not surprising that Putnam, who is much more explicitly indebted to, and influenced by, the classical pragmatists, should find so much in common with McDowell. He thoroughly endorses McDowell's claim that what Kant calls spontaneity and what Sellars calls the "logical space of reasons" is essentially and intrinsically normative. Furthermore, Putnam praises McDowell for independently showing the truth of direct realism—the type of realism that Putnam finds in James. McDowell tells us "there is no ontological gap between the sort of thing one can mean, or generally the sort of thing one thinks truly, what one thinks is what is the case" (McDowell 1996: 27).

Here I think it is appropriate to explicitly acknowledge the relevance of the later Wittgenstein for a pragmatic way of thinking. I certainly do not want to suggest that Wittgenstein was a pragmatist. If there ever was a thinker who wasn't any kind of "ist" it surely is Wittgenstein. But I don't think that it is an accident that many contemporary thinkers who do identify themselves with the pragmatic tradition are drawn to the later Wittgenstein. Earlier I cited Putnam's remark that for the pragmatic way of thinking, "practice is primary." Wittgenstein, more than any other twentieth-century philosopher, has brought out the nuances and the variety of human practices—especially linguistic practices. I can indicate the significance of Wittgenstein's reflections concerning practices by turning to the work of McDowell's colleague, Robert Brandom.

At a time when the journal article has become the favored form of philosophic writing, Brandom has written a closely argued book of 741 pages. To round out this phase of my discussion of pragmatic themes, I want to focus on a single but central theme of *Making It Explicit.* The title of his opening chapter is "Toward a Normative Pragmatics" (Brandom 1994). In this chapter Brandom tells a story whose main characters are Kant, Frege, and Wittgenstein. He argues that it was Kant who initially brought out the normative character of concepts and rationality. Building on Kant, Frege makes a sharp distinction between *justification*—where assessments of correctness of propositional contents are involved—and *causation.* It is Wittgenstein, however, who shows that norms are embedded in practices. They are implicit in social practices. Indeed, the explicit formulation of rules itself presupposes norms implicit in practices. We make these norms explicit. Brandom's larger aim is to clarify what it means to be a rational creature. In a manner that echoes the classical pragmatists, Brandom tells us "Being rational is being bound or constrained by norms." Brandom also is influenced by the Kantian-pragmatic theme in Sellars and Wittgenstein. Wittgenstein shows us why unless we acknowledge the role of implicit norms in linguistic practices we cannot adequately account for our capacity to follow rules. In a recent paper, "Pragmatics and Pragmatisms," Brandom succinctly states his primary thesis: "Some norms are implicit in practices—in what practitioners actually do—rather than explicit in the form of rules that say what the norm is" (Brandom 2002). The power of Brandom's book is that he seeks to justify this general thesis in exhaustive detail—to show precisely how norms are implicit in social practices, and how they influence what we say and do. He seeks to show how his normative pragmatics leads to, and is compatible with, an inferential semantics. Although Brandom does not include Peirce in his narrative of the emergence of normative pragmatics, I would argue that Peirce not only plays a vital role in this narrative but anticipates the main thesis about norms being implicit in practices. We even find the anticipation of an inferential semantics in Peirce in his reflections on "leading principles."

I feel that, as I am coming to the end of this chapter, I am barely just beginning. This is only a fragment of what I want to say. That is why I hope to write a book in which I can fully develop and justify the thesis that our century is "The Pragmatic Century." So, in conclusion, let me outline what I would like to show in detail. Here I have focused on a series of thinkers, Sellars, Putnam, McDowell, and Brandom, who are frequently identified as "analytic philosophers" in order to show how they exemplify a pragmatic way of thinking. In my larger project, I also want to focus on some developments in contemporary Continental philosophy—especially German philosophy—where we find a similar dialectic at work. I am referring to the work of Karl-Otto Apel, who is largely responsible for the introduction of Peirce in Germany, and who has developed his own version of a transcendental pragmatics; Jurgen Habermas, who has appropriated Peircian, Meadean, and Deweyean themes into his own creative synthesis, and whose understanding of deliberative democracy bears a strong affinity for John Dewey's ideal of democracy; and Hans Jonas, the German sociologist who has not only written one of the best studies of George Herbert Mead but who has one of the finest understandings of the creative fertility of the American pragmatic tradition. The renewed interest in Mead, and especially the way in which Mead's understanding of the genesis of intersubjectivity and sociality has influenced contemporary discussions of communicative rationality and intersubjectivity, deserves special attention. I also would like to explore some of the striking affinities (as well as some of the differences) between the pragmatists' rejection of all forms of epistemological and metaphysical foundationalism and the critique of the "metaphysics of presence" in Derrida. Important similarities even exist in the way in which Derrida has recently discussed what he calls the "democracy to come" and Dewey's ideal of creative democracy.

But it is not just that the pragmatic way of thinking cuts across the so-called analytic-Continental divide; it is also essential to see how the pragmatic esprit and the pragmatic way of thinking have influenced other domains of culture, including our understanding of religious experience. The classic American thinkers were never antireligious. Indeed, they sought to recover the integrity of religious experience from dogmatism and fundamentalism. Let me remind you that in the very essay in which James introduced pragmatism, he sought to apply the pragmatic approach to clarify and test the religious hypothesis by showing its relevance to our concrete practical experience. And finally, I also would like to discuss the work of those thinkers who, at a time when the classic pragmatic thinkers were neglected and marginalized, sought to keep this tradition alive—philosophers such as John E. Smith, John McDermott, and Max Fisch.

In 1954, when I was a graduate student at Yale, I had the good fortune to participate in a reading group of Dewey's *Experience and Nature* that was organized by a young assistant professor, John E. Smith. It was that experience that opened my eyes to the vitality and fertility of the pragmatic tradition and inspired me to write my dissertation, "John Dewey's Metaphysics of Experience." Yale was also the institution where Paul Weiss, the co-editor of the *Collected Papers of Charles Sanders Peirce*, taught. And many graduate students had a serious interest in Peirce. My first book, a collection of articles by Dewey entitled *John Dewey: On Experience, Nature, and Freedom*, was published in 1960. In the Introduction to that book I wrote: "There is a felt need for reunion in philosophy, for new perspective and vision that is informed by the lessons of careful analysis. In this search for new directions, there is much to be learned from John Dewey, who sought to unite speculative imagination with a sensitive concern for the variety of human experience and the specific 'problems of men'" (Bernstein 1960). During the decade of the 1950s, when pragmatism had reached its low point among professional philosophers, I felt that the day would come when philosophy would catch up with the pragmatists. Now, almost half a century later, I feel completely vindicated. Pragmatism originally burst upon the philosophic scene at the turn of the twentieth century. As we look forward to fresh philosophic developments in this new century, we are witnessing an exciting and a lively flourishing of pragmatic themes. Philosophically, the twentieth century has been "The Pragmatic Century."

References

Bernstein, Richard J. 1960. Introduction. In *John Dewey: On experience, nature, and freedom*, ed. Richard J. Bernstein, ix–xlvii. New York: Liberal Arts Press.

Brandom, Robert. 1994. *Making it explicit.* Cambridge, MA: Harvard University Press.

———. 2002. Pragmatics and pragmatisms. In *Hilary Putnam: Pragmatism and Realism.* Ed. James Conant and Urzula M. Zeglen, 40–59. New York: Routledge.

James, William. 1977. Philosophical conceptions and practical results. In *The writings of William James*, ed. John McDermott, 345–61. Chicago: University of Chicago Press.

———. 1977. *A pluralistic universe.* Cambridge, MA: Harvard University Press.

McDowell, John. 1996. *Mind and world.* Cambridge, MA: Harvard University Press.

Peirce, Charles Sanders. 1931. *Collected papers of Charles Sanders Peirce.* Ed. Charles Hartshorne and Paul Weiss. Cambridge, MA: Harvard University Press.

Putnam, Hilary. 1991. A reconsideration of Deweyean democracy. In *Pragmatism in law and society*, ed. Michael Brint and William Weaver, 217–43. Boulder, CO: Westview Press.

———. 1994. *Words and life*. Ed. James Conant. Cambridge, MA: Harvard University Press.

———. 1999. *Cogito: Key philosophers in conversation*. Ed. Andrew Pyle. New York: Routledge.

Rorty, Richard. 1979. *Philosophy and the mirror of nature*. Princeton, NJ: Princeton University Press.

Wittgenstein, Ludwig. 1978. *Philosophical investigations*; the English text of the third edition. Trans. G. E. M. Anscombe. New York: Macmillan.

Theses on Bernstein

William D. Hart

> In *The American Evasion of Philosophy* (1989), Cornel West offers an unusually broad view of the pragmatist tradition. Far from restricting himself to the usual trinity of Peirce, James, and Dewey, West includes the life and thought of W. E. B. Du Bois. In thus expanding the pragmatist canon to encompass a major body of critical reflection on "race" and racism in America, West also poses a challenge to anyone contemplating a revival of pragmatism today. We are challenged to cast a net wide enough to catch not only the concerns of Stanley Fish, Hilary Putnam, and Richard Rorty but also what Du Bois famously called "the problem of the color line," a problem certain to outlast the twentieth century and a crucial test for the pragmatist enterprise of using social intelligence to guide social practice.
>
> The most important lesson for those proposing to revive pragmatism today is this: There is not one pragmatism, but several. We had better know which of them we want to revive.
>
> —Nancy Fraser[1]

My original intention was to write a commentary on various themes in Richard Bernstein's provocative book *The New Constellation: The Ethical-Political Horizons of Modernity/Post-Modernity* (1992). It soon became apparent that to write that I would have to track a set of interrelated questions—the Question Concerning Technology, the Jewish Question, and questions of *phronēsis* and *praxis*—that snakes its way through that book *and* through Bernstein's recent work. I could not imagine doing this task without exploring the ways that pragmatism serves as my inspiration and critical guide. My goal, I resolved, was to restate what Bernstein has said with as much fidelity as I could and to say *with as little presumption and rancor as possible* what he did not say but ought to have said. A standard narrative essay, I thought, would serve these purposes well. But the complexity and heterogeneity of Bernstein's work seems both to invite and to resist that form. Thus my approach is a compromise between the expansiveness and continuity of a narrative essay and the concise, pithy form of Marx's "Theses on Feuerbach." For if philosophers have interpreted the world, in various ways, then Bernstein seeks to change it.

I

According to Bernstein, the chief defect of most theories of rationality—those of Nietzscheans, Heideggerians, Weberians, and French poststructuralists included—is that reason's otherness, non-identity, and difference are extirpated, forgotten, and excluded. These theories of rationality, according to Bernstein, constitute a grand (though heterogenous) narrative of reason-induced peril: of a will to truth that nihilistically consumes itself, of a forgetfulness of Being whose technological, "Enframing" essence endangers us,[2] of a purposive rationality that imprisons us in iron cages, administered societies, and the carceral archipelago. This narrative conceals, however, the otherness of rationality, those competing traditions in which reason is non-identical with itself. If I understand Bernstein correctly, he accuses this hydra-headed Nietzschean and post-Nietzschean discourse of reason of a forgetfulness of the dialogical and communicative strand in the history of rationality. While identifying dialogical rationality preeminently with the American pragmatist tradition, he traces the roots of such rationality to Plato's early Socratic dialogues. Bernstein is determined to guard this dialogical notion of rationality from too close an association with Habermas's notion of communicative rationality. He does so not because he wishes to exclude Habermas from this tradition but rather to protect this competing tradition of dialogical and non-identical rationality from the defects in Habermas's version and from the mind-numbing controversies about the possibility of distortion-free communication that it generated.[3] Thus he looks backward to Dewey and Peirce, who never imagined that dialogue lacked pregnant silences, sharp words, and misunderstandings that signal the provisional and revisable nature of this kind of reason. Thus he commends the suspicions of Nietzscheans and post-Nietzscheans, especially their critique of false dialogue, of closed, inward-looking notions of "we," and of reason as the violent imposition of commonality (Bernstein 1992: 38–41, 45–52). But Bernstein will not allow himself to be carried to the hysterical extreme of thinking that sameness by definition, by some metaphysical necessity that only Derrida and his crew can understand, is evidence of violence, and that the search for common, communicatively mediated ground is the leading edge of enlightened terror.

II

Bernstein traces the horrendous consequences of this grand narrative of reason-sponsored peril in the post-Nazi era writings of Martin Heidegger. Through a close reading of "The Question Concerning Technology" and "The Letter on Humanism," which supplement, in the Derridian sense, Heidegger's earlier questioning of Being, Bernstein discloses what Heidegger conceals. Hidden in Heidegger's elaborate word play are the difference between moral knowledge (*phronēsis*) and technical knowledge (*technē*) and the difference between human agency (*praxis*) and the divinity of poetic revealing (*poiesis*). Furthermore, in Heidegger's questioning of technology, the democratic character of *phronēsis* is absorbed by the aristocratic character of *Denken*, of meditative thinking. On this view, human destiny lies in the hands of poets and thinkers. Practical wisdom (*phronēsis*) and political action (*praxis*)—that is, the capacities of ordinary people—can play no role in saving mortals from the "Enframing" essence of technology. Enframing (*Gestell*) is a form of revealing. It is the whence, the nature, or Being of beings. It is a partial answer to the question, why is there something rather than nothing? Enframing is the process through which some things and eventually everything, including humans, is made available for use, as a "stockpile in service to, and on call for, technological purposes." Enframing prevents things/beings, including humans, from appearing as what they are, in their essential dignity.[4] The essence of technology is "an orientation toward efficiency" (Feenberg 1999: x) that obscures poetic revealing. This act of concealing is the supreme danger. Humans are powerless to save themselves from this dangerous destiny, except insofar as they watch over Being, the process of revealing-unconcealing, like a shepherd watches over sheep. Or, as Heidegger puts it, "human reflection can ponder the fact that all saving power must be of a higher essence than what is endangered, though at the same time kindred to it" (Heidegger 1993: 339). Thus Heidegger tells a grim story in which there are only two options: either the divinity of poetic revealing-unconcealing, where "Only a god can save us," or the Enframing of technology, which reduces humans, the earth, and the fullness thereof to a vast standing reserve of used and reusable parts (Heidegger). What makes this story particularly grim is not the fact that a great thinker displays a troubling lack of nuance, where nuance is what careful judgment requires, but the ethical-political blindness that this lack of judgment encodes. In a related but different context Hannah Arendt called this the banality of evil. Thus Heidegger is silent, in the sense that he will acknowledge no responsibility about his role in the Third Reich, whose Enframing, technological essence is no different, he thinks, than motorized agriculture and thus as big a threat to "man's essential nature" and dignity as a meditative thinking being. "What calls forth thinking here," according to Bernstein, "is Heidegger's own understanding of a type of meditative thinking that *anesthetizes* us to the frightful contingencies of human life and death, that is so obsessed with the 'real' danger, the 'real' plight that it can dismiss the difference between motorized agriculture and mass murder as 'nonessential'" (Bernstein 1992: 133).

Here, Bernstein contends, is a decisive difference between Heidegger and pragmatists:

> For the pragmatists turn our attention to how we can think about our *praxis,* and how we can foster a sense of solidarity and community among human beings. This is why the notion of a critical community without any absolute beginning points or finalities is so fundamental for them—a type of community in which there can be an overcoming of the "eclipse of public life." *Our dialogue, and communicative transactions, is not only with Being itself, but with other human beings.* (Bernstein 1986: 219; emphasis added)

If "questioning is the piety of thought," then what happened to Heidegger? How could he have forgotten the difference, that is, failed to properly judge—not merely the ontological but the ethical-political—difference between Being and human beings? That Heidegger forgot our dialogical relation not only with Being but with human beings, according to Bernstein, reveals a loud silence: a silence that "is resounding, deafening, and damning" (Bernstein 1992: 136). Following Hannah Arendt, I call evil Heidegger's forgetfulness of human beings, even though she dithered on this issue and refused to make this call.

III

Here is Bernstein quoting Arendt's reply to Gershom Scholem's sharp critique of her book *Eichmann in Jerusalem: A Report on the Banality of Evil*:

> It is indeed my opinion now that evil is never "radical," that it is only extreme, and that it possesses neither depth nor any demonic dimension. It can overgrow and lay waste the whole world precisely because it spreads like a fungus on the surface. It is "thought-defying," as I said, because thought tries to reach some depth, to go to the roots, and the moment concerns itself with evil, it is frustrated because there is nothing. (Bernstein 1996: 167)

The banality of evil is a much-debated idea. Arendt authored this idea, perhaps as Bernstein suggests, under the unacknowledged inspiration of Karl Jaspers (Bernstein 1996: 147–48). As a former student of Heidegger's during the 1920s, and as a German Jew who was forced to flee the Nazi death machine, Arendt faced squarely the issue of catastrophic evil, what Heidegger, who rejected moral language, called the supreme danger. Like Heidegger, she associates this danger/evil with a failure to think. Unlike her teacher, she also views catastrophic evil as an ethical-political failure. Or, as Bernstein suggests, she tries to fudge the difference between evil as an intellectual failure, a failure to think, and evil as a moral failure, a failure to judge rightly. What precisely is the relation among evil, thinking, and judging? Bernstein raises serious questions about Arendt's success in answering this question. Specifically, how does thinking, which subsumes particulars under universals, relate to the ability to judge particulars directly, without the aid of universals? If, as Arendt argues, thinking liberates the capacity to judge, then how does she account, Bernstein asks, for the deleterious effects (such as licentiousness and cynicism) that the thinking of Socrates, the paradigmatic thinker, had on Alcibiades and Critias? More important, why did not Heidegger's thinking liberate his judgment concerning Hitler and Nazism? And why did not Arendt's thinking liberate her judgment about Heidegger? Most important, how does she account for the ability of *some* people to think and judge rightly under circumstances in which *most* people do not? Why, to put this question starkly, did Anton Schmidt,[5] a sergeant in the German army, defy the Nazi death machine by rescuing Jews, while Eichmann ensured that the death machine ran as efficiently as possible (Bernstein 1996: 173–76)? Bernstein does not answer the questions that he so ably poses and that Arendt left unanswered. But the effort to answer these questions, it seems to me, is a worthy one. If they remain unanswered, the reason should not be that of a perverse piety, which celebrates ineffability and abjures the piety of asking questions and searching for answers. For in attempting to answer these questions, we may better understand just how precious and fragile judging and acting are and why the rage against an imperial, self-identical, and violent rationality—whether called "humanism" or "Enframing"—should not be confused with a rage against ethical and political intelligence. From the Nazi Holocaust and before to Rwanda and after, mass killing is not a failure of theoretical reason (what we can know) or of meditative thinking and poetic imagination but a failure of moral judgment and political action.

IV

Bernstein poses virtually the same question to Freud, "Can one so neatly and rigorously distinguish the religion of Judaism from the essential nature of Jewishness?," that he did to Arendt, "Can one so easily separate Judaism from Jewishness?" In both cases, the reason for the question is the same: Arendt and Freud profess to be both godless and Jewish. How can this be? How can Freud be cavalier if not indifferent to the "rituals, ceremonies, narratives, customs, and cultural practices" (Bernstein 1998: 2; 1996: 28) of Judaism and profess to be Jewish? In a complex effort to do justice to the radical play of blindness and insight in *The Man Moses and the Monotheistic Religion*,[6] Bernstein shows how Freud does a better job of thinking through the relation between Judaism and Jewish identity than Arendt does. Bernstein criticizes Arendt for not considering the religious significance of being a Jew, her distinction between "'Judaism' or 'Jewish substance' and 'Jewishness'" being inadequate, and for the unargued assumptions in the very notion of a godless Jew (Bernstein 1996: 27). The great merit of Freud, in contrast and among others, is that he provides a provocative answer (whether a compelling answer I leave to others) to a question that Arendt barely asks.

According to Bernstein, *The Man Moses and the Monotheistic Religion* should be seen as an answer to the question that Freud posed in the preface of *Totem and Taboo* nearly three decades earlier. Here is Bernstein quoting Freud:

> No reader of [the Hebrew version of] this book will find it easy to put himself in the emotional position of an author who is ignorant of the language of holy writ, who is completely estranged from the religion of his fathers—as well as from every other religion—and who cannot take a share in nationalist ideals, but who has yet never repudiated his people, who feels that he is in his essential nature a Jew and who has no desire to alter that nature. If the question were to be put to him: "Since you have abandoned all these common characteristics of your country-men, what is there left to you that is Jewish?" he would reply: "A very great deal, and *probably its very essence.*" He could not now express that essence clearly in words; but some day, no doubt, it will become accessible to the scientific mind. (Bernstein 1998: 1)

Despite his concern about speaking prematurely, Freud answers his own question by providing an expanded account of the emergence of monotheism from Totemism, whose foundational event, whether real or imaginary, was the murder of the primal father. On this account, according to Bernstein, Freud discovers a repetitive pattern: "murder of the primal father, murder of Moses, murder of Christ. The memory-traces of this 'transfigured' event persist, and it is evoked by the repetition of the trauma of the primal murder. The trauma is both forgotten (repressed) and remembered (re-lived)" (Bernstein 1998: 77). It is this double movement of forgetting and remembering, each leaving its trace in the other, which Bernstein cites as among Freud's greatest insights. For this interplay enables Freud to illuminate the relations between Christian anti-Semitism, the unparalleled assault on the Jewish people by the Nazis, and the essence of Jewishness.

Recall Freud's creative appropriation of Darwin's speculations about a primal horde. Once upon a time, in this Darwinian state of nature, there was a father (or alpha male) who maintained an unconstrained monopoly on sexual access to all of the females in the horde. He enforced this monopoly through the threat of castration and murderous violence, which prevented his sons (or subdominant males) from gratifying their desire. One day the jealous brothers decided to make common cause, so they murdered their father and consumed his body. This created a tremendous sense of guilt and ambivalence in the brothers, who both loved and hated their father. Each of them admired and envied the father (which is why they identified with him by cannibalizing his body), and each longed to take his place as the alpha, senior male, and the new lord of the horde. But prudence dictated a renunciation of this desire, for to act on this desire would lead to a Hobbesian "war of all against all." This renunciation was institutionalized in the prohibition of murder and incest, the very foundations of justice and morality. Here also lies the foundation of religion, since Totemism is based on the ritual reenactment (though displaced onto the totemic animal) of the murder and consumption of the primal father. The price of instinctual renunciation is anger, guilt, and ambivalence. Such, in bald outline and with many gaps, is Freud's account of the emergence of civilization, morality, law, and religion (Freud 1995: 882–87; 1961: 99–100; 1967: 168).

Freud detects the same anger, guilt, and ambivalence in Christian anti-Semitism and in Nazism that he did in the primal horde. The junior male, Christianity, wants what the senior male, Judaism, has.[7] The senior male's desire is the junior male's desire, which produces a guilty, ambivalent anger toward his rival. Thus Christianity is always in the business of one-upping Judaism. Moses brings the law, but Jesus fulfills it. Moses feeds the liberated Hebrews with bread from heaven, but Jesus is the bread of life. Moses lifts up the bronze serpent on a pole to cure a deadly snakebite, but Jesus goes further: lifted on the cross, he cures the deadly poison of sin (Paul 1996: 17, 20, 36, 200–202, 212). The same competitive rivalry drives Nazism. The Nazi celebration of the so-called pagan revival of polytheistic religion is an expression of hostility toward the instinctual renunciation that the monotheistic religions demand. While I am somewhat skeptical, this sounds like a fascinating line of inquiry. If only Bernstein had done more with it.

What remains to be answered is Freud's question about the essence of Jewishness: an essence that is compatible with godlessness, with an indifference to the ceremonies, rituals, customs, and cultural practices associated with Judaism. What then is the essence of Jewishness? That essence, according to Bernstein, is epitomized in the phrase "*Der Fortschritt in der Geistigkeit*," which he says is difficult to translate but has been variously translated as "The Advance in Intellectuality" or "The Progress in Spirituality." This intellectual and spiritual progress, driven by instinctual renunciation, which is rooted in the murder of Moses, which is a repetition of the murder of the primal father (the return of the repressed), is the essence of Jewishness. "This is the enduring legacy of Mosaic monotheism—a legacy which Freud believed held the Jewish people together, and enabled the Jews to survive through centuries of persecution. It is a legacy that is at once intellectual, spiritual, and ethical; a legacy which outlasts the *religious* teachings of Judaism; a legacy with which Freud proudly identifies" (Bernstein 1998: 31, 84). What is fascinating about Bernstein's interpretation is that it suggests a way of identifying with the "essence" of a theistic religious tradition, its latent rather than manifest essence, while affirming one's godlessness and indifference to most of its creeds and rituals. This is what Freud's *The Man Moses and the Monotheistic Religion*, on Bernstein's interpretation, appears to have achieved.

V

If Freud thinks of Nazism in psychoanalytic terms as an angry, guilty, ambivalence that is driven by the instinctual renunciations that Judaism demands, then Derrida splits the difference between Freud's account and Arendt's quasi-organic account of Nazism as a pernicious growth. Or at least that is what he appears to do. According to Derrida, "Nazism was not born in the desert. We all know this, but it has to be constantly recalled. And even if, far from any desert, it has grown like a mushroom in the silence of a European forest, it would have done so in the shadow of big trees, in the shelter of their silence or indifference but in the same soil" (Derrida 1986: 109). This is as clear a statement as one will find in the writings of Derrida. For his writings on the Jewish question, what the Nazis thought was a "final solution" to that question, and on the question concerning Heidegger's complicity (for surely he helped cultivate the "big trees" under which Nazism grew[8]) are as obscure, circuitous, and elusive as his other writings. What are the ethical-political consequences of this style? This is the question I take Bernstein to be asking when he writes, "After all we can well understand the ambiguities that allowed the Nazis to brutalize Nietzsche's texts. But can we even imagine that they might have done the same to the texts of—say—John Dewey?" (Bernstein 1992: 190). I will return to Bernstein's question after briefly considering his account of Derrida's ethical-political horizon.

There is something uncanny, Bernstein argues, about the writings of Derrida, which remind us of Freud's famous essay on that topic.[9] Derrida makes our search for an *archi*-original, absolute starting point tremble, our centers wobble, and our foundations unstable. Like a Socratic gadfly, he irritates. He is as irritating as insightful; indeed, this play of irritation and insight is methodical and irremediable. He casts aspersions on the idea of taking an ethical-political position, but his writing, Bernstein contends, is full of moral passion and Levinasian-sounding motifs such as responsibility. Bernstein takes these as signs of the ethical-political horizon of everything that Derrida writes. One "lesson" that Bernstein takes from Derrida's work is that "there is no 'boundary-fixing' that cannot itself be questioned" (Bernstein 1992: 184). Beliefs must be fixed, as Peirce would say, but they can always be questioned, for all of our claims are subject to criticism and revision. Does this mean that Derrida is a quasi-pragmatist? I do not think that Bernstein would go that far, even though Derrida takes apart (or deconstructs) the stark contrast between foundations and chaos that feeds the either-or logic of what Bernstein calls the "Cartesian anxiety." However, Derrida's skepticism seems to cut deeper than that of pragmatists; he seems to be a more relentless inquirer, less comfortable with provisional claims, more afraid that those claims will become the new dogma. In this respect, he seems very unpragmatic, since pragmatists are generally comfortable with claims they have no good reason to doubt. Yet there is something arresting about this relentless thinker-questioner named Derrida, about the idiosyncratic way he tries to keep the road of inquiry open. The question I take Bernstein to be asking is whether the ethical-political price of Derrida's idiosyncratic mode of inquiry is too high.

We are now in a position to consider Bernstein's earlier question: to what extent is Derrida responsible for the reception, mis-reception, and uncomprehending reception of his texts? Does he bear some responsibility for the bad (ethical-political) uses to which his texts have been put in the same way that Nietzsche, because he is ambiguous, esoteric, and otherwise fails to make his ideas clear, bears some responsibility for the way the Nazis read his texts? I do not want to be misunderstood. Bernstein is not suggesting that Derrida's failures, whatever they may be, are equivalent to the failures of Nietzsche. Nor does he claim that moral responsibility can be assigned to either of them or to any writer in a straightforward, unmediated, and noncontroversial way. Our words can always be used against us, against what we reflectively take our intentions to have been. What I do take Bernstein to be saying is that certain norms are constitutive of dialogical, communicative, or pragmatic rationality. We are responsible before the other and to the other for making our ideas clear. Perfect transparency is an unattainable goal; it is a virtual if ever receding reality. But it is a goal nonetheless. We should seek simplicity *and clarity* while distrusting them. To the extent that we fail to make our ideas clear, are carried away by rhetorical playfulness, or are seduced by esoteric modes of discourse, are we responsible, however mediated and qualified, for the way our words are used? This is true despite the fact that our use of the word "black" can be read as "white" in some possible world, on some ingenious reading. There are no remedies for that kind of "genius." We should honor the subjects of such genius and distrust them. We should honor them because they make us think differently, which might contribute, in time, to the formation of more excellent habits of judging and acting. We should distrust them because they distract us from doing what we ought to do, here and now, according to our best ethical-political judgment. Our best judgment is the best we will ever have, for the perfect, as conservatives rightly argue, is the enemy of the good and the best. And there is no path to the better except through the best.

Gillian Rose puts a sharper point on Bernstein's critique of Derrida's ethical-political horizon, which makes that horizon more threatening and less attractive than Bernstein thinks. It is not merely Derrida's style that is troubling but his anti-metaphysical metaphysics, which is related to his style and to his tortured defense of Heidegger. According to Rose, Derrida ontologizes violence. Violence is "of spirit"; spirit is flame, a conflagration. "[W]hether one speaks for Nazism or strives to oppose it, both are equally terrifying contaminations" (Rose 1993: 61). Spirit, which enflames and potentially reduces everything to ashes, is the whence of both. As Rose observes, "This stipulation would deflect investigation from Heidegger's defense of Nazism as a 'spiritual force' by attributing any conceivable basis for such investigation to a 'metaphysics of subjectivity,' which is extended to cover 'all the pitfalls of the strategy of establishing demarcations,' 'for example, democracy or—human rights'" (Rose 1993: 61). Derrida's strategy, she argues, "disqualifies all thinking." It becomes impossible to politically discriminate between inclusive and exclusive political ideas. Both are equally contaminated with the ontological violence of Spirit (Wood 1993: 62). This is a flanking maneuver in which primordial, incendiary, and violent Spirit is the condition for the possibility of both apology and critique. Derrida conflates Nazism and the critique of Nazism and embeds their mutual contamination in the very notion of human rights. This maneuver is constitutive of Derrida's apology for Heidegger and is comparable to Heidegger's inability to see the difference between mechanized agriculture and genocide. Thus Spirit is to Derrida what Enframing is to Heidegger. In both cases, difference is sunk in an ethical-political pit of indifference and the unwillingness to differentiate.

VI

If how we write is an ethical-political imperative, which demands that we make relevant distinctions, unmake irrelevant distinctions, while seeking maximal clarity, then there is a certain genius in the crystal-clear prose—relatively speaking—of Richard Rorty. Perhaps no one does a better job of honoring that genius and distrusting it than Bernstein. He distrusts Rorty's claim that he is a Deweyan pragmatist, an advocate of the creative—radical—democracy that Dewey imagined. On Bernstein's view, Rorty conflates liberalism and democracy, thus obscuring the difference between and within these terms. He plays a rhetorical game that does not help a careful critic make distinctions that she may want to make. If some form of liberalism is constitutive of radical change, as Dewey contends, then Rorty consecrates a form of liberalism that Dewey condemns as "irrelevant and doomed" (Bernstein 1992: 233). If most forms of liberalism represent a middle position between authoritarianism and radical, egalitarian democracy, then Rorty's pragmatism[10] is a middle position between positivism, relativism, and emotivism, on the one side, and Deweyan pragmatism, on the other.

Bernstein charges Rorty with using rhetorical strategies that "tend to close off serious/playful conversation about liberalism and democracy" (Bernstein 1992: 253). His wit and rhetorical genius obscure the deep tensions in his work: between denying an epistemological given and presupposing a historical given, between calling for open inquiry and arguing for an emotive-fideistic-absolutist notion of final vocabularies, between horror at cruelty and the cruelty and sophistry of redescription, between the democratic-pragmatic virtue of fallibilism and the aristocratic-Nietzschean virtue of irony. Moreover, his use of the pronoun "we" exemplifies a pulverizing, homogenizing, egocentric blindness that led Foucault, Derrida, and others to be overly suspicious (indeed, disastrously suspicious) of "we sentiments" in the first place (Bernstein 1992: 235–36, 244, 247–49). Not everyone is convinced by Bernstein's criticism. According to David Hall, Bernstein's criticism would be telling "only if it could be shown that there is an alternative to beginning with 'me' on the way to a construction of 'we.'" One must show that Rorty's use of "we" presupposes rather than invites consensus. Hall's conclusion, as I understand it, is that Rorty's ethnocentrism, his use of "we," is an ever-expansive and, in principle, infinitely inclusive "we" (Hall 1994: 14, 182–83). Bernstein might retort that Rorty is not sufficiently attentive to the gap between principle and practice and the perverse ways that ideology fills the gap, transforming principles into "ideological weapons of death."[11] To put the best pragmatist spin on Rorty's use of "ethnocentrism," one might think of it by analogy to Peirce's principle of conservation and Gadamer's use of prejudice. Ethnocentrism, like conservatism and prejudice, is the place from which we necessarily begin. To recognize our starting point is to gain some leverage on it. But we should not exaggerate that leverage, which is what Rorty and Bernstein do consistently, according to Stanley Fish. He accuses Rorty and Bernstein of "the critical self-consciousness fallacy or antifoundationalist theory hope." This is

> the fallacy of thinking that there is a mental space you can occupy to the side of your convictions and commitments, and the hope that you can use the lesson that no transcendent standpoint is available as a way of bootstrapping yourself to transcendence (on the reasoning that since we know that "we cannot hope to escape our prejudices, we can be on guard against those prejudices and better able to see things clearly"). (Fish 1999: 305)

On the contrary, says Fish. For even

> if you believe that your convictions have their source not in ultimate truths or foundations but in contingent traditions of inquiry and are therefore revisable, that belief, in and of itself, will not render you disposed to revise your convictions or turn you into a person who enters into situations provisionally and with epistemic modesty. You can give all the standard answers to all the pragmatist questions and still be an authoritarian in the classroom, a decided conservative in cultural matters, or inclined to absolutes of theology. (I am, in differing degrees, all three.) (Fish 1999: 300)

While characteristically strong, Fish's critique of fallibilism is anything but fishy. What makes our strongest convictions strong is precisely their resistance to criticism and revision, not as a matter of principle but of practice. These beliefs possess us every bit as much as we possess them. Nothing is likely to count as evidence against them. No one is likely to persuade us that those who hold opposing views on these matters are not dangerous, evil, and even deadly (Fish 1999: 101–105.) Fish cannot merely be dismissed as a font of rhetorical bile. That description may be correct, but it is not true. For Fish's argument about the sort of convictions that people would rather kill and die for than change is the ultimate test case for pragmatic fallibilism.

Having said this, I am still prepared to trot out the usual Peircean and Deweyan line that we are better positioned to criticize and revise our own ethnocentric, conservative, and prejudiced beliefs than those who loudly, absolutely, and blindly decry such beliefs and thus knowingly or unknowingly resist acknowledging, criticizing, and revising their own preunderstandings. And we are better off than the subjects of the nonfallibilistic pragmatism that Fish advocates. I am confident in this view because Fish is clearly mistaken. He confuses what may or may not be possible for a particular agent (who may or may not be able to criticize and revise her or his beliefs under particular circumstances) with the relative, incremental, and cumulative effects of fallibilism as a social practice. Fallibilism is not an artifact of our ability to introspect, that is, to survey what Rorty calls the Cartesian-Lockean mental theater (Fish 1999: xxii-xxiii). On the contrary, fallibilism is a public art, an artifact of our intersubjective ability to interpret signs, and to revise our beliefs, our habits of action accordingly. Thus fallibilism may be a form of piety and a form of hope, but it is more than a self-deluding, pious hope or a new form of transcendentalism.

If fallibilism is more than a pious hope, then what about Rorty's notion of irony? Rorty supplements, in the Derridian sense, the Peircean and Deweyan notion of fallibilism with his own, distinctive notion of irony. On Bernstein's view, Rorty does not adequately address the tensions between irony and liberalism. But the tensions between irony (as ordinarily conceived) and democracy are even greater. As an essential part of satire, irony teaches us to look down, often down our noses, at others. Irony (in Swift, Nietzsche, and most esoteric writers) is for those who have the ears to hear and who are in the know. The rest of us won't get it. For Irony speaks above our heads or between lines that we cannot read. Granted its typically aristocratic abode, can irony have democratic uses? Can we think of irony as a rhetorical strategy for leveling up as well as one that keeps others down? If the case could be made for a democratic use of irony, then we creative, radical, egalitarian democrats would look down in an effort to level up. On this view, the witty and wicked irony of Rorty might be a potent democratic tool. But this requires further thought. For now I can only make this argument in the subjunctive mood, since I cannot distinguish Rorty's irony (perhaps he can) from what Peirce called "paper doubt."

VII

Audible in much of what Bernstein writes is Dewey's refrain: "Philosophy recovers itself when it ceases being a device for dealing with the problems of philosophers and becomes a method, cultivated by philosophers, for dealing with the problems of men" (Dewey 1981: 95). In his eleventh thesis on Feuerbach, Marx made a similar point: "Philosophers have only *interpreted* the world, in various ways; the point, however, is to *change* it" (Marx 1978: 145). Bernstein's work is an attempt to remain faithful to this radical imperative. With more verve and insight than anyone else, he has engaged the issues that a less insular and more cosmopolitan pragmatism must address. He has cultivated the tradition without being trapped by it. Where Rorty remains obsessed by the epistemological tradition, with an endless round of circumvention, deconstruction, and evasion, Bernstein makes an effort to go beyond the obsession with objectivism and relativism to a notion of praxis that stands somewhere between Marx and Dewey. Still, we can ask, without being cantankerous, just how successful has he been? Consider the following passage from Bernstein's 1982 essay "What Is the Difference That Makes a Difference? Gadamer, Habermas, and Rorty":

> Dewey is one of Rorty's heroes but Rorty does not follow Dewey in his socio-political critiques of the "problems of men." But although Rorty himself has not practiced the type of socio-political critique that became so central for Dewey, he expresses deep sympathy with it. Rorty, too, is an apologist for those very democratic virtues that were so central for Dewey and which he sought to make concrete. There is an important difference of emphasis here between Rorty and Habermas—one which also reveals the common ground that they share. For Rorty's descriptions of what characterizes the socio-political practices of our time are rather "thin" when compared with the "thick" descriptions of Habermas (or even with the highly illuminating analyses of micro-practices by Foucault). If, as Rorty tells us, the legacy of the pragmatists is to call for a change of orientation on how we can best cope with the world, how we should live our lives so that we can "combine private fulfillment, self-realization, with public morality, a concern with justice," then this demands a critical analysis of the *conflicts* of the social and cultural practices that shape our lives. (Bernstein 1986: 88–89)

To what extent is Bernstein vulnerable to his own critique? To what extent has he failed to put forward a "thick" historical narrative, such as those of Marx, de Beauvoir, and Du Bois, that engages the complexities of politics and culture (West 1993: 127)? This is another way of asking the question, what does the pragmatism of Alain Locke have to do with Bernstein? Locke was an African American philosopher. A student of Josiah Royce, he was also influenced by the pragmatism of William James. He tried to address, pragmatically, the problem of white supremacy and racial identity at the beginning of the twentieth century. "If many of Locke's insights derive from his pragmatism, his lectures [on race] present a strand of pragmatist thought that differs importantly from the mainstream of the movement" (Harris 1999: 17). While he shared Kallen's, Bourne's, and Dewey's interest in regulating group difference in twentieth-century America, he did not share their understanding of what this meant. For the problem, as they saw it, was that "of harmoniously orchestrating the cultural differences of immigrant groups, a view largely irrelevant to Negroes and to the struggle against racism" (Harris 1999: 17). In contrast, "Locke understood group difference in the light of power, domination, and political economy. Thus, unlike the pragmatist mainstream," he realized that cultural identity was double edged (Harris 1999: 17). It might cut against interests of a dominated group, but it could cut in favor of their interests as well. "Locke represents, in sum, another pragmatism" (Harris 1999: 17).

Since Locke's pioneering diagnostic efforts, white supremacy has undergone many metamorphoses. And yet this distinctively American problem remains a problem about which pragmatists and other American philosophers—Royce, Du Bois, Locke, and Cornel West excluded—have been strangely and scandalously silent. We are still silent. Can Bernstein's Deweyan pragmatism help us deal with the "American Dilemma" of white supremacy, with perhaps the most persistent and insistent problem of men and women on the eve and at the beginning of the third millennium? And what about other problems? If we pragmatists, as Nancy Fraser observes, are to avoid a charge, which is too often true, of soft pedaling "the 'hard facts' of power and domination," which hide in a soupy pluralism and in the thin broth of an imaginary holism, then what kind of inquiry must we pursue (Harris 1999: 4–5)? What are the special responsibilities of philosopher-critics in a powerful and privileged nation-state such as ours? How does what we do as philosopher-critics relate to the international division of labor, power, and status, especially when strategies for dealing with this problem often conflict with efforts to address the same kind of divisions at home? These are difficult questions. That we ask such questions is a measure of Bernstein's success. He has raised our expectations (a great achievement) and given us much to think about.

Notes

1. Nancy Fraser is among the most insightful and provocative of the politically oriented pragmatists. See her article "Another Pragmatism: Alain Locke, Critical 'Race' Theory, and the Politics of Culture," in *The Critical Pragmatism of Alain Locke*, ed. Leonard Harris (Lanham, MD: Rowman & Littlefield, 1999), 3, 18.

2. Perhaps I exaggerate. According to Bernstein, in "*Heidegger's Silence?: Ethōs and Technology* it is important to realize that Heidegger's narrative of the epochal history of Being which has culminated in the holding sway of *Gestell* is not simply a story of decline—even though there is a powerful strand in his thinking that tempts us to read him in this way. To give in to this temptation is to misread him." See Richard Bernstein, *The New Constellation* (Cambridge, MA: MIT Press, 1992), 116. Bernstein is undoubtedly correct. Heidegger's narrative of decline, like the Christian story of the Fall that it mimics, is subservient to a story of redemption. Heidegger's story is about the grandeur of *Dasein*, of mortals, which has been darkened and thus obscured by the essence of technology.

3. Stanley Fish, in *The Trouble with Principle* (Cambridge, MA: Harvard University Press, 1999), skewers what he regards as Bernstein's Habermasian view. See the chapter "Truth and Toilets."

4. See David Farrell Krell's introduction to "The Question Concerning Technology" in *Martin Heidegger: Basic Writings*, ed. David Farell Krell (New York: HarperCollins, 1993), 1–35. Also see William Lovitt's introduction to Martin Heidegger, in *The Question Concerning Technology and Other Essays*, ed. William Lovitt (New York: Harper and Row, 1977), xiii–xxxix.

5. In May 2000, the German government renamed a military base—formerly named in honor of General Guenther Ruedel, who had long been held as a World War II hero—in honor of Anton Schmidt. This is one more step in Germany's effort to accept responsibility for the Nazi Holocaust.

6. *Moses and Monotheism* is the usual translation of this title. Bernstein regards his translation as more accurate.

7. Compare this analysis, in which Christianity's rivalry with Judaism exemplifies mimetic desire, with Rene Girard's claim (1977, 1986, 1987) that Christianity overcomes this violence-inducing desire.

8. The rest of the passage from which I take this quotation reads: "I will not list these trees which in Europe people an immense black forest, I will not count the species. For essential reasons, the presentation of them defies tabular layout. In their bushy taxonomy,

they would be the names of religions, philosophies, political regimes, economic structures, religious or academic institutions. In short, what is just as confusedly called culture, or the world spirit" (Jacques Derrida, *Of Spirit: Heidegger and the Question*, trans. Geoffrey Bennington and Rachel Bowlby [Chicago: University of Chicago Press, 1986], 109–10).

9. See Sigmund Freud, "The Uncanny," in *The Standard Edition of the Complete Psychological Works of Sigmund Freud*, ed. James Strachey (London: The Hogarth Press and the Institute of Psycho-Analysis, 1955), vol. 17, 217–52.

10. Rorty's liberalism is evident in many texts. Among the most explicit are "Postmodern Bourgeois Liberalism," in *Objectivity, Relativism, and Truth: Philosophical Papers, Vol. 1* (New York: Cambridge University Press, 1991), 197–202, "The Priority of Democracy to Philosophy," in *Objectivity, Relativism, and Truth: Philosophical Papers, Vol. 1* (New York: Cambridge University Press, 1991), 175–96, and *Achieving Our Country: Leftist Thought in Twentieth Century America* (Cambridge, MA: Harvard University Press, 1999).

11. For a powerful example of how ideology perverts liberal principles, see Franz Hinkelammert, *Ideological Weapons of Death: A Theological Critique of Capitalism* (1986).

REFERENCES

Arendt, Hannah, 1983. *Eichmann in Jerusalem: A report on the banality of evil.* New York: Penguin USA.

Bernstein, Richard J., 1986. *Philosophical profiles.* Philadelphia: University of Pennsylvania Press.

———. 1992. *The new constellation: The ethical-political horizons of modernity/postmodernity.* Cambridge, MA: MIT Press.

———. 1996. *Hannah Arendt and the Jewish question.* Cambridge, MA: MIT Press.

———. 1998. *Freud and the legacy of Moses.* Cambridge, U.K.: Cambridge University Press.

Derrida, Jacques. 1986. *Of spirit: Heidegger and the question.* Trans. Geoffrey Bennington and Rachel Bowlby. Chicago: University of Chicago Press.

Dewey, John. 1981. *The philosophy of John Dewey.* Ed. John J. McDermott. Chicago: University of Chicago Press.

Feenberg, Andrew. 1999. *Questioning technology.* London: Routledge.

Fish, Stanley. 1999. *The trouble with principle.* Cambridge, MA: Harvard University Press.

Fraser, Nancy. 1999. Another pragmatism: Alain Locke, critical race theory and the politics of culture. In *The critical pragmatism of Alain Locke*, ed. Leonard Harris. Lanham, MD: Rowman & Littlefield.

Freud, Sigmund. 1955. The uncanny. In *The standard edition of the complete psychological works of Sigmund Freud*, ed. James Strachey, vol. 17, 217–52. London: The Hogarth Press and the Institute of Psycho-Analysis.

———. 1961. *Civilization and its discontents.* The standard edition. New York: W.W. Norton & Company.

———. 1967. *Moses and monotheism.* Trans. Katherine Jones. New York: Vintage Books.

———. 1995. *The basic writings of Sigmund Freud.* Trans. and ed. A. A. Brill. New York: The Modern Library.

Girard, Rene. 1977. *Violence and the sacred.* Trans. Patrick Gregory. Baltimore, MD: Johns Hopkins University Press.

———. 1986. *The scapegoat.* Trans. Yvonne Freccero. Baltimore, MD: Johns Hopkins University Press.

———. 1987. *Things hidden since the foundation of the world.* Trans. Thomas Bann. Stanford: Stanford University Press.

Hall, David L. 1995. *Richard Rorty: Prophet and poet of the new pragmatism.* Albany: State University of New York Press.

Heidegger, Martin. 1977. *The question concerning technology and other essays.* Ed. William Lovitt. New York: Harper and Row.

———. 1993. *Martin Heidegger: Basic writings.* Ed. David Farrell Krell. New York: HarperCollins.

Hinkelammert, Franz. 1986. *Ideological weapons of death: A theological critique of capitalism.* Maryknoll, NY: Orbis Books.

Marx, Karl. 1978. *The Marx-Engels reader.* Ed. Robert C. Tucker. W. W. Norton and Company.

Paul, Robert A. 1996. *Moses and civilization.* New Haven, CT: Yale University Press.

Rorty, Richard. 1991. *Objectivity, relativism, and truth: Philosophical papers, vol. 1.* New York: Cambridge University Press.

———. 1999a. *Achieving our country: Leftist thought in twentieth century America.* Cambridge, MA: Harvard University Press.

———. 1999b. *Philosophy and social hope.* New York: Penguin Books.

Rose, Gillian. 1993. Of Derrida's spirit. In *Of Derrida, Heidegger, and spirit,* ed. David Wood, 56–72. Evanston, IL: Northwestern University Press.

West, Cornel. 1989. *The American evasion of philosophy: A genealogy of pragmatism.* Madison: University of Wisconsin Press.

———. 1993. *Keeping faith.* New York: Routledge.

Richard J. Bernstein's Response to William D. Hart

When Warren Frisina and Sheila Davaney initially approached me about having a symposium dedicated to my work, I was at once flattered and a bit apprehensive. Frequently such symposia (especially when the author is present) turn into "polite" occasions for praising an author for his or her virtues and glossing over serious faults. My first reaction upon reading the papers delivered at the symposium was to cross out all references to "Bernstein," to substitute the pronoun "I," and to publish the articles under my own name! I was originally impressed—and continue to be impressed—by the hermeneutic sensitivity of the authors. They have made a very serious effort to understand what I was saying—to understand me better than I understand myself, to see connections in my work that I was hardly aware of—and to locate fault lines. I learned a great deal about myself, and about how different aspects of my writings are related to each other. The deepest desire of any writer—at least *this* one—is to be understood, even when objections are raised. This collection of articles eminently succeeds in that task. I have always believed that the first and most difficult task is to try to understand what is being said and why—or to use a Hegelian turn of phrase—to elicit the "truth" in what is being said. This is the necessary condition for any fruitful dialogue and critique. And this is what I have sought to practice in my writing on a wide range of thinkers and problems.

William Hart illustrates the intellectual virtues that I admire in his chapter "Theses on Bernstein." He ranges over a great deal of my work—from my critical encounters with Arendt, Freud, Heidegger, Derrida, and

Rorty to my understanding of pragmatism. His characterizations of my views are both fair and judicious. I have never dealt directly with Stanley Fish and his criticisms of fallibilism, but Hart articulates the very objection that I would make against Fish. Fish confuses what may be the possible or the actual state of mind of someone who may (or may not) be able and willing to criticize and revise her or his beliefs "with the relative, incremental, and cumulative effects of fallibilism as a social practice." Peirce originally came up with the idea of fallibilism because he was acutely aware of how tenaciously we—as *individuals*—cling to our most cherished ideas and commitments. Peirce and the pragmatists have always understood what they are fighting against—the desire to cling to security, certainty, and unquestioned authority. This is why a self-critical community of inquirers plays such a fundamental role in Peirce's—and the pragmatists'—understanding of inquiry. When we witness the growing attractiveness of forms of fanaticism and uncritical fundamentalism that are so appealing (whether these fundamentalisms are Christian, Jewish, Islamic, or secular), then the ethical-political project of developing pragmatic fallibilistic *practices* becomes even more urgent and demanding. Fallibilism can sound "pious" when we ignore the deep and dangerous tendency of human beings to hold on to what they *take* to be unquestioned truths. Clinging to absolutes is not only epistemologically misguided, it is politically dangerous. Freud teaches us the difficulty of trying to live in a way that takes seriously the unavoidable contingencies and ambiguities of everyday life. One of the great insights of Louis Menand's *The Metaphysical Club* is to grasp how much of the pragmatic fallibilistic spirit was developed in reaction to the terrible consequences of the clinging to absolutes that was so characteristic of the mentality of the Civil War. Fallibilism is not merely a doctrine about the character of human knowledge and inquiry. It is primarily an ethical-political orientation. Furthermore, I fully share the fundamental conviction of my good friends Richard Rorty and Hilary Putnam that there is nothing incompatible about having strong and deep commitments, and advocating a thoroughgoing fallibilism. Getting beyond the Cartesian Anxiety means that the strength of one's commitments—even being prepared to die for one's ideals—has nothing to do with epistemological certainty and with a craving for absolutes.

Finally, I would like to deal with Hart's "gentle criticism." Frankly, I think he is a bit too gentle. He opens his chapter by referring to the broad sense of the pragmatic tradition invoked by Cornel West—one that includes in this tradition W. E. B. Du Bois, the famous student of William

James, and Alain Locke, who was so important for the Harlem Renaissance. I agree with Hart that there has been a tendency to marginalize such figures when dealing with the pragmatic tradition. Doing so impoverishes our understanding of pragmatism. I also agree with Nancy Fraser that there is not *one* pragmatism, but several, and that "we better know which of them we want to revive." But there is a much more serious criticism that can and should be raised against the pragmatic thinkers when this is limited to such "canonical" figures as Peirce, James, Dewey, and Mead. Dewey and Mead were most directly concerned with social issues, and with taking seriously the task of the thinker to illuminate and guide social reform. But it is striking how little attention they paid to what was—and still is—the most intractable social question in the United States—the question of race. Universal democratic education, the status of immigrant populations, the need for union representation, and even poverty and economic reform loom much larger in their thinking than proposals about eliminating racism. Of course, there is plenty of evidence that pragmatists were not indifferent to issues of racial discrimination and the need for fostering practices of democratic tolerance. But racism—in all of its ugly forms—was never fully thematized. This has been a blind spot, and it is important that it should be noted and sharply criticized. A pragmatic orientation is not a set of dogmas. It is an orientation that invites and requires self-criticism. It is important that others who take pragmatism seriously should face the tangled questions of race and racism better than the classical pragmatic thinkers. But we should not neglect the resources in the pragmatic tradition for confronting these problems. We should not forget that one of the sources of inspiration for the early civil rights movement and the famous Port Huron Statement was Dewey's radical participatory democratic idea. His unwavering faith in a democracy is one that includes *all* human beings. It is still relevant today as a normative horizon—or, as he would phrase it, "a moral way of life" that ought to be dedicated to eliminating racism. Pragmatists should be sensitive to their blind spots and weaknesses. And there is certainly a pragmatic need today to find fresh ways to think about, and to combat, the entrenched forms of racism and its pernicious social consequences.

References

Menand, Louis. 2001. *The metaphysical club: A story of ideas in America.* New York: Farrar, Straus, and Giroux.

Engaged Pluralism

Between Alterity and Sociality

Vincent Colapietro

The Question of Pluralism

Richard J. Bernstein's distinguished career exemplifies in a truly singular way what he identified in "Pragmatism, Pluralism, and the Healing of Wounds," his Presidential Address to the Eastern Division of the APA, as "engaged fallibilistic pluralism" and, more simply, "engaged pluralism" (Bernstein 1992b: 336).[1] Even earlier in "Metaphysics, Critique, and Utopia," his Presidential Address to the Metaphysical Society of America (MSA), he claimed, "Such an engaged pluralism does not mean giving up the search for truth and objectivity" (Bernstein 1988: 271). Such pluralism does however mean giving up the quest for absolutes. It also means tarrying with the negative[2] and engaging with the other (see, e.g., Bernstein 1992b, chapter 3).

The question of pluralism is first and foremost a problem of men and women in the concrete circumstances of their everyday lives (cf. Bernstein 1965: 66–67). It can be transformed into an abstract intellectual puzzle, but in its lived form this question is a human problematique of far-reaching and deep-cutting significance (cf. Bernstein 1987: 201).[3] To some extent, this problematique is rooted in the sociality of human beings, regardless of culture or epoch: it presses upon us simply by virtue of our humanity (since to be human is to be social, to live amid others) (Bernstein 1981, 1987, 1998b). To perhaps a greater extent, however, this problematique is rooted in the ethos of late modernity (see, e.g., Giddens 1990). It presses upon us, at this time, more intensely, insistently, and disconcertingly than it has asserted itself in the past.

Let me, as subsections of this opening section, (1) frame the question of pluralism in reference to the interplay of sociality and alterity and (2) present Bernstein's response to the challenge posed by this aspect of our lives, paying explicit attention to the rival forms of pluralism from which he dissociates himself. It will become evident that Bernstein's engaged pluralism is, at bottom, a critical engagement with the concrete predicament of human beings, especially as this predicament is shaped by the forces of late modernity (or nascent postmodernity).[4] One of its defining features is the extent to which this pluralism is historically inflected and informed (Bernstein 1987: 214–17; 1992b: 116; 1988: 262–64).

As a pluralist, Bernstein takes great pains to avoid reifying contingent historical conditions into necessary ontological structures. But he takes equal pains to avoid the insular relativism inherent in so many fashionable forms of the pluralistic orientation, that is, the type of historicism or relativism wherein "it is asserted that different historical periods are so different and alien to each other that they do not share anything in common" (Bernstein 1987: 214). What are, arguably, invariant facets of the human condition are honestly considered by him, but always with a sensitivity to the crucial differences made by historical epoch. This is nowhere more manifest than in Bernstein's consideration of sociality and alterity.

SOCIALITY, ALTERITY, AND DIALOGUE

Our lives are always already bound up with those of others in ways, and to a degree, largely exceeding our comprehension or appreciation. In short, our humanity is bound up with our sociality. But sociality is not even remotely another name for harmony, much less for homogeneity. It designates rather our being with others such that alterity is both a defining trait of even the most rudimentary forms of human sociality and a continuous challenge to cultivate ever more humane forms of human life. The give-and-take by which we become human is a paradigm of the encounter between self and other, since the identities of both self and other are never given fully or finally in advance of this give-and-take.[5] Rather the identities are worked out in dialogue, in the creative tension between sociality and alterity. But every creative tension is also a destructive one. Ancient rituals of symbolic sacrifice bear eloquent witness to the human necessity of divesting ourselves of something precious and even integral: self-overcoming cannot help but be, to some degree, self-destruction. The self can become through dialogue other than who she or he was, but this is typically an arduous and a painful transformation.[6] In one sense, then, alterity is given along with sociality; in another, it is achieved through an ongoing, transformative encounter of self and other.

Sociality indicates a plurality of selves and, hence, a plurality of projects, perspectives, and pursuits. It too is, at once, a datum and an achievement. For humans to be with one another involves a nexus of connections, some of these connections being constitutive of the persons enmeshed in these relationships. Sociality is a datum because natality is our origin: we are not only born of others but also utterly dependent upon them in ways that mark us for life.[7] Sociality is, however, an achievement, because the determinate forms of human togetherness sustain themselves by working against genuine plurality.

Engaged pluralism is, thus, both an acknowledgment of the inescapable plurality of human perspectives and an affirmation of the ideal of a plurality of selves standing to one another in their radical and irreducible alterity.[8] The realization or, better, approximation of this ideal demands an ongoing, transformative, critical dialogue in which sociality becomes a celebration of alterity. Yet the tolerance and openness requisite for such dialogue stops far short of endorsing anything or accepting everything. It must be, in a word, critical—discerning, discriminating, attuned to those differences that truly make a difference and thus not in the least inclined to become indiscriminate in its praise or undiscerning in its encounters with alterity. A genuine encounter with others invites and perhaps even demands an ever more discerning appreciation of alterity. Apart from such discernment, it is problematic whether the other has been encountered.

Drawing the Requisite Distinctions

In the expressions "engaged fallibilistic pluralism" and "engaged pluralism," the qualifiers (*engaged* and *fallibilistic*) are significant, for they indicate that pluralism is open to a plurality of quite different interpretations and enlisted in the service of rival orientations. Indeed, these interpretations do not necessarily cohere, just as these orientations do not necessarily coalesce. Insistence on pluralism often simply means the acceptance of the absence of such coherence or coalescence, consensus or fusion, as not only the original but also the insurmountable situation in which political actors, intellectual inquirers, and all other human beings in their various engagements are required to fight for their divergent objectives. For participants engaged in some undertaking of consequence, too quick and facile an acceptance of such "pluralism" effectively means abandonment of the undertaking. Even if the criteria and norms whereby we evaluate whether one interpretation is better than another are themselves open to conflicting interpretations and evaluations, some interpretations are better than others—even though some alternative, incommensurable interpretations continue to exert equal attraction or compel the rational assent of equally competent interpreters. Meta-interpretations (interpretations of what the process of interpretation demands or allows) are either integral parts of the open-ended, self-conscious interpretations of engaged interpreters or fifth wheels (cf. Smith 1992: 100). No matter how fast such wheels spin or how fascinating such spinning proves, they contribute nothing to the movement of thought. The possibility or (in some cases) necessity of moving from an interpretation of a given work to that of the interpretive process itself makes the question of pluralism more complex. It leaves open the most basic questions: Is this interpretation of a given text better than that interpretation? What forms of interpretation are most fruitful or insightful? What sort of training and discipline assists persons in becoming creative and insightful interpreters?

The engaged pluralist is, accordingly, committed to preserving the critical distinctions, though she or he acutely realizes that the meaning and even bases of these distinctions can never be secured once and for all. The commitment to these distinctions necessitates distinguishing the forms of pluralism from one another, since some of these forms obliterate or undermine the critical distinctions necessary for self-critical conduct (Bernstein 1988: 269–71; 1992b: 335–36). To ensure such distinctions as accuracy and inaccuracy, fidelity and infidelity, truth and falsity, other distinctions need to be drawn.

Some of these distinctions pertain to pluralism, hardly a univocal term. Thus Bernstein identifies a handful of diverse positions likely to be called by the same name; this makes evident the need for modifiers.[9] There is "a *fragmenting* pluralism where the centrifugal forces become so strong that we are only able to communicate with the small group that already shares our own biases, and no longer even experience the need to talk with others outside of this circle" (Bernstein 1992b: 335). One consequence of such pluralism is that those who are outside of this circle are judged by these insiders to be not truly engaged in a given pursuit or practice. There is also "a *flabby* pluralism where our borrowings from different orientations are little more than glib superficial poaching" (Bernstein 1992b: 335). There is, in addition, "*polemical* pluralism." This is a masked intolerance making use of pluralism (i.e., the appearance of tolerance) as a Trojan horse; once inside the walls of the city, the polemical "pluralist" sheds the (dis)guise of pluralism and advances the comprehensive truth of a single perspective. And there is *defensive* pluralism. This is to be a ruse to be left alone "to do one's own thing" without being ever in the position to be held accountable by others. It works by paying lip service to others "doing *their* own thing" while remaining convinced there is nothing valuable to be learned from them (Bernstein 1992b: 336).

The pragmatic tradition to which Bernstein appeals in his APA address and other writings embodies, however, a quite different form of philosophical pluralism than the ones just distinguished. It represents "an *engaged fallibilistic pluralism*" (Bernstein, 1992b: 336).[10] It emerges from the perspective of participants truly engaged in a practice in and through which they define themselves. Such participants cannot stand completely aloof from the practices in which they are implicated; nor can they as such participants be indifferent to the utterances of their co-participants. For the religious believer, the experimental inquirer, and the democratic citizen (to take but three examples), the cautions, criticisms, advice, and suggestions of some others carry the force of a provisional yet weighty authority. To treat these as negligible is almost always to act irresponsibly; indeed, to act responsibly means, more often than not, to act responsively to the cautions, criticisms, advice, and suggestions of other participants, at least, those equally or more competent than oneself.

Engaged pluralism entails critical dialogue. To some extent, it is but another name for such an exchange. Hence, Bernstein drives this point home when he asserts that engaged pluralism "demands an openness to what is different and other, a willingness to risk one's prejudgments, seeking for common ground without any guarantee that it will be found. It demands—and it is a strenuous demand—that one tries to be responsive to the claims of the other" (Bernstein 1988: 271). Such openness stands in marked contrast to the adversarial style of so much academic philosophy. The other is approached as an opponent or, at least, as a potential source of error or confusion. The point is not to be taken in by the other, that is, "the aim is to locate specifically what is wrong in the opponent's position, to expose its weaknesses" (Bernstein 1992b: 337). The advantages of this style do not compensate for the deafness or blindness it tends to induce: "in being primarily concerned with exposing weaknesses, with showing the absurdities in what is taken to be mistaken, we can be blind to what the other is saying and to the truth that the other is contributing to the discussion" (Bernstein 1992b: 337). In contrast to the model of adversarial confrontation, that of dialogical encounter "begins with the assumption that the other has something to say to us and to contribute to our understanding" (Bernstein 1992b: 337). This means that one's initial impulse is trying not to sniff out weaknesses and confusions but to discern the animating insights and fruitful implications of what the other is claiming. The adversarial style is most effective in avoiding error, whereas the dialogical model is most useful in approximating truth (cf. James 1956).[11] Most of even our most secure insights are only rough approximations, in principle, open to continuous revision (Bernstein 1971; cf. Peirce 1935); hence, it is always more appropriate for the engaged fallibilist to speak of the approximation, rather than the attainment, of truth.

Properly understood, there is—and must be—an agonistic dimension of dialogical encounters. Conflict is an unavoidable consequence in such encounters,[12] since honesty is one of the necessary conditions. Indeed, dialogue in Bernstein's sense is as much as anything else "a way to clarify our disagreements," a means to sharpen our comprehension of just where—and why—our thinking diverges from each other's (Bernstein 1992b: 337–38).

Let me, accordingly, take this occasion to consider one of Bernstein's questions and also one of his affirmations, in the hope of clarifying a possible disagreement. The question concerns at one level the interpretation of Peirce and at another the ideal of consensus. The affirmation concerns a task identified by Bernstein himself.

In "Metaphysics, Critique, and Utopia," Bernstein appeals to pragmatism and to Peirce in particular for insights into fallibilism. But he also raises "critical questions about Peirce's own understanding of inquiry" (at the center of this understanding being an uncompromising acknowledgment of human fallibility). Bernstein alleges, without qualification,

> Peirce does believe that ideally there will be a convergence of opinions. "We can ascertain by reasoning how things really and truly are; and any man, if he have sufficient experience and he reason enough about it, will be led to the one True conclusion"

> [Peirce 1935: 5:384]. But in the twentieth century there have been many challenges to the convergence thesis—even in scientific inquiry. Hilary Putnam, for example, claims "there is no more evidence that science converges to one final world view than there is that literature or morality converge to one final world view. . . . Frequently this lack of convergence has been viewed as a "scandal"—as a sign of a deficiency or worse—an indication of the arbitrariness of metaphysical speculation [or even scientific investigation]. But a lack of convergence need not and should not be interpreted in this manner. Our perspectives may be limited and we may never entirely rid ourselves of all our prejudices and prejudgments, but our linguistic horizons are always open to what is different and other. A lack of convergence does not lead to despair, but to a commitment to critical encounter and dialogue. (Bernstein 1988: 269)

Here Bernstein calls into question the very ideal of consensus as a constitutive norm or goal of interpretation and even investigation. He seems to do so on the basis of (or in the name of) both history and pluralism. Traditional ideals of agreement, consensus, fusion of horizons, and convergence of opinions are not everywhere desirable, much less possible. This seems incontrovertible. But questions are surely in order regarding the questioning of these ideals, if only to help us specify the contexts, reasons, and respects in which these ideals should not be allowed to animate and direct our endeavors and exchanges. In particular, the forces of advertising play a pervasive, persistent, complex, obvious, *and* subtle role in at once undermining the creditability of consensus as an ideal and fostering conformity on a truly global scale. Hence, the questioning of the ideal of consensus should not be done in abstraction from the historical circumstances in which uncoerced rational agreement is so effectively contested or discredited.[13] Indeed, the ideal of mutuality so deeply rooted in Bernstein's engaged pluralism might require an even more subtle understanding of the ideal of consensus than the one he has articulated so far. In any event, my own sense is that Peirce is better than the thinker who on many occasions made incautious claims represented by the text quoted by Bernstein. In some of Peirce's own formulations, the ideal of consensus is not a fated outcome but a regulative ideal. In turn, he explicitly identifies this ideal with hope, the refusal to succumb to the despair of ever escaping the contingencies and distortions of our biases and prejudices. The function of this ideal is to project an other against which our present understanding and knowledge will in all likelihood prove deficient.

It is also my sense that, quite apart from Peirce, the ideal of consensus plays a more pervasive and fruitful role than Bernstein's questioning allows us to discern.[14] His own questioning—his critique of this ideal—might draw its strength partly from what he not only refuses to acknowledge but also outright challenges (see, e.g., Bernstein 1992a, 834).

Let us turn from Bernstein's questioning of consensus to one of his affirmations, a point to be discussed much more briefly. He emphasizes, the task of critique (responsibly undertaken) "demands that we honestly and imaginatively articulate and defend the ideals that are the basis of critique" (Bernstein 1992a, 839). Yet this is a task that he has not carried out in sufficient depth or detail. The origin, status, and interconnections of the ideals animating and directing his own critiques of particular philosophers and social practices have been left all too implicit, though the names of humanity, agency, freedom, and a host of other ideals are robustly affirmed at certain critical junctures. Even so, more needs to be said, especially given Bernstein's own affirmation.

My own critical engagement here with the actual articulation of Bernstein's engaged pluralism is simply an attempt to trace out trajectories in his own texts. Tracing out such trajectories and working out the implications of our diverse commitments, inherited and otherwise, are definitive of the pluralism being advocated here. That is, the engaged pluralist is an implicated agent working out of diverse, intersecting histories.[15] But such agents do not only work out of such histories; by virtue of the demands, confusions, and conflicts inherent in, and truly constitutive of these defining histories, they are forced to own up to and also to work through these histories (Colapietro 2002). These histories are complexly related to one another; at times they mutually support, while at other times they destructively contest, one another.

It would be instructive to examine Bernstein's own project as an attempt to own up to and work through several of the histories in which he is implicated and by which he is defined, though hardly imprisoned. Despite his emphasis on the finitude, partiality, and fallibility of human rationality, there is on Bernstein's part a modest yet an undeniable affirmation of the capacity of rational agents to transcend, in some manner and measure, their contingent circumstances and cultural biases. This is, to be sure, a transcendence in history, not a transcendence of history. It is achieved by working through, in detail, the impasses, fixations, and *apo-*

rias so characteristic of so much of our defining histories. For example, such transcendence can be won by working through the impasse between objectivism and relativism, or the fixation on apodictic certainty, or the *aporias* generated by the indeliminable demands of reflexive criticism.[16] Let us, then, turn to a consideration of Bernstein's project precisely as an attempt to work out of two apparently disconnected histories, that of institutional philosophy in the United States and that of American Judaism.[17] But, first, let us frame this consideration in light of his understanding of critique, since this understanding underwrites his conception of philosophy and characterizes the manner in which he tries to work out of the traditions to be examined below.

Critique, Affirmation, and Acknowledgment

It is significant that in his Presidential Address to the APA ("Pragmatism, Pluralism, and the Healing of Wounds") and in his critiques of Martin Heidegger, Jürgen Habermas, Michel Foucault, and Jacques Derrida, Bernstein affirms the continuing validity of American pragmatism. His creative appropriation of insights from a wide array of analytic philosophers and European thinkers clearly bears the stamp of his pragmatic commitments. Bernstein is certainly more than a pragmatist, for his encounters with other traditions have transformed pragmatism into something other than what it has ever been—something more hermeneutically sophisticated, historically attuned, widely dialogical, deeply critical, thoroughly fallibilistic, truly tough minded, and insistently other focused than the versions of pragmatism articulated by either earlier or contemporary advocates. Bernstein's robust affirmation of the continuing vitality and relevance of pragmatism should not incline us to overlook the extent to which his dialogical pluralism has transformed, in his case, the pragmatic orientation.

In his first book, Bernstein stressed: "Dewey stands as a challenge to make philosophy relevant to the 'problems of men [and women]'" (Bernstein 1967: 175).[18] Bernstein's career is nothing less than a response to this challenge. At the same time, his manner of responding makes it clear that he feels even more intensely than Dewey the plea voiced in Dewey's own "Philosophy and Civilization." The plea implicit in this essay is made explicit at its conclusion; it is "a plea for the casting off of that intellectual timidity which hampers the wings of imagination, a plea for speculative audacity, for more faith in ideas" (Dewey 1988b: LW 3: 10). In a manner and measure unmatched by Dewey, Bernstein is a speculatively audacious philosopher. In the end, however, his conception of philosophy is very close to the one championed by Dewey.

Closely linked to this, Bernstein's conception of rationality is also akin to the one advocated by Dewey. For both thinkers, reason is above all else an interrogative, dialogical affair (cf. Colapietro 1999). There are nonetheless affirmations integral to the incessant questioning characteristic of human reason; so too there is the acknowledgment that dialogue is not always possible. These affirmations pertain to the bases of criticism and thus the task of dialogue itself. "Because our affirmations do not rest upon fixed foundations and are not gratuitous 'decisions,'" Bernstein observes in "The Resurgence of Pragmatism," "it becomes vital that they be articulated, debated, and publicly discussed" (Bernstein 1992a: 839). If our critiques undermine the authority or validity of our affirmations, then they undermine themselves. "We must recognize," Bernstein insists, "that there cannot be any critique without some sort of affirmation" (Bernstein 1992b: 318). There is no necessity to affirm fixed universal standards of critique; even so, "a focus on context, specificity, and locality does not mean we can avoid facing up to our affirmations" (Bernstein 1992b: 318). Accordingly, our critiques are responsible only when we are willing to own up to "what we are affirming when we engage in critique" (Bernstein 1992b: 318). But just as critique derives from affirmations, however unstated or unacknowledged, so our affirmations inevitably invite scrutiny and examination, at some fateful juncture. We say, for example, that in the name of security we are undertaking this military campaign or instituting these domestic safeguards, but is security truly being served by such measures and, moreover, might the ideal of security not eclipse in this case more weighty or compelling ideals? Thus both the honest critique and acknowledgment of our authorizing affirmations are required. "We need," in other words, "to maintain a vigilant *double* attitude where we are at once aware of the need for affirmation and that any affirmation can be called into question" (Bernstein 1992b: 318).

At certain critical junctures, then, it is imperative to own up to our affirmations. This cannot be accomplished in a solitary or an arbitrary way; it is rather a communal and rational endeavor. As just noted, it is vital that our affirmations be publicly expressed and defended. The necessity for dialogue in these (and, indeed, other) situations does not, however, guarantee its possibility. In some circumstances, we are forced to acknowledge that dialogue is, provisionally, impossible. This acknowledgment concerns a candid assessment of the actual circumstances in which mutual interrogation is destined to take place. In the name of dialogue itself, it might be necessary to break off the conversation or even to exclude certain interlocutors.

> Sometimes what is required to communicate—to establish a reciprocal "we"—is rupture and break—a *refusal* to accept the common ground laid down by the "other." It is extremely easy to pay lip service to recognizing and respecting genuine plurality, difference, otherness, but nothing perhaps is more difficult than to achieve this in practice—and such practice is *never* completely stable or permanent. It is a self-deceptive illusion to think that the "other" can always be heard in a friendly [or even barely civil] dialogue. (Bernstein 1992b: 52)

There is nothing either naïve or fatalistic, facile or nihilistic, about the vision of rationality being adumbrated and indeed exemplified by Bernstein's various critical engagements with distinct historical figures and diverse intellectual movements. Just as his fallibilism is crucially different from any species of dogmatic skepticism, his contextualism far removed from any version of reductive relativism, and his pragmatism quite distant from any stripe of crude instrumentalism or superficial practicalism, so his dialogical conception of rationality stands at a far distance from any sentimental endorsement of dialogue or romantic appeal to *logos.* Bernstein is not only a speculatively audacious philosopher, he is also an indefatigably critical thinker whose own affirmations and acknowledgments, assertions and arguments, are always, in principle, open to review and thus to revision, even to rejection. No better evidence can be offered for his engaged pluralism.

"Knowledge is in the end based," Wittgenstein contends, "on acknowledgment" (Wittgenstein 1972: 378). This is likely true of much else besides knowledge. In any event, the upshot of this section is that, for Bernstein, both our own affirmations and critiques depend upon a certain form of acknowledgment—a willingness to own up to and then to work through the affirmations implicit in our critiques and the flaws inherent in our affirmations.[19] An aspect of this task is that of owning up to the traditions in and through which one has forged one's sensibility, character, and intelligence. Reason as an interrogative, dialogical capacity is born of being impelled to respond to the questions of others and, more basically, to take into account the insistent presence and irreducible otherness of other selves (cf. Bernstein 1992b: 72). Bernstein agrees with Derrida (and thus disagrees with Levinas) that "if the other was not recognized as ego, its entire alterity collapses"; "the other as alter ego [as other self] signifies the other as other, irreducible to *my* ego, precisely because it is an ego, because it has the form of the ego" (quoted in Bernstein 1992b, 72). Owning up to the otherness of others often invites the challenge of owning up to the alterity within the ego itself (cf. Kristeva 1991). But it always demands coming to terms with the social and thus historical practices, the intergenerational and hence traditional activities, incorporated in our psyches in the form of affective, cognitive, and conative habits. In brief, it means owning up to the traditions that, in a sense, own us (cf. Gadamer 1975: 324; Ricoeur 1980).

TRADITION, CONTINUITY, AND REPRESSION

Bernstein's writings are, in effect, reports of his critical engagements with diverse perspectives, philosophical and otherwise. Near (perhaps at) the center of these engagements is a concern for tradition somewhat unusual for so secular a philosopher. For my purposes, two texts in particular are especially pertinent for exploring this aspect of his project. One of these texts is an essay, the other a monograph. The former concerns a philosophical movement, the latter an unsurpassed investigator of the human psyche. The movement is one that is distinctively American, the text "The Resurgence of Pragmatism." The investigator is one who is problematically Jewish, the text *Freud and the Legacy of Moses* (Bernstein 1998a). At the center of "The Resurgence of Pragmatism" is a re-narration of American pragmatism in which Willard von Orman Quine, Wilfrid Sellars, Donald Davidson, and several others are deftly woven into the complex tapestry of a still unfinished work (Bernstein 1992a, 817). At the center of Bernstein's monograph on Freud's own monograph about Freud and monotheism is a meditation on the actuality and dynamics of tradition, religious and otherwise.

Whereas the author of "The Resurgence of Pragmatism" is animated by an irenic and synechistic impulse driving toward showing the *continuity* between, on the one side, Peirce, James, Dewey, and Mead, and on the other, Quine, Sellars, Davidson, Putnam, and Rorty, that of *Freud and the*

Legacy of Moses is more attentive to rupture, disruption, and even repression. But there is for Bernstein in both texts a keen appreciation of the extent to which the continuity of any tradition can never be preserved or recovered by a simple return to founding figures or originary events. Indeed, founding figures such as Moses might be figural fabrications. This is partly the burden of Sigmund Freud's *Moses and Monotheism.*

Despite the appearance of irrevocable rupture, the dominant tradition of academic philosophy in the United States, even when analytic paradigms exerted their most exclusionary influence, was more vitally and intimately continuous with earlier philosophical traditions, in particular, classical American pragmatism, than any side realized. So, at least, Bernstein argues; and it is significant that narration is integral to the argument. Despite the appearance of historical continuity, the persistence of Judaism is a site wherein what Freud identified as "the return of the repressed" is inescapable. Thus this persistence depends on the ability of the members of a tradition in some manner both to reenact the traumas being repressed *and* to work through some of the more debilitating or destructive consequences of such repression. "What is communicated from one generation to the next," Bernstein stresses, "is not only what is explicitly stated or what is set forth by precept and example, but also what is unconsciously communicated" (Bernstein 1998a: 59). This makes of any tradition a complex interplay of conscious and unconscious memory traces (see, e.g., Bernstein 1998a: 58). In turn, this makes of our task—that of comprehending the traditions in and through which our sensibility, conceptuality, and thus psyches have taken shape—nothing less than psychoanalysis, in some sense (but a sense akin to that of Freud's project, however different in detail, rhetoric, and objective). Quite simply, "[u]nless we pay attention to these dynamics of transmission, we will never understand the receptivity (and resistance) to a living tradition" (Bernstein 1998a: 59). Bernstein goes so far as to assert, "What is most vital in a tradition is not just what is *preconscious,* but what is genuinely *unconscious.* An adequate understanding of tradition requires us to account for the gaps and ruptures in the transmission of tradition" (Bernstein 1998a: 63).

The manifest ruptures and gaps in academic philosophy in the United States are, at this juncture in our essentially contentious history (histories?), less important than the almost imperceptible continuity between analytic philosophy and American pragmatism. The remarkable continuity of the Jewish people as a self-conscious community committed to preserving in ceremonial memory its founding figures and originary events should not divert our critical attention from the repressed traumas partly animating and structuring the intergenerational renewal crucial for any living tradition.

I have misgivings about Bernstein's re-narration of academic philosophy in the United States. Principally, my reasons are that too much past bullying is covered over, and too much persisting marginalization of those working outside of the analytic tradition is left unchallenged. It is time to heal wounds, but many philosophical pluralists in both the broadly intellectual and narrowly ideological sense are still suspicious that the acceptance of pluralism by analysts is purely strategic. That is, it is an example of what Bernstein calls "defensive pluralism." Unquestionably, the word "pluralist" in the mouths of many academic philosophers who define themselves in reference to classical American figures or Continental authors is also disingenuous, since they mean by this term anything but analytic philosophy. To stop short of such a vital and central tradition of contemporary philosophy is to betray one's lack of pluralism. But institutional power and prestige are still today distributed unevenly in ways advantageous to analytic philosophy, but certainly not its rival traditions. Distinctions are required. Analytic philosophy as a philosophical tradition is to be valued and extended, but as an academic ideology operating to denigrate or delegitimate alternative traditions, it is to be exposed and contested. Bernstein's re-narration pays insufficient attention to this crucial distinction. The attraction of philosophers in the United States to such thinkers as Peirce, James, Dewey, on the one side, and Heidegger, Derrida, on the other, is enough to disqualify these individuals from serious attention by "mainstream" philosophers.

Our attractions are revealing, so it is not surprising that they serve so often as the basis for judgment, dismissive and otherwise.[20] At the outset of *Freud and the Legacy of Moses,* Bernstein recalls, "Freud was deeply attracted to the figure of Moses." This attraction eventually turned into something more arresting and insistent: "In his final years, he [Freud] was literally obsessed with 'the great man' Moses and his vexed legacy—a legacy that is rooted in the past, shapes the present, and extends its influence to the future" (Bernstein 1998a: ix). It would hardly be warranted to suggest that, in turn, Bernstein is obsessed with Freud and *his* vexed legacy of psychoanalytic theory. But it does seem reasonable to register his fascination with Freud. Moreover, it is relevant to our inquiry to follow out the analogy one step farther: Bernstein's critical engagement with Freud's writings bears a strong resemblance to Freud's psychoanalytic interpretation of Moses's traditional status and historical actuality. In Bernstein's judgment, "the most important part of the story that Freud tells [in *Moses and Monotheism*] has to do with his struggle to articulate what he [Freud] passionately believed to be the essence of (his) Jewishness, the key to Jewish survival, and the deep psychological reasons for anti-Semitism" (Bernstein 1998a: ix).

In order for Freud to come more fully to terms with himself, with his singular psyche in its convoluted depth, he had to come more directly to terms with the tradition of Judaism and thus with the figure of Moses. Apparently, something analogous holds for Bernstein himself: in order for him to come more honestly to terms with his dialogical self, he had to come more explicitly to terms with the tradition of Judaism. But in his case this confrontation is mediated by the figure of Freud. There can be, at least for this philosopher, no simple return to even a living tradition encompassing some of the most brilliant minds in human history. The return (if this is even the right word here) must be circuitous. The movement of Bernstein's thought circles through Freud's own circling re-narration of who Moses was and, even given its conclusion (Moses was most likely not a Jew but an Egyptian), what Moses yet means for the tradition of Judaism. In a sense, the figure of Moses upon this retelling stands not only for the hidden other but also the repressed identity of the agonistic other who in time has become an exemplary ancestor (cf. Kristeva 1991: 181, 192).

Bernstein takes Freud in *Moses and Monotheism* to be answering a question Freud "posed for himself in the Hebrew translation of *Totem and Taboo*" (Bernstein 1998a: ix). There Freud confesses he not only abandoned the religion of his ancestors but also is estranged from what he takes to be the spirit of any religion. In light of this, he presses upon himself the question, what then is left to you that is truly Jewish? While Freud's answer is perhaps surprising, it is unquestionably instructive: "A very great deal, and probably its very essence" (quoted in Bernstein 1998a: x). Bernstein's hypothesis is that Freud's answer to the question of his Jewishness and, hence, to the question regarding the "essence" of Jewishness itself is to be found in Freud's *Moses and Monotheism* or, as Bernstein prefers to translate the original title of the German work, *The Man Moses and the Monotheistic Religion* (Bernstein 1998a: x).

As already indicated, I take Bernstein in *Moses and the Legacy of Freud* to be addressing the question of his own Jewishness but in a manner self-consciously mediated by Freud. Matters are, however, even more complex than this. For not only is Bernstein's critical engagement with the Jewish tradition mediated by the father of psychoanalysis but also his return to Freud is mediated or, at least, conditioned by Yosef Hayim Yerushalmi's *Freud's Moses: Judaism Terminable and Interminable* (Bernstein 1998a: x). Freud's reading and critique of Judaism are thereby placed in dialogical tension with Yerushalmi's interpretation and criticisms of Freud. Bernstein is convinced that just as "Freud does not do full justice to the meaning of Judaism and Jewishness" (Bernstein 1998a: xi), so "Yerushalmi obscures and distorts some of Freud's most creative and fertile suggestions" (Bernstein 1998a: x; cf. 91). Even so, Bernstein's *Freud and the Legacy of Moses* concludes with a dialogical missive to the author of *Freud's Moses,* the final chapter of Bernstein's monograph entitled "'Dialogue' with Yerushalmi." It takes the form of a letter, beginning with the salutation "Dear Yosef Hayim Yerushalmi." Bernstein explains this rhetorical strategy and, in particular, its somewhat ironic connection to the structure of Yerushalmi's own book:

> Yerushalmi's *Freud's Moses* . . . concludes with a "Monologue with Freud." Yerushalmi acknowledges that this monologue is a "fiction." He adopts this rhetorical strategy because he feels "an inner need to speak to you directly and to have an audience eavesdrop, as it were" (Yerushalmi 1991: 81). I have appropriated a variation of this strategy in order to sharpen my differences with Yerushalmi's interpretation of *The Man Moses and the Monotheistic Religion.* Of course, the Freud that Yerushalmi addresses in his "monologue" is dead, but Yerushalmi is very much alive. My primary intention is not to criticize Yerushalmi, but rather to bring out the full power as well as the challenge presented by Freud's interpretation of Moses, monotheism, and the essential character of the Jewish people. (Bernstein 1992b: 139, note 1)

Bernstein's rhetorical strategy and its underlying motivation are, however, related to the Talmudic *le-didakh,* far more an existential stance than a discursive pose. In Freud's Moses, Yerushalmi explains that *le-didakh* (an Aramaic word meaning "according to you") more amply "signifies that for the sake of the discussion and its effort to ascertain the truth, one party will provisionally accept the assumptions of the other, and they will go on from there" (Yerushalmi 1991: 83). He offers this explanation in the context of his "Monologue with Freud." This makes of the concluding chapter of *Freud's Moses* something more than a monologue, for the voice of Freud is not only allowed but also invited and encouraged to articulate and defend what, according to you "Dear and most highly esteemed Professor Freud," is the truth about Moses and, by implication, about Judaism ("Moses was not a Hebrew but an Eygptian. He learned his monotheism from Ikhnaton. He gave the new religion to our forefathers, who subsequently rebelled and killed him" [Yerushalmi 1991: 84]). Yerushalmi is in effect saying to Freud (and the tone throughout this chapter is personal and respectful): According to you, Moses was an Egyptian and Judaism a repression of his identity. Let us provisionally accept this, for the sake of ascertaining the truth—for the sake of a dialogical encounter in which irreducibly different voices can be heard in their radical alterity.

Just as Bernstein's *Freud and the Legacy of Moses* concludes with his "'Dialogue' with Yerushalmi," so this chapter itself ends with a recollection of what binds the participants in this dialogue into a community, however fragile or provisional. Specifically, it ends with a recollection of *le-didakh* and, in this connection, with Yerushalmi's insistence that his interpretation of Freud's argument is preparatory and preliminary:

> I have tried to take seriously [Bernstein stresses in the concluding paragraph to this concluding chapter, quoting here in full] your declaration that *Freud's Moses* is a "prolegomenon," and that your primary purpose has been to open a serious discussion, not to close it. There is, and can be, no finality to agonistic but friendly *le-didakh.* It is itself a symbol of the survival and hope of the Jewish tradition. (Bernstein 1998a: 116)

But, in a modified form, the advocacy of dialogue interrupted but interminable is also the symbol of the vitality and hope of the Socratic tradition.

Hence, Bernstein (like Freud) embodies his own Jewishness in a life self-critically taking the form of a personal, critical address—according to you (*le-didakh*)—though his principal interlocutors are not Talmudic scholars or rabbinical commentators but philosophical inquirers, most often ones only distantly concerned with religious questions, at least in their traditional theological form. For example, Bernstein in *Praxis and Action: Contemporary Philosophies of Human Activity* (1971) is, in effect, saying: *according* to Hegel and Marx, Kierkegaard and Sartre, Peirce and Dewey, Charles Taylor and a host of other analytic philosophers, human action is to be interpreted and evaluated in this way. Such a critical engagement with diverse perspectives is indispensable to glimpsing whatever truth is accessible to us, but only when each approach is sympathetically inhabited and extended (i.e., only when each one is provisionally accepted as an indispensable intellectual resource).

THE QUESTION OF HOPE

The point of disagreement between Bernstein and Yerushalmi regarding Freud's relation to Judaism concerns, at bottom, the question of hope (West 1993). Yerushalmi judges Freud to have abandoned hope and thereby any link to Judaism. But Bernstein takes this to be a misinterpretation. However tempered and tutored by the harsh events leading up to 1939, the year of Freud's death as well as Hitler's invasions of Bohemia, Moravia, and Poland, there is in Freud's psyche an inextinguishable vibrancy and vitality. These traits are intimately connected to an abiding faith in experimental intelligence and, moreover, to the hope that the exercise of such intelligence would be ameliorative and, indeed, reparative. The felt need to repair a broken world and to rebuild amid haunting ruins gives some weight to Freud's claim that, even in his secularity, he remained a Jew. What remained of his Jewishness might arguably be nothing less than the essence of Jewishness (Bernstein 1998a: x), the willingness to stand firm in one's own tradition *as a means of* embracing the other, for the sake of protecting concrete others in their irreducible alterity.[21] As a very old man, ravaged by cancer and living in exile, Freud's vitality should still be sensed. After meeting him very near his death, Virginia Woolf wrote in her diary on Sunday, January 29, 1939:

> Dr Freud gave me a narcissus [sometimes a flower is not just a flower!]. Was sitting in a great library with little statues at a large scrupulously tidy shiny table. We like patients on chairs. A screwed up shrunk very old man: with a monkey's light eyes, paralyzed spasmodic movements, inarticulate: but alert. On Hitler. Generation before the poison will work out. About his books. Fame? I was infamous rather than famous. . . . Difficult talk. An interview. Daughter and Martin helped. Immense potential, I mean an old fire now flickering. When we left he took up the stand What are *you* going to do? The English—war. (Woolf 1984: 202)

This is hardly the portrait of a man dying of and, simply, in despair. It is the glimpse of a man enduring unabated physical pain and emotional anguish, but challenging others to carry on the fight against Hitler. On this score, then, Bernstein's judgment seems more accurate and fair than Yerushalmi's assessment.

For traditional religious believers, to be Godless is to be hopeless. Despair is from their perspective truly a sickness unto death; it makes of life a hardly living death. Since the Godless can so effectively mask such despair from themselves, one of the tasks of defenders of religions such as Judaism and Christianity is to unmask these strategies of self-deception. But for Godless Jews such as Freud, the question of hope is separable from the question of God, though not from thorny questions concerning humanizing traditions. Hence, in response to Yerushalmi's charge, Bernstein asserts:

> This is not "hopelessness," and it certainly is not "un-Jewish." In the spirit of the prophetic tradition that Freud so admired, it is an expression of a profound hope. Indeed, if I were asked, while standing on one foot, to say what *The Man Moses and the Monotheistic Religion* is about, I would not hesitate to say it is about hope and the promise of Jewish survival. (Bernstein 1998a: 116)

But if hope is given to us, it is not given for us. We must be hopeful for those who are destined to inherit the world we have ourselves inherited and, as the responsibility of receiving this behest, we have repaired—or failed to make more humane and hospitable. The human world is ineluctably a broken world; accordingly, our abiding task is reparation. Of even more pressing concern, we must be hopeful for those who are despairing. It is significant, then, that Bernstein in his impassioned defense of Sigmund Freud quotes the dark eloquence of Walter Benjamin: *Nur um der Hoffnungslosen willen ist uns die Hoffnung gegeben* (It is only for the sake of those who are without hope that hope is given to us) (Bernstein 1998a: 115).

For Bernstein no less than Freud, the question of hope is bound up with that of rationality. The rage against reason so characteristic of so much contemporary thought expresses a pervasive *Stimmung*. The mood is partly one of suspicions regarding the innocence and neutrality of the historically accredited forms of human rationality. These suspicions are, ironically, reasonable: given the histories in and through which reason has defined itself, we have grounds for being suspicious of covert complicities with dark forces and destructive tendencies. So, Bernstein does not hesitate to stress:

> We must learn again and again to hear what Weber, Adorno, Heidegger, and their successors are telling and showing us. But we must resist the temptation to be seduced by "arguments" of necessity, destiny, and ineluctable decline. We must resist those essentialist stories [especially when disguised as historicist narratives] of the history of Western rationality that see it as only ending in hidden forms of violence and despairing nihilism. For then we would surely be enclosed in the darkness of forgetfulness and betrayal. (Bernstein 1992b: 52)

But how can we most effectively resist such stories and avoid such enclosure? Tellingly, Bernstein's suggestion is a recollection of what one of his own most valued interlocutors claims: "communicative reason operates in history as an avenging force" (quoted in 1992b: 52). As Jürgen Habermas also states, reason has "a stubbornly transcending power, because it is renewed with each act of unconstrained understanding" and with "each moment of living together in solidarity" (Bernstein 1992b: 52–53).

But this makes of communicative (or dialogical) reason a tradition, an intergenerational practice renewed in circumstances inevitably threatening its distortion, disfigurement, and even destruction. In reference to Hans-Georg Gadamer, Bernstein seems to endorse the hermeneutic conception of human rationality. He too appears to hold, "Reason itself becomes effective when it is historically embodied in tradition" (Bernstein 1998a: 62; cf. Smith 1992: 86). If human rationality is an individual capacity, it is because such rationality is a deep-rooted cultural inheritance and an open-ended reflexive project.

Richard J. Bernstein's critical engagement with diverse perspectives and rival approaches is, in my judgment, undertaken principally to bring one or another aspect of dialogical reason into sharp focus. The darkness of contemporary history does not convince him of the inevitability of nihilistic despair. One of his most characteristic and forceful affirmations is the pragmatic upshot of his nuanced reflection on "The Rage against Reason": "A *practical* commitment to the avenging *energeia* of communicative reason is the basis—perhaps the only honest basis—for hope" (Bernstein 1992b: 53). Since dialogue is not always possible, violence is not always avoidable. But it is infantile to suppose that the occasional unavoidability of violence proves the utter impotence of reason. Like all other things human and historical, rationality is broken. In virtually all of its actual manifestations, it is fractured and fragmented, disfigured and maimed. Since the work of reparation is inescapable, the need for dialogue is interminable. Bernstein's acceptance of the lack of any finality to the "agonistic but friendly *le-didakh*" is not in the least contradicted by his affirmations, especially since one of his innermost affirmations is the interminable process of reflexive criticism. Hence, "we must continually ask, 'What precisely is being criticized—and critique in the name of what?' This demands that we honestly and imaginatively articulate and defend the ideals that are the basis of critique" (Bernstein 1992a: 839). Of course, the bases of our critiques are themselves susceptible to criticism, though not all at once and also not from a transcendental perspective secured apart from our defining commitments to various historical practices (e.g., democratic pluralism or experimental investigation). That is, criticism is insufficiently critical if it is not insistently reflexive. Such criticism is, inescapably, an enactment of tradition. History has a way of showing how, *in time,* the most self-consciously rebellious thinkers or figures unwittingly ensure the continuity of the tradition against which they are rebelling, whereas the most self-consciously conservative defenders of a tradition are by virtue of the strength of their resistance to alteration unconsciously bearing witness to what the tradition at its heart has repressed.

Bernstein's re-narration of the recent history of American philosophy and that of the ancient history of the Jewish people helps us see the extent to which ascertaining the truth entangles us in histories with decisive trajectories yet no fated outcomes. The tradition of re-narration has myriad, intertwined roots. When renewed humanely and imaginatively, as it is by Bernstein, traditions of re-narration can emancipate us from certain fixations from the past, by disclosing previously undetected sites of repression. We are not so much condemned to live—and, thus, to think—between alterity and sociality as we are continuously called to address or engage others, by the innovations and provocations as well as affirmations and critiques of others (indeed, simply by the presence of others). As Bernstein has dialogically addressed others, we might in turn address him: *"According to you,* we might tell a very different story about the development of academic philosophy in the United States—or the deconstruction of the Jewish tradition from a Freudian perspective—or the restructuring of social and political thought in the middle decades of the twentieth century—or the newly appearing constellation of themes, criticisms, and moods defining our cultural moment—or the still largely intractable impasse between objectivism and relativism—or a number of other vital, pressing matters." Attending to the details of these re-narrations assists us in acquiring the resources for working through the impasses, fixations, and *aporias* so characteristic of Western culture in late modernity.

Just as narration is integral to the form of argument being elaborated here, so re-narration is inseparable from the only form of freedom worthy of our solicitude. The force of the argument is, of course, to be found in the details of the re-narration. Even if one is not persuaded by a particular re-narration (as I am largely skeptical of Bernstein's retelling of the story of philosophy in America, at least as found in such writings as "The Resurgence of Pragmatism"), one can only be impressed by the range of erudition and depth of sympathy, the clarity of his expositions and charity of his interpretations, the justice but also the force of his critiques. In the end, however, Socratic philosophy can only be *ad hominem* (cf. Johnstone: 1959) in the sense that it is addressed to persons possessing a certain type of character because shaped by a certain form of life. Such philosophy must be, if it is to be true to itself (i.e., faithful to the inspiration of Socrates), addressed to other persons in their historical circumstances. But the right of anyone to address others is contingent upon that individual's willingness to hear others out.

The question of hope transposes itself and becomes the hope of questioning, the hope of continuing to pose meaningful, orienting, and fruitful questions. Social conditions and moral qualities are as vital to sustaining this hope as are intellectual ability and rhetorical sophistication (Bernstein 1992b: 339; 1981; Rorty 1982: 172–75).

Has any contemporary philosopher better exemplified the ideal of "engaged fallibilistic pluralism"—the willingness to hear out so many diverse and demanding authors—than Richard J. Bernstein?[22] Has anyone done more to advance the cause of a self-critical, tough-minded pluralism than this eloquent advocate of dialogical reason? Has anyone done more for the healing of the wounds in academic philosophy and, of far greater significance, for the facilitation of dialogue across cultural boundaries? Is there any contemporary philosopher in whom the question of hope is addressed more modestly yet persuasively, simply by embodying the *ēthos* of critique in so exemplary, humane, and hopeful a manner (cf. Bernstein 1992b: 165–66)?[23]

NOTES

1. It is evident that *fallibilistic* is, for Bernstein, always implied in the more economical, elegant expression. In fact, this qualifier is the one explicated by him, whereas the modifier *engaged* receives little explication.

2. This is an allusion to a famous passage in the Preface to Hegel's *Phenomenology of Spirit*: "Death, if that is what we want to call this non-actuality, is of all things the most dreadful, and to hold fast what is dead requires the greatest strength. . . . But the life of Spirit is not the life that shrinks from death and keeps itself untouched by devastation, but rather the life that endures it and maintains itself in it. It wins its truth only when, in utter dismemberment, it finds itself. It is this power, not as something positive, which closes its eyes to the negative, as when we say of something that it is nothing or is false, and then, having done with it, turn away and pass on to something else; on the contrary, Spirit is this power only by looking the negative in the face, and tarrying with it. . . . This power is identical with . . . the Subject" (Hegel 1981: 19). Bernstein's engaged pluralism is partly rooted in the Hegelian critique of "disengaged" or "uncoupled" skepticism. As he explains in "Metaphysics, Critique, and Utopia," he means by this expression "the type of skepticism that Hegel contrasts with the dialectical activity of determinate negation" (Bernstein 1988: 259). Such skepticism is abstract in contrast to what Hegel understood as the labor of the negative, the concrete work of determinate negation. In one of his earliest books, *Praxis and Action* (Bernstein 1971), he displayed a sharp and subtle appreciation of the power of the negative in its Marxian as well as Hegelian form. See also "Negativity: Themes and Variations" in Bernstein 1986. Sigmund Freud, a figure to be considered in reference to Bernstein's *Freud and the Legacy of Moses* (Bernstein 1998a), exemplified the strength to tarry with the negative. This is an important reason to focus on him here.

3. I use the term *problematique* rather than problem as a way of suggesting an existential, social condition demanding critical assessment and historical narration. In my sense, we are enveloped and defined by a problematique; it is part of who we are.

4. What Bernstein wrote of Paul Weiss regarding the problem of the one and the many applies with equal force to Bernstein himself regarding the problematique of pluralism: "It is the mark of genuine thinkers to possess and be possessed by a single thought that shines like a star and radiates throughout their work and the pathways they pursue. . . . With nuanced subtlety he has persistently pursued the theme of the one and the many. Explicitly or implicitly, it is evident in everything he has written and is manifested in the entire range of his concerns whether they deal with the most speculative metaphysical and ontological issues or the most intimate aspects of human life" (Bernstein 1987: 200).

5. In *The Public and Its Problems*, Dewey stresses, "To learn to be human is to develop through the give-and-take of communication an affective sense of being an individually distinctive member of a community; one who understands and appreciates its beliefs, desires, and methods, and who contributes to a further conversion of organic powers into human resources and values. But this transition is never finished" (Dewey 1988a: LW 2: 332).

6. A passage from Hegel quoted by Bernstein in *Praxis and Action* (1971) is especially pertinent here. What Hegel is claiming about Spirit (*Geist*) might be even better claimed about humanity (indeed, Marx's insight is that Hegel's penetrating account of *Geist* is a mystified account of humanity): "The transition of its potentiality into actuality is mediated through consciousness and will. These are themselves first immersed in their immediate organic life; their first object and purpose is this natural existence as such. But the latter, through its animation by Spirit, becomes infinitely demanding, rich, and strong. Thus Spirit is at war with itself. It must overcome itself as its own enemy and formidable obstacle. Development, which in nature is a quiet unfolding, is in Spirit a hard, infinite struggle against itself" (Bernstein 1971: 19).

7. Though I borrow this word from Hannah Arendt, I use it in a sense closer to an emphasis in Dewey's writings than to hers, though I suppose this emphasis is connected, however remotely, to hers. "The activities of the group are already there [when any individual arrives as a newborn], and some assimilation of his own acts to their pattern is a prerequisite of a share therein, and hence of having any part in what is going on. Each person is born an infant, and every infant is subject from the first breath he draws and the first cry he utters to the attentions and demands of others" (Dewey 1983: MW 14: 43) "In the life of an individual, instinctive activity comes first. But an individual begins life as a baby, and babies are dependent beings. Their activities could continue at most for only a few hours were it not for the presence and aid of adults with their formed habits" (Dewey 1983: MW 14: 63). "In short, the *meaning* of native activities is not native; it is acquired. It depends upon interaction [or transaction] with a matured social medium" (Dewey 1983: MW 14: 63).

8. What Dewey asserts about democracy might with equal justice be said of plurality (indeed, perhaps there is here only a verbal difference, two different words being used to indicate the same thing): "Regarded as an idea, democracy is not an alternative to other principles of associated life. It is the idea of community life itself. It is an ideal in the only intelligible sense of an ideal: namely, the tendency and movement of some thing which exists carried to its final limit, viewed as completed, perfected" (Dewey 1988a: LW 2:328).

9. I will focus on these distinctions as they are drawn in his Presidential Address to the APA ("Pragmatism, Pluralism, and the Healing of Wounds" [Bernstein 1992, Appendix]). But those distinctions drawn in his Presidential Address to the MSA ("Metaphysics, Critique, and Utopia" [Bernstein 1988]) are not clearly the same set of distinctions with (in several instances) different names, though there is some overlap.

10. In "Metaphysics, Critique, and Utopia" Bernstein notes that his pluralism is an attempt to address the question, "How are we to deal with the multiplicity of perspectives and interpretations in a decentered world?" (Bernstein 1988: 271). He goes on to stress that this attempt "leads to the type of pluralism I want to advocate—an engaged pluralism. And I believe it is the type of pluralism that has been characteristic of what is best in our own American philosophic tradition. One accepts the fallibility of all inquiry and even the lack of convergence of metaphysical speculation. One accepts the multiplicity of perspectives and interpretations. One rejects the quest for certainty, the craving for absolutes, and the idea of a totality in which all differences are finally reconciled. But such a pluralism demands an openness to what is different and other, a willingness to risk one's prejudgments, seeking for common ground without any guarantee that it will be found. It

demands—and it is a strenuous demand—that one tries to be responsive to the claims of the other. Such an engaged pluralism does not mean giving up the search for objectivity and truth. . . . But the quest for truth and objectivity is not to be confused with the quest for absolutes" (Bernstein 1988: 271; cf. Bernstein 1992b, 336–37).

11. "Believe truth! Shun error!—these, we see, are two materially different laws; and by choosing between them we may end by coloring differently our whole intellectual life. We may regard the chase for truth as paramount, and the avoidance of error as secondary; or we may, on the other hand, treat the avoidance of error as more imperative, and let truth take its chance" (James 1956: 18). "Our errors are surely not such awfully solemn things. In a world where we are so certain to incur them in spite of all our caution, a certain lightness of heart seems healthier than this nervousness on their behalf. At any rate it seems the fittest thing for the empiricist philosopher" (James 1956: 19).

12. Of course, this conflict need not be expressed, much less explored. Civility often requires leaving differences implicit. But dialogical civility frequently demands the courage to mark points of significant disagreement.

13. "The whole originality of pragmatism, the whole point in it, is," according to William James, "its use of the concrete way of seeing. It begins with concreteness and returns and ends with it" (James 1978 [1909]: 115–16). But, arguably, the most effective way of rendering matters concrete is by contextualizing, by offering thick contextualizations in which the multiple facets of historical affairs are identified and related to one another as well as seemingly remote affairs (e.g., the rise of analytic philosophy and the politics of the Cold War). The thickness of our narratives therefore depends on the multiple dimensions of the historical contexts taken into account by these narrations. Such considerations prompt me to question whether Bernstein's revisionist story of academic philosophy in the United States is sufficiently thick.

14. There are, claims Jacques Derrida in an essay to which Bernstein has paid considerable attention ("Structure, Sign, and Play in the Discourses of the Human Sciences"), "two interpretations of interpretation, of structure, of sign, of play. The one seeks to decipher, dreams of deciphering a truth or an origin which escapes play and the order of sign, and which lives the necessity of interpretation as an exile. The other, which is no longer turned toward the origin, affirms and tries to pass beyond man and humanism, the name of man being the name of that being who . . . has dreamed of full presence, the reassuring foundation, the origin and end of play" (Derrida 1978: 292). But there are multiple interpretations of interpretation, just as the name of man is far from a univocal sign meaning only the being who dreams of being led out of the ceaseless journeying imposed by hermeneutic exile and thereby led into the promised land of full presence. The critique of humanism is made easy, all too easy, by the violent reduction of this polysemous signifier to a single meaning. So, too, the questioning of the ideal of consensus is made too easy by drawing an all too sharp distinction between investigative practices aiming at this ideal and interpretive ones dispensing (or suspending) this ideal. While it may be the case that consensus is not the overarching, constitutive goal of every form of inquiry, let alone every genre of interpretation, it may nonetheless play a crucial yet subordinate role in a wide variety of our interpretive and investigative practices—indeed, a more extensive and important role than is acknowledged in the self-understanding of contemporary practitioners. In other words, this self-understanding may be, in crucial respects, self-deceptive.

15. The ideal of pluralism being championed by Bernstein demands engagement with both the past in its persistent actuality and the future in its nascent presence. In his own words, "We are not only thrust backward, but forward. 'He' must always engage in a double battle. Philosophy becomes thin and is in danger of losing its identity when it forgets its past, when it gives up trying to grapple with both the strangeness and familiarity of what is 'other' and alien. But it also becomes thin when it is seduced into thinking that the appeal to tradition [to the past and history] is sufficient to answer its questions" (Bernstein 1992b: 28). The distinction between thick and thin has its roots in (among other authors) William James (see James 1971, with Introduction by Richard J. Bernstein: 186, 278).

16. "Now control," as C. S. Peirce notes, "may itself be controlled, criticism itself subjected to criticism; and ideally there is no obvious definite limit to the sequence" (1935, vol. 5: 422). In an unpublished manuscript, Peirce ventured: "if any criticism is beyond criticism (which may be doubted) it is the criticism of criticism itself" (Peirce 1902).

17. Focusing on these two histories is less arbitrary than it might seem to some readers. After all, Bernstein is a professional philosopher who has secured an international reputation in, at least, the academic world. In other words, this is part of who he most significantly is. In obvious and subtle ways, he also is (like Sigmund Freud) a person who in a self-conscious and self-critical way has worked through and continues to work through his relationship to Judaism.

18. This statement carries an allusion to one of Dewey's most famous assertions: "Philosophy recovers itself when it ceases to be a device for dealing with the problems of philosophers and becomes a method, cultivated by philosophers, for dealing with the problems of men" (Bernstein 1960: 66–67).

19. As I am using the term here, *acknowledgment* does not so much designate a third process or task, alongside critique and affirmation, as it indicates a phase or moment in a single endeavor. Critique, affirmation, and acknowledgment are not separable undertakings of achievements; they are, rather, more or less clearly distinguishable aspects of any critical or reflective engagement. My "addition" of acknowledgment to the two terms emphasized by Bernstein both makes more explicit than he does an important dimension of critical engagement or dialogue and connects this activity with Freud's insights into the processes of *working through* loss, anxiety, conflict, and other traumatizing events and experiences.

20. My own attraction to Freud's writings has aroused suspicions in those who otherwise appear to respect my judgment and intelligence.

21. In *Hannah Arendt and the Jewish Question* (1996), Bernstein makes two points of great relevance to this characterization of Judaism. First, he strenuously challenges the tendency to dissociate Judaism from Jewishness (Bernstein 1996: 27–30, 184–88). My own sense is that to be a Jew is to be a self-conscious member of a community of memory, sharpened and sustained by communal rituals of formal recollection (cf. Bernstein 1998a: xi), rooted in scriptural narratives, even though in some cases this membership is maintained by an extremely attenuated relationship to these rituals of recollection (cf. Yerushalmi 1991; Bernstein 1998a: 87–88). Moreover, to be a Jew is to be a self-conscious

member of a community of hope, in particular, hope for the reparation of the world (cf. Yerushalmi 1991; Bernstein 1998a: 95). (I borrow from Josiah Royce the distinction between these two forms of community—a community of memory and one of hope.) It may even be that the sense of kinship felt by religiously deracinated and avowedly Godless Jews with this community remains alive, because one's self-understanding of how one is living incorporates, *mutatis mutandis*, a sensibility and character defined by recollection and reparation as both self-imposed obligations and historically rooted imperatives.

Second, Bernstein is careful in this study to highlight Arendt's misgivings about the very strong tendencies within Zionism to transform this movement into an exclusive ideology. Pointedly, she stresses, Arendt castigated her fellow Zionists for their failure to face up honestly to [or to *acknowledge* uncompromisingly] the need for direct Arab-Jewish negotiation and cooperation. She warned against growing Jewish nationalism and chauvinism" (Bernstein 1996: 182). This makes of past and present betrayals of the noble ideal of embracing the other, for the sake of protecting concrete others in their irreducible alterity, nothing less than the deepest betrayal and desecration of the Jewish tradition. The vitality and validity of this noble tradition are best discerned in resisting the temptation to transform the other into the enemy and, in turn, in fostering the moral imagination and courage needed to transform actual enemies into civil co-inhabitants.

22. In one of his *Essays in Radical Empiricism* (published in a Dutton edition along with *A Pluralistic Universe*, with an Introduction by Richard J. Bernstein), William James suggests: "Philosophy always turns on grammatical particles. With, near, next, like, from, toward, against, because, for, through, my" (James 1971: 26). My discussion of Bernstein's project turns also on such words, especially hearing someone out, working through, owning up to the affirmations implicit in our critiques and, in turn, the flaws inherent in our affirmations. Not only life but also thought is, first and foremost, in the transitions, especially those enabling us to counteract Cartesian anxieties, false dichotomies, entrenched dualisms, and skeptical despair.

23. Bernstein concludes "Foucault: Critique as Philosophic *Ēthos*" by quoting from a late interview with Michel Foucault, one in which the French thinker acknowledges what animates his own investigations, genealogies, and critiques:

> I insist on this difference [between discussion and polemics] as something essential: a whole morality is at stake, the morality that concerns the search for the truth and the relation to the other.
>
> In the serious play of questions and answers, in the work of reciprocal elucidation, the rights of each person are in some sense immanent in the discussion. They depend only on the dialogue situation. The person asking the questions is merely exercising the right that has been given him: to remain unconvinced, to perceive a contradiction, to require more information. . . . As for the person answering the questions, he too exercises a right that does not go beyond the discussion itself; by the logic of his own discussion he is tied to the questioning of the other. (Quoted in Bernstein 1992b, 165–66)

Foucault's affirmation of the morality implicit in the logic of dialogue is an acknowledgment of what engaging in "the serious play of questions and answers" demands of its participants. One of Bernstein's own most characteristic affirmations is an even more straightforward, emphatic acknowledgment of these demands. This acknowledgment is, in effect, a pragmatic clarification of the meaning of his *engaged* pluralism: what engagement practically means is the resolute willingness to engage in an ongoing process of reciprocal elucidation, questioning, and challenge.

REFERENCES

Bernstein, Richard J. 1965. Action, conduct, and self-control. In *Perspectives on Peirce: Critical essays on Charles Sanders Peirce,* ed. Richard J. Bernstein, 66–91. New Haven, CT: Yale University Press.

———. 1967. *John Dewey.* New York: Washington Square Press.

———. 1970. In defense of American philosophy. In *Contemporary American philosophy,* ed. John E. Smith, 293–311. London: George Allen & Unwin.

———. 1971. *Praxis and action: Contemporary philosophies of human activity.* Philadelphia: University of Pennsylvania Press.

———. 1981. Towards a more rational community. In *Graduate Studies, Texas Technical University,* ed. Kenneth L. Ketner et al., 115–20. Lubbock: Texas Tech University Press.

———. 1986. *Philosophical profiles: Essays in a pragmatic mode.* Philadelphia: University of Pennsylvania Press.

———. 1987. Human beings: Plurality and togetherness. In *Creativity and commonsense,* ed. Thomas Krettek, 200–17. Albany: State University of New York Press.

———. 1988. Metaphysics, critique, and utopia. *Review of Metaphysics* 42 (December): 255–74.

———. 1989. Pragmatism, pluralism, and the healing of wounds. *Proceedings and addresses of the American Philosophical Association* 63/3: 5–18.

———. 1991. The lure of the ideal. In *Peirce and law: Issues in pragmatism, legal realism, and semiotics,* ed. Roberta Kevelson. New York: Peter Lang.

———. 1992a. The resurgence of pragmatism. In *Social Research* 59:4 (Winter): 813–40.

———. 1992b. *The new constellation: The ethical-political horizon of modernity/postmodernity.* Cambridge: MIT Press.

———. 1996. *Hannah Arendt and the Jewish question.* Cambridge: MIT Press.

———. 1998a. *Freud and the legacy of Moses.* Cambridge: Cambridge University Press.

———. 1998b. Community in the pragmatic tradition. In *The revival of pragmatism: New essays on social thought, law, and culture,* ed. Morris Dickstein, 141–56. Durham, NC: Duke University Press.

Bernstein, Richard J., ed. 1960. *John Dewey: On experience, nature, and freedom.* Indianapolis, IN: Bobbs-Merrill.

Colapietro, Vincent. 1998. Entangling alliances and critical traditions: Reclaiming the possibilities of critique. *The Journal of Speculative Philosophy* 12:2: 114–33.

———. 1999. Peirce's guess at the riddle of rationality: Deliberative imagination as the personal locus of human practice. In *Classical American pragmatism: Its contemporary vitality*, ed. Douglas R. Anderson, Carl R. Hausman, and Sandra B. Rosenthal, 15–30. Urbana and Chicago: University of Illinois Press.

———. 2002. *Fateful shapes of human freedom: John William Miller and the crisis of modernity.* Nashville, TN: Vanderbilt University Press.

Derrida, Jacques. 1978. *Writing and difference.* Trans. Alan Bass. Chicago: University of Chicago Press.

Dewey, John. 1983. *The middle works of John Dewey, vol. 14 (1899–1924).* Ed. Jo Ann Boydston. Carbondale and Edwardsville, IL: SIU Press. Cited as MW 14.

———. 1988a. *The later works of John Dewey, vol. 2 (1925–1927).* Ed. Jo Ann Boydston. Carbondale and Edwardsville, IL: SIU Press. Cited as LW 2.

———. 1988b. *The later works of John Dewey, vol. 3 (1927–1928).* Ed. Jo Ann Boydston. Carbondale and Edwardsville, IL: SIU Press. Cited as LW 3.

Freud, Sigmund. 1939. *Moses and monotheism.* Trans. Katherine Jones. New York: Vintage.

Gadamer, Hans-Georg. 1975. *Truth and method.* New York: Seabury Press.

Giddens, Anthony. 1990. *The consequences of modernity.* Stanford, CA: Stanford University Press.

Hegel, G. W. F. 1981. *Phenomenology of spirit.* Trans. A. V. Miller. Oxford: Oxford University Press.

James, William. 1956. *The will to believe and other essays in popular philosophy.* New York: Dover.

———. 1971*Essays in radical empiricism and a pluralistic universe.* Introduction by Richard J. Bernstein. New York: E. P. Dutton.

———. 1978. *The meaning of truth.* Cambridge, MA: Harvard University Press. First published in 1909.

Johnstone, Jr., Henry W. 1959. *Philosophy and argument.* University Park: Pennsylvania State University Press.

Kristeva, Julia. 1991. *Strangers to ourselves.* Trans. Leon S. Roudiez. New York: Columbia University Press.

Lear, Jonathan. 1998. *Open minded: Working out the logic of the soul.* Cambridge, MA: Harvard University Press.

MacIntyre, Alasdair. 1977. Epistemological crises, dramatic narrative, and the philosophy of science. *The Monist* 60: 453–71. Reprinted in *Paradigms and revolutions: Appraisals and applications of Thomas Kuhn's philosophy of science.* Notre Dame: University of Notre Dame Press, 1980, 54–74.

———. 1985. Relativism, power, and philosophy. In *Proceedings and address of the APA*, Newark, Delaware, 5–22. Reprinted in *After philosophy*, ed. Kenneth Baynes et al., 385–411. Cambridge: MIT Press, 1987.

Peirce, C. S. 1902. MS 598: Reason's rules. As identified by Richard S. Robins in Annotated Catalog of the Papers of Charles S. Peirce. Amherst, MA: University of Massachusetts Press, 1967.

———. 1935. *The collected papers of Charles Sanders Peirce,* vols. 5 and 6. Ed. Charles Hartshorne and Paul Weiss. Cambridge, MA: Belknap Press of Harvard University Press.

Ricoeur, Paul. 1980. *Hermeneutics and the human sciences: Essays on language, action, and interpretation.* Trans. J. B. Thompson. London: Cambridge University Press.

Rorty, Richard. 1982. *Consequences of pragmatism.* Minneapolis: University of Minnesota Press.

———. 1999. *Philosophy and social hope.* London: Penguin Books.

Segal, Hanna. 1995. *Psychoanalysis, literature and war: Papers 1972–1995.* Ed. John Steiner. New York: Routledge.

Smith, John E. 1983. *The spirit of American philosophy.* Rev. ed. Albany: State University of New York Press.

———. 1992. *America's philosophical vision.* Chicago: University of Chicago Press.

West, Cornel. 1993. *Keeping faith: Philosophy and race in America.* New York: Routledge.

Wittgenstein, Ludwig. 1972. *On certainty.* Trans. Denis Paul and G. E. M. Anscombe. New York: Harper & Row.

Woolf, Virgina. 1984. *The diary of Virgina Woolf, vol. V (1936–1941).* Ed. Anne Olivier Bell and Andrew McNeillie. London: Hogarth Press. Philadelphia: University of Pennsylvania Press.

Yerushalmi, Yosef Hayim. 1991. *Freud's Moses: Judaism terminable and interminable.* New Haven, CT: Yale University Press.

Richard J. Bernstein's Response to Vincent Colapietro

I have always learned from the writings of Vincent Colapietro. I have felt a special affinity for his work for several reasons. He has a profound and subtle understanding of what is best in the American pragmatic tradition. He also shares a serious interest in a creative dialogue with recent developments in Continental philosophy. Many years ago, I criticized Peirce's understanding of the self and of human individuality. I argued that there were deep, unresolved tensions in Peirce, and that his various claims about the self did not really hang together. But when I read Colapietro's monograph on Peirce (which was, in part, written as a response to my criticisms of Peirce), I came to the conclusion that he was right—that Peirce's reflections on the self are more subtle and complex than I had originally claimed. Although I still feel that there are unresolved problems in Peirce, this is a good example of how one can learn from one's critics. There is another feature of his writing that impresses me. In his chapter he gives a succinct account of the engaged fallibilistic pluralism that I have advocated. His account is sharper, more focused, and more vigorous than my attempts to specify the meaning of engaged pluralism. I also find his discussion of *Freud and the Legacy of Moses* the most perceptive that I have read. He gets right to the heart of the matter.

In the final section of his chapter, he critically examines my narrative account of the development of philosophy in America. He claims that I have stressed the continuity of American philosophy, and that I have glossed over the rupture that took place when analytic philosophy burst forth as the only "legitimate" game in town. Colapietro may be right. I was a graduate student at Yale during a time (1950s) when the *ideology* of analytic philosophy was at its height. For fifty years I have witnessed the power plays, snippiness, and downright hostility that many analytic philosophers have expressed to other philosophers and other ways of "doing" philosophy. I was fortunate, however, to study with two of the most prominent (and intellectually generous) analytic philosophers of the twentieth century: Carl G. Hempel and Wilfrid Sellars. I studied with Hempel during my first year as a graduate student at Yale, before he went to Princeton. And I had the good fortune, as a junior faculty member at Yale, to sit in on many of Sellars's classes (Sellars being one of my intellectual heroes). I have always made a distinction between the narrow-minded *ideology* of some analytic philosophers and the *philosophic* contributions of analytic philosophy. The former is distasteful and occasionally stupid, although unfortunately still too powerful and prevalent. Departments and positions in our profession are still defined by such categories as analytic and Continental philosophy. Many excellent analytic philosophers have never even read a word of any nineteenth- or twentieth-century Continental philosopher. And I suspect that the overwhelming majority of students who have received their PhDs in philosophy during the past few decades have never seriously studied the classical American pragmatic thinkers. I do not want to deny that a history of academic philosophy in America has to come to grips with this phenomenon, how it came about, and how it is institutionally maintained. Although I know all of this, I have always been impressed by a different phenomenon that has received far less comment. This is the way in which many of the most interesting and creative philosophers ignore or transcend these ideological divides. When Thomas Kuhn tells us that hermeneutics is relevant to his reflections on the structure of scientific revolutions, when Jürgen Habermas draws on speech act theory and American pragmatism to develop his communicative theory of rationality, and when Dieter Henrich and Manfred Frank engage the "analytic" literature on subjectivity and self-consciousness, we witness creative philosophic crossings that have little to do with the analytic ideology. And this tendency seems to be increasing, as evidenced by the recent work of Robert Brandom, John McDowell, and Bernard Williams. Analytic ideology still has a very strong influence on the philosophic profession, but frankly, I find this ideology boring and philosophically uninteresting. It still has a pernicious influence. On a more positive note, I suggest that there are ways of reading the analytic contributions to philosophy—evidenced by Sellars, Rorty, and Brandom—that display genuine philosophic continuity with the classical pragmatic tradition. This is what I have tried to show in my chapter "The Pragmatic Century."

Let me turn to Colapietro's perceptive remarks about hope and my circuitous encounters with the Jewish tradition. I admire Freud as a thinker, but I am also very uneasy with the way he treats his own Jewishness. He has raised profound questions about the transmission and dynamics of a religious tradition. His emphasis on the *Fortschritt der Geistigkeit* tells us as much about Freud's Enlightenment commitments as it does about the Jewish tradition. I also find unsatisfactory the facile way in which Arendt wants to distinguish Jewishness from Judaism. My interest in Freud's and Arendt's reflections on Judaism and Jewishness has been in the context of different ways of making sense of the idea of a secular Jew. I do not claim that I have worked out a more adequate understanding of what it means to be a secular Jew. This is still a journey of discovery for me.

Finally, I want to turn to what Colapietro says about hope. Until I read his chapter, I did not realize how much the appeal to hope plays in all of my writings. Unlike Rorty, who speaks of "ungrounded hope," my commitment to hope (like Dewey's) is based on a *reasonable* faith. Colapietro phrases the point eloquently when he writes: "The question of hope transposes itself and becomes the hope of questioning, the hope of continuing to pose meaningful, orienting, and fruitful questions. Social conditions and moral qualities are as vital to sustaining this hope as are intellectual ability and rhetorical sophistication." If you don't mind my "stealing" from you, I would use this as an epigraph for all of my writings.

References

Bernstein, Richard J. 1998. *Freud and the legacy of Moses.* Cambridge: Cambridge University Press.

Bernstein and Rorty on Justification by Faith Alone

Nancy K. Frankenberry

> A very popular error: having the courage of one's convictions; rather, it is a matter of having the courage for an attack on one's convictions!
>
> —Nietzsche, *Musarionausgabe*

What I intend by the somewhat provocative title of this chapter is an examination of the conflict of narratives between Richard Bernstein and Richard Rorty on the topic of "justification," a matter that has exercised the religious imagination for quite a bit longer than it has exasperated philosophical anti-foundationalists. Both Bernstein and Rorty share a repudiation of foundationalism, the vain quest for beliefs that are certain in themselves and that in turn support the beliefs derived from them in an extended system of knowledge. But they differ in their estimations of how far pragmatists need to go in providing justifications for their convictions. It is Richard Bernstein who has long been the voice of philosophical moderation—measured, judicious, and rightly suspicious of false dichotomies, entrenched either/or extremes, and insufficiently warranted positions. He has championed the role of reason, argumentative rigor, and the giving of good reasons for one's convictions, much in the spirit of Catholicism's historical commitment to the integral importance of reason in arriving at and defending faith. By comparison, he has tended to view the reformation figure, Richard Rorty, as bordering on reckless fideism. Engaged in the production of meritorious works, Rorty makes a characteristically Protestant appeal to justification by faith alone when it comes to the basic convictions for which Bernstein wants more rational defense. To theologically attuned readers of the American philosophical scene, it could appear that Bernstein plays Erasmus to Rorty's Luther, Rahner to Rorty's Barth, and David Tracy to Rorty's George Lindbeck. I think this gets Rorty wrong in terms of the justificatory loci available to neopragmatism, but nearly right in terms of the philosophy of religion Rorty has sketched to date. The first part of this chapter is devoted to defending Rorty against certain criticisms Bernstein has made and the second part to analyzing what might be thought of as the "indulgence" Rorty dispenses to the priesthood of all believers, making every religious man his own prophet, in private, at least. My concern is that this indulgence only encourages the popular error Nietzsche complained of about those who have the courage of their convictions, but not the courage to criticize their own convictions.

I

In two important chapters of *The New Constellation: The Ethical-Political Horizons of Modernity/Postmodernity*, Bernstein asks whether the "aestheticized pragmatism" advocated by Rorty is adequate, especially for ethics and politics.[1] In the first essay, he depicts Rorty's defense of liberal democracy as little more than an apologia for the status quo and concludes that Rorty's thinking exhibits a blatant "proto-positivist" strain (Bernstein 1992: 236). In the second essay, he concentrates on a critique of the ethical-political horizons of Rorty's 1989 *Contingency, Irony, and Solidarity* in which he detects a "vulgar emotivism" and a "fideistic absolutism" (Bernstein 1992: 278). These are strong epithets—even for two veterans of the University of Chicago! Having positioned Rorty's pragmatism at an extreme pole, Bernstein takes him to be telling us that there is not, and cannot be, any rational grounding of basic ethical-political norms, that decision and commitment are the only basis for our ultimate affirmations, and that all rational justification is a futile project (Bernstein 1992: 7). Simply because justification cannot be thought of as a matter of deduction from indubitable premises, it does not follow, Bernstein insists, that we cannot critically evaluate competing political arguments. Particularly in a liberal democracy in which we are faced with conflicting and incompatible practices, "we need to confront the issues of which practices are to be favored and which are to be modified or eliminated" (Bernstein 1992: 241). But Rorty's rhetoric falsely dichotomizes, as though the only choices are either to appeal to what is local and ethnocentric or else to fixed, permanent, ahistorical foundations (Bernstein 1992: 242). The real work, Bernstein points out, consists in eliminating pernicious forms of ethnocentric appeals and promoting *less* pernicious forms. To do this, we need to be able to distinguish between better and worse forms of intolerance, and to do that we need reference to criteria or standards of one kind or another. This problem cannot be settled simply by pointing to practices, if we do not know what counts as a "better" or "worse" practice. The pragmatist appeal to social practices, historical consensus, or shared beliefs only describes controversies, but does not help solve them.

As Bernstein formulates the problem that Rorty took up in *Contingency, Irony, and Solidarity*, it could serve equally as a statement of the central preoccupation of most philosophy of religion and liberal theology today: "how to enhance our liberal convictions, make them 'look good,' *and* learn the lesson that the culture of irony has taught us, that there is no non-circular argument for justifying our historically contingent beliefs" (Bernstein 1992: 266). While he clearly sees that Rorty aims not to ground liberalism philosophically, but only to make it look attractive, Bernstein nevertheless is not convinced that this rhetorical strategy can succeed in outflanking relativism. To Bernstein, "Rorty clearly looks like a relativist for he is constantly telling us there are no neutral criteria for evaluating competing incommensurable vocabularies" (Bernstein 1992: 270). If this is relativism, I might add, most contemporary schools of philosophy of religion and theological method embrace it. Both political philosophy and religious philosophy currently face a similar challenge of situating their discourse in a more moderate space between the extreme either-or of objectivism and relativism. Pragmatism—with its long-standing critique of absolutes and dualisms—seeks to advance just such a space, one that Bernstein eloquently advocated in *Beyond Objectivism and Relativism* and best summarizes in a passage in *The New Constellation*:

> One of the major themes in philosophy during the past 100 years—from Peirce through Sellars and Quine to Rorty—has been that it is a mistake to think we can (or need to) give strong foundational justification in any area in human inquiry. But this doesn't mean that we can't distinguish better from worse reasons when we are evaluating a scientific hypothesis or the interpretation of a poem—even if what are to count as "good reasons" are themselves historically conditioned and contestable. (Bernstein 1992: 277)

Reading Rorty in this light, the force of Bernstein's critique in 1992 was threefold. First, Rorty had rightly critiqued the strong, foundationalist sense of rational justification, but this did not rule out the weaker sense of justification as reason giving in support of beliefs, and on this Rorty had not done enough. Second, Bernstein thought that Rorty had so radicalized his claims about contingency, historicism, and nominalism that he ran the risk of removing any scope for human agency and intentional action. "Projects formulated to eliminate cruelty might just as well have the opposite result" (Bernstein 1992: 277). When it is contingency "all the way down," Bernstein worried, not only would there be no motivation for acting one way or another, but Rorty's rhetoric of liberal hope would offer no more reason for hope than despair. "For there is no *reason* to expect that anything we do is more likely to bring us closer to this utopia than to its opposite" (Bernstein 1992: 277).

Finally, highlighting the concept of universality that "Rorty plays fast and loose with," Bernstein stated what he saw as the unresolved tension in Rorty's thought in the strongest terms: "The 'logic' of Rorty's strategy comes down to making the adoption of a vocabulary a matter of taste about which there can be no rational debate. Rorty's conviction concerning the contingency of all vocabularies begins to look like old-styled vulgar emotivism" (Bernstein 1992: 278). Going further, Bernstein advised that rather than advocating a liberal pluralistic openness, Rorty may really be advancing a "fideistic absolutism" in which none of our central beliefs can be even minimally warranted rationally. On this reading, "when doubts are raised about one's final vocabulary the only response that is appropriate," Bernstein wrote, is "Here I stand (and I hope you will also stand here)" (Bernstein 1992: 278–79).

In these essays, as well as in his earlier classic review of *Philosophy and the Mirror of Nature,* Bernstein's criticisms, hesitations, and suspicions proved prescient.[2] Soon a host of critics, from both the Left and the Right, were calling into question aspects of Rorty's writings first identified by Bernstein.[3] Even so, Bernstein was not prescient enough to anticipate the evolving replies Rorty would make to such criticisms in a series of publications throughout the 1990s. Covering the full register of venues open to a public intellectual in the tradition of Dewey, Rorty's writings spanned magazines, popular and highbrow journals, book reviews, distinguished lectureships, and professional journals of philosophy. Taken in its entire sweep, this body of work both delineated and defended the politics and social hopes that Bernstein had found "thin" (Bernstein 1986: 89), in comparison to those of Habermas or Foucault, and provided detailed arguments in reply to such philosophers as Hilary Putnam, Crispin Wright, John Searle, Charles Taylor, Robert Brandom, and John McDowell concerning the question of truth (Rorty 1998a).[4] While still picking the same highly professionalized nits he had in 1979, Rorty had also done a lot of what he called "pedagogic, drum-beating, and popularizing work" (Rorty 1998a: 9).

One has only to read *Achieving Our Country: Leftist Thought in Twentieth-Century America* (Rorty 1998b) to see that, far from espousing an ironism that slides into cynicism, as Bernstein feared, Rorty relishes a national pride that would rejuvenate "pure joyous hope" and mobilize the political Left in pursuit of Whitman's and Dewey's dreams for America's secular and pragmatic strivings. The moral compass of Rorty's pragmatism, which seemed to elude Bernstein's 1992 commentary, emerged in the autobiographical "Trotsky and the Wild Orchids" (Rorty 1993: 29–50) and became more evident in Rorty's essays about feminism, cultural difference, human rights, Havel, and social hope (Rorty 1998a).

By century's end, it began to look as though Rorty had done just what Bernstein urged him to do by way of explicating the norms that govern the social practice of justification and clarifying the characteristics of the consensus that we do have, morally and politically, around American liberal democracy. In his 1990s' writings, Rorty does not come across as the poster boy for old-fashioned Cold War liberalism or status quoism, nor is he nailing his theses to the door and relying on justification by faith alone. While his arguments on behalf of liberal democratic values do highlight the contingency of liberal institutions and continue to make clear that public hope has no guarantees to rely on, that is a sign of their fragility not of Rorty's nihilism. The rest of history, we are acutely aware, could conceivably be ruled by cosmopolitan torturers like Orwell's O'Brien. But the fact that liberal values are not metaphysically grounded or permanently shored up only makes them transient and revisable, like everything else in the human adventure. It does not make their adoption arbitrary or relative in a crippling sense. Anyone who still thinks that the charge of relativism can be made to stick against Rorty should read his elegant essays "Relativism: Finding and Making" and "Pragmatism, Pluralism, and Postmodernism" (in Rorty 1999), both aimed at a wide audience, along with the more technical papers in Part I of his *Truth and Progress* (1998a), aimed at a variety of contemporary philosophers.[5] In the latter collection, Rorty gives especially clear arguments in "John Searle on Realism and Relativism" and

"Charles Taylor on Truth" to show why pragmatism's repudiation of such ideas as representation, realism, and correspondence does not entail relativism of truth.

While the intricacies of Rorty's recent work cannot be encompassed here, I believe he can be read as successfully navigating between what Bernstein identified as the twin shoals of "objectivism and relativism," thereby offering a viable, indeed an exemplary, postmetaphysical position. Encapsulating the trajectory of a century of pragmatism, I would further suggest that the apparent relativism or fideism of Rortyan neopragmatism can be checked by Davidsonian doctrines and, likewise, the apparent formalism of Davidsonian doctrines can be supplemented by Rortyan pragmatist considerations. The major difference between Davidson and Rorty pivots not on "truth" but on "justification," which Rorty from time to time assimilates to truth and Davidson sharply distinguishes from the topic of truth. Much of what critics object to in Rorty's (and William James's) slippery way with "truth" might be obviated by substituting "justified" or "not justified" in place of "true." Putting Davidson's views on truth and meaning to work in the gaps Bernstein finds in Rorty's version of pragmatism, we can also better expose the intricate set of arguments that lurks behind what Jeffrey Stout has called Rorty's "pithy little formulae" (Stout 1988: chapter 11).

In the narrative Rorty tells of the trajectory of a century of pragmatism, the rise of deconstruction and poststructuralism in Continental philosophy converged with the best accounts of postanalytic philosophy. And with the contributions of Quine, Sellars, and Davidson (we could add Rorty as well), analytic philosophy converged with the American pragmatist tradition begun by Peirce, James, and Dewey. Rorty has acknowledged that his sense of "pragmatist" might be a tad "idiosyncratic"—but it is, I find, exceptionally beguiling and tightly coherent. "Forget Sellars on picturing," he advises, and "Dewey on scientific method, Wittgenstein on nonsense, and Nietzsche on big strong warriors" (Rorty 1995: 69). Repackaging what is left, he can construct a narrative that pairs Putnam and Peirce, Nietzsche and James, Davidson and Dewey, and Sellars and Wittgenstein.

According to this story, Davidson's contribution to pragmatism is to add a nonrepresentationalist philosophy of language to go with Dewey's nonrepresentationalist account of knowledge (see Rorty 1986: 333–68; cf. Rorty's Introduction to Murphy 1990). The significance of this is hard to overestimate. By dropping representations, we can dispense with what

Dewey called "the whole epistemology industry" whose distinctions gave rise to a long history of artificial problems: skepticism, subjectivism, and relativism. Another name for pragmatism's anti-representationalism is holism, a way of still having your cake even after dividing it for specific purposes.

Bernstein registered his general sympathy with this narrative in his 1995 article on "American Pragmatism: The Conflict of Narratives" (see Bernstein 1995: 54–67).[6] Depicting pragmatism's capacious inclusion of a plurality of origin stories and contested views, he endorsed Rorty's metanarrative about pragmatism according to which Quine, Sellars, Davidson, and Putnam are seen as continuing, rather than radically breaking from, pragmatist themes. Like a number of other critics, Bernstein considered Rorty's interpretation of Davidson to be as "original" as his readings of Quine and Sellars, but he could still conclude that Rorty has "effectively shown how Davidson's own version of holism, and his demythologizing of 'truth' can be related to, and integrated into, a continuous (albeit contested) pragmatic legacy" (Bernstein 1995: 63). This suggests that Bernstein understands the way in which Rortyan neopragmatism, relying on Davidsonian arguments, *does* evade relativism as to truth, even while emphasizing the relativity of justifications to social and historical contexts.

Donald Davidson, for his part, having been recruited as a pragmatist *malgré lui*,[7] explained in a 1994 interview: "I would say nobody seems to me to have done as well in seeing what my overall picture is than Rorty. Even though Rorty and I think of things in quite a different way, he has made an effort to follow what I was up to, and it seems to me he gets the main thing right" (Davidson 1994: 26). More recently, in a 1999 response to Rorty's essay, "Is Truth a Goal of Inquiry? Donald Davidson versus Crispin Wright," Davidson not only helped clarify some of the confusion Rorty has sown but also identified what may be the source of Richard Bernstein's initial complaint. "Much of the time," Davidson explains, "Rorty appears to endorse the view that truth and justification are identical: pragmatists are 'suspicious of the distinction between justification and truth,'" he said, quoting Rorty (Davidson 1999a: 17–19). In that case, since Rorty also thinks justification is a norm, Davidson wonders why he does not conclude that truth is a norm. But of course he knows better. Among other problems, the idea that truth is a norm would only invite the impossible God's-eye view that can never be applied. Still, there is an important difference between justified beliefs and true beliefs, and Rorty signals this difference when he calls attention to the "cautionary" use of the concept of truth (Rorty 1986: 334–35). As Davidson acknowledges, the distinction between truth and justification therefore *does* matter to practice, despite the difficulty of applying it. Indeed, Rorty confesses to weaseling on this distinction, and of having tried to reduce truth to justification. In a recent unequivocal statement, however, he affirms that truth is absolute:

> Truth is, to be sure, an absolute notion, in the following sense: "true for me but not true for you" and "true in my culture but not in yours" are weird, pointless locutions. So is "true then, but not now." . . . Davidson has helped us realize that *the very absoluteness of truth is a good reason for thinking "true" indefinable and for thinking that no theory of the nature of truth is possible.* It is only the relative about which there is anything to say. (This is why the God of orthodox monotheists, for example, remains so tiresomely ineffable.) (1998a: 2–3, emphasis in original)

On the other hand, for both Rorty and Davidson, justification *is* relative. It is relative to such conditions as the availability of evidence, the expense of obtaining it, the audience, the standards of evidential support, and so on. But truth is not relative in those ways, and so Davidson can say: "I applaud Rorty for not going along with many of his followers who would say that it is" (Davidson 1999a: 18). Davidson himself has shrewdly disavowed all attempts to treat truth epistemologically rather than semantically and therefore can agree with Rorty that truth is not a goal of inquiry. Finding evidence to justify our beliefs is a goal of inquiry, and there is then nothing more we can do in trying to "firm up our convictions." Truth is not an additional norm that can be called in, checked with, and used to bestow greater or lesser justification. Yet truth is "pretty much the same goal" as justification. Davidson points out that we are bound to think (not always correctly, however), that the more evidence we have the more apt we are to be right. "People who invest on the basis of inside information on the stock market," he says, "certainly believe so" (Davidson 1999a: 17–18).

Cash value aside, if we separate justification and truth, following Davidson, then truth is best taken as a primitive. A purely logical explication of our knowledge of truth can be given in terms of Tarski's T-sentences. That is to say, according to Davidson: "Truth is as clear and basic a concept as we have. Tarski has given us an idea of how to apply the general concept (or try to apply it) to particular languages on the assumption that we already understand it; but of course he didn't show how to define it in general (he proved, rather, that this couldn't be done). Any further attempt to explain, define, analyze or explicate the concept will be empty or wrong" (Davidson 1990b: 135).

Assuming that truth can take care of itself, we still need to see why the pragmatist notion of justification as consisting in social practices not only differs from a careless slide into relativism but also, by a combination of inference and causation, gives us all we have to go on, and all we need. This could be accomplished ("if we had world enough and time") in the following three steps: (1) rehearsing the arguments against the Myth of the Given (Sellars), the Myth of the Museum (Quine), and the Two Dogmas of Empiricism (Quine) in order to eliminate the standard empiricist and rationalist methods of justification; (2) rehearsing the arguments against the Third Dogma of Empiricism (Davidson) in order to undermine the crucial distinction (scheme-content) that relativistic versions of truth employ; and (3) drawing out the implications of Triangulation (Davidson) to show that the holism resulting from (1) and (2) is not an idealistic form of coherentism.

The first step combines the outcome of Quine's attack on a version of the structure-content distinction in "Two Dogmas of Empiricism" (1953) with Sellars's attack on the idea of givenness in *Empiricism and the Philosophy of Mind* (1997). Quine's arguments led to the conclusion that the distinction between "true by virtue of the meanings of words" and "true by virtue of facts in the world" had to be replaced by the notion of a single web of beliefs, and this is reinforced by Sellars's conclusion that "all awareness is a linguistic affair." Accepting both sets of arguments effectively nullified both traditional empiricism's and rationalism's pictures of knowledge and its justification.

The second step adds Davidson's criticism of the scheme-content distinction (1984) and of the correspondence theory of truth (1990a). If Sellars blurred the distinction between intuitions and concepts, and Quine blurred the distinction between synthetic and analytic truths, then it was Davidson who delivered the final blow to traditional empiricism by dissolving the dualism of scheme and content, of organizing system and something waiting to be organized. Once all three dogmas are rejected, there is no sense to any strong meaning of objectivity, and therefore no foundation or ground to provide an imagined alternative against which pragmatist "muddling through" might be measured and found wanting.

The combined effect of the Quine-Sellars-Davidson critiques requires us to reject, as Rorty does, any position or project that attempts to draw a general line between what is made and what is found, what is subjective and what is objective, what is mere appearance and what is really real. These intellectual distinctions may sometimes have useful applications, for particular purposes and interests, but there is no reason to hypostatize them into a picture that confers priority to the subjective over the objective, or to mind's power over world's constraint—*or the converse.* Especially when we see that we are unable to give any content to the appearance-reality distinction, that is, to "things as they appear to us," versus "things as they are, independent of human inquiry," skeptical worries lose their point and relativist charges have nothing to stick to.[8]

Dropping, then, the distinctions between scheme and content, theoretical and observational statements, results and data, or subjective belief and objective evidence, we can think of justification in terms of the coherence of a particular belief with other beliefs rather than as correspondence with the world or with matters of fact. The third step in the set of arguments I am canvassing concerns the kind of holism that is left after the standard empiricist and rationalist arguments have been eliminated. If a belief coheres with a significant body of coherent beliefs, then it can be considered justified. Holism thus offers not a coherence theory of truth but coherence among propositional attitudes as the best *test* for justification. Mutual support is all we have, and all we need. Without any way to distinguish between statements "made true" by experience and those "made true" by conceptual understandings of meanings, we would have to say with Davidson: "Nothing, . . . no *thing*, makes our sentences or theories true: not experience, not surface irritations, not the world, can make a sentence true" (Davidson 1984: 193).[9] Positively stated, the only thing that can be a reason for holding a belief is another belief.[10]

Does this mean the world is "well lost," or that holism forfeits "being in touch" with reality? Not at all, according to Davidson, who limns the lines of support in a triangulated set of relations among speaker, interpreter, and the world determining contents of thought and speech.[11] Triangulation figures in Davidson's philosophy as a reminder that no one of these three corners can be lost, dropped, or out of touch from the other two. Neopragmatism, as a holism, not only affirms coherence as the best *test* of the justification of inferential relations among our beliefs but also holds that coherence is not *quite* all we have: there is also causation, or what Davidson calls the world's "causal sway," over our beliefs as a totality.

The world's causal sway over our belief system is such that we can say, if we like, that there are constraints imposed on the conversationalist view of knowledge; however, nothing principled can be said about those constraints in general. A gap still yawns between "constraints" that are causal and "justifications" that are linguistic. Stimuli cause speakers to make certain statements, but the world does not make those sentences true. Of course, once the line between world's constraint and mind's power has been blurred, it would be equally wrong to assert a primacy of thought or language (idealism) or of unmediated world (realism). Precisely because we are related to the world in causal terms, in "unmediated touch," as Davidson puts it, pragmatism can dispense with such epistemic intermediaries as representations, sense-data, intuitions, and other *tertia.*

The problem of justification now gets formulated, after Sellars, Quine, Davidson, and Rorty, as a holistic matter, in which what is the "given" that serves to "ground" something else is always unstable and depends on our purposes as we shift, inferentially and causally, back and forth around the triangle that relates speaker, other language users, and world. Only in piecemeal fashion do we manage to see which beliefs support and are supported by others within a coherent web. At times the distribution of truth-values over the sentences we share with others may have to give way, but so too might other beliefs currently held fast. Which ones yield to others and which ones are allowed to stand firm is a matter of choice and changing purposes. If I find, for example, that my belief in human fallibility does not cohere well with my belief in papal infallibility, then which belief shall I relinquish? No rational device exists for eliminating the elements of contingency, or agent-dependent choice, in this matter. Sooner or later, one might suppose, I will run into major disruptive incoherence in my overall web of beliefs if I opt for papal infallibility. But perhaps not. If my powers of compartmentalization are highly developed, or my deference to authority deeply ingrained, then self-deception may be easier to practice.[12]

To sum up, it is hard to see how pragmatists could improve on Rorty's pithy little formula: "Nothing counts as justification unless by reference to what we already accept, and there is no way to get outside our beliefs and our language so as to find some test other than coherence" (Rorty 1979: 178; cf. Davidson 1986: 324, 331). Justification, in the most general sense, is simply a matter of being able to give good reasons for beliefs. What count as good reasons or standards of "better" and "worse" are produced by social practices. But the pragmatist appeal to "social practices" is not the same thing as urging the formation of "consensus." Along with the language that we acquire socially, we learn criteria for linguistic usage. The set of criteria that are favored by a community at any particular time will be variable and contingent. We accept these criteria not because they are self-evident but because we share a social practice, embedded in a common human genome and general host environment. Based on complicated bodies of evidence, discussion of arguments, and answered objections, we may come to a consensus, but the consensus is the result of successful social practices and is itself a factor in the ongoing revisable conversation. Most often, it is not because of any consensus that we consider a belief well justified; rather, we form the consensus because we have good reasons for that belief.

It should now be clear how the charge of relativism against Rorty can be given a nuanced reply. Recall that Bernstein traced the problem chiefly to Rorty's three interrelated claims in *Contingency, Irony, and Solidarity* that "no final vocabulary can be grounded in something more fundamental, that anything can be made to look good or bad by redescription, [and] there are no constraints on the invention of new vocabularies" (Bernstein 1992: 279). Qualifying each of these themes in light of Davidsonian doctrines, I would interpret them in the following ways. First, as long as "final vocabularies" are not treated like so many "conceptual schemes" that are incommensurable and untranslatable, thus inviting truth relative to the scheme, no problem of relativism arises. Rorty himself has consistently treated alternative vocabularies more like alternative *tools* than conceptual schemes. Tools are neither true nor false, but useful or inefficient. Only sentences may be true or false. At the level of vocabularies or theories, the evaluative question is whether they perform a useful function. Rational justifications for preferring one vocabulary over another have to do with their utility, and explanations of their acquisition have to do with causes.

Second, when Rorty has wanted to dodge matters of truth, he has tended to rely upon the amusing method of invidious comparison and redescription to make his points look good and his opponents look bad, as though all else is pointlessly "metaphysical." But being made to "look good" (or bad) by redescription is a rhetorical trick, not necessarily a truth-claim. Insofar as truth-conditions pertain, not just "anything" can be made to look good or bad. The point is not that there are no rational arguments against the Holocaust or against Stalin, but that there are no *philosophical refutations* that Nazis or Stalinists accept. Nor does it seem that Rorty thinks his "redescriptions" have no truth-conditions. Since at least 1994 he has been willing to say that "when I put forward large philosophical views I am making 'claims to truth' . . . rather than simply a recommendation to speak differently" (Rorty 1994: n. 16).[13]

Third, inventing new vocabularies may very well be constrained in wholesale ways but not in any retail way that can be known in advance. Constraints there are, but these are typically holistic. "Nobody's language has ever been or ever will be unconstrained by the world," Rorty acknowledged in a 1995 reply to critics, "and . . . nobody will ever be able to be interestingly specific about what these constraints are and how they work" (1995: 194).[14] In keeping with the Sellars-Quine-Davidson separation of the causal story from the justificatory story, some people have to work at changing human vocabularies in order to signal intellectual progress, or to effect conceptual change, or to forge linguistic reformation. Rortyan "redescriptions" are not simply issued as *dicta* without supporting reasons and attractive narratives, and the emphasis on "conversation," far from being an effete and a languid art limited to intellectuals, presupposes a social give-and-take familiar to everyone on one level or another. After all, not just any redescription will do if it cannot be shown to be persuasive, and some conversational tacks are inappropriate or unconvincing. Our peers will *not* let us get away with just anything. (Just *try* getting away with the idea that Abraham Lincoln is not really dead, said William James.) In the edifying conversation Rorty envisions replacing Philosophy, one does have to hold one's own against objections, answer challenges, and entertain criticism from opposing voices—all part of standard justificatory practices.

This discussion of justification has been quite general and programmatic, but it is indicative of another difference between Bernstein and Rorty. Dropping the facetious Catholic-Protestant analogy, and descending now into crass mercantilism, I could characterize the difference between these two pragmatists as the difference between a retail merchant and a wholesale supplier. In answer to the leading question of Bernsteinian pragmatism, "how do you justify your ethical-political convictions?," Rortyan pragmatism offers general and programmatic criteria at the wholesale level: utility, coping, human flourishing. Going to Rorty for justificatory loci is like going to the grocery to get food that is "nourishing." It does not exactly narrow it down. Cereal? Meat? Vegetables? Popsicles? We could "cope" with all of the above, and more. Every aisle has something "useful." Bernstein has rightly raised the question as to what the goods will cost us at the retail level.

On the whole, however, Bernstein and Rorty have even more in common than their celebrated interpretations of American pragmatism or their talent for building bridges between Anglo-American thought and Continental philosophy. The spirit of Bernstein's decisive critique of Cartesian anxiety and of the excesses of objectivism seems remarkably close to Rorty's ironist, who doubts even her own favored vocabulary as final. The deeply moral aspect of ironism asserts itself in the difficult work of not absolutizing one's own vocabulary as final and trying to hold one's most entrenched convictions tentatively and fallibilistically. What else is Peirce's principle of fallibilism than a secularized version of the "Protestant principle," with its suspicion from Luther to Tillich of giving ultimate commitment to anything less than ultimate? This spirit embues the work of both Bernstein and Rorty.

Indeed, in the last analysis, Bernstein's own answer to the question of justification takes the form of recommending the very same variety of strategies that abounds in Rorty's writings—"argumentation, narrative, imagining new possibilities, articulating visions of what we take to be desirable" (Bernstein 1992: 319). These are the measures, he tells us, still open to those who have learned, in Hannah Arendt's words, to think without banisters. Like Rorty, Bernstein knows that "such a bricolage will not satisfy those who hanker after something more solid, foundational, and secure—those who dream of some sort of conclusive grounding" (319). But what gospel has ever promised anyone that?

II

Having helped keep Rorty's boat afloat while it is being repaired in this manner, I turn now to his philosophy of religion as given in two papers to date, "Religious Faith, Intellectual Responsibility, and Romance" (Rorty 1997) and "Pragmatism as Romantic Polytheism" (Rorty 1998c). In recent years Anglo-American philosophy of religion has been overtaken by a variety of nonfoundationalist experiments (postliberal narrative theology; the basic belief apologetic; Wittgensteinian fideism) that appears to retreat into a new confessionalism.[15] The view that no understanding is foundational has been confused with the view that all understanding is tradition bound, paradigm dependent, and community relative, according to particular conceptual schemes that are just given, as though peoples' religious beliefs are deterministically caused and stand in need of no criticism or holistic relation to other propositional attitudes that may contradict them. This development has produced a kind of upside-down foundationalism with a new Myth of the Given.

For example, in the hands of Alvin Plantinga and his followers, antifoundationalism has been used to undermine the very idea of the need to provide justification of a certain set of religious beliefs. The result is that religious believers are allowed to hold, in good epistemic conscience, beliefs that they cannot justify. Fideists and fundamentalists, the fatuous and the fanatical alike, exempt themselves from serious criticism and dialogical engagement on the basis of this philosophy of religion. Does a pragmatist philosophy of religion offer a vantage point for critique of such practices, or does it too acquiesce in the ongoing fideism of our times?

This is not the occasion for an in-depth analysis of Rorty on religion.[16] Here I will highlight only two questions of immediate interest. First, does Rorty's "romantic utilitarianism" bring a pragmatist philosophy of religion too close for comfort to functionalism? Second, where is the inducement for religious folk to have, as Nietzsche would want, the courage to *critique* their own religious convictions? These questions are not easy to answer in connection with Rorty's work, in part because religion figures in not one but two ways in his writings, corresponding to both a public and a private set of concerns—or, better, to a Historical Stage and a Private Podium. In the first treatment, he leaves no doubt that religion is already circling the drain. In the second treatment, he assigns religious beliefs to the realm of private self-invention, requiring no justification to others.

Religion on the historical stage reflects Rorty's anti-authoritarianism and follows a concise metanarrative that might be called a History of How the West Was Weaned—first from God and then from other, quasi-divine authorities:

> [O]nce upon a time we felt a need to worship something which lay beyond the visible world. Beginning in the seventeenth century we tried to substitute a love of truth for a love of God, treating the world described by science as a quasi divinity. Beginning at the end of the eighteenth century we tried to substitute a love of ourselves for a love of scientific truth, a worship of our own deep spiritual or poetic nature, treated as one more quasi divinity. (Rorty 1989: 22)

Contingency means that Western intellectuals have now arrived at the point where we no longer worship anything, "where we treat *nothing* as a quasi divinity, where we treat *everything*—our language, our conscience, our community—as a product of time and chance" (Rorty 1989: 22; emphasis in original). The successive de-divinization of monotheism, metaphysics, and science (as attempts to say what the world *really* is) ends with the substitution of poetry for religion. Monotheism yields to polytheism, as philosophical realism yields to pragmatism. Both of the former projects gave a sense of importance to "something out there with which to get in touch"—either Reality or the Divine. Both urged us to humble ourselves. An opponent of patriarchal authoritarianism in any form, Rorty ties his narrative to a description of various changes in self-image, on the part of Western humans, as we have come out from under the authority of any Supreme Narrator, whether God or Science or Reason or Nature. In the long transition out of Platonism and into pragmatism, we have gradually de-transcendentalized all of our absolutes and begun the work of democratizing our forms of human community. Philosophy no longer seeks the redemptive power of Truth "out there," and religion is better off seeking the Romance of diverse, even conflicting, ideals and forms of private self-perfecting.

Polytheism, in the twist given it by Rorty, stands for the idea that "there are diverse, conflicting, but equally valuable forms of human life," but there is "no actual or possible object of knowledge that would permit you to commensurate and rank all human needs" (Rorty 1998c: 23). As a species of romantic utilitarianism, polytheism shares with the Romantic movement, two centuries ago, a hope that religion, having died as dogma, might be reborn as art, in Rorty's case as literature. The utilitarian contribution owes more to John Stuart Mill than to Bentham and adds the suggestion that the obligation to justify one's beliefs arises only when one's habits of action interfere with the fulfillment of others' needs. In this light, Rorty offers a rigorous defense of Dewey's tolerance for religious belief, revealing atheism, or at least Nietzsche's aggressive version, to be "unnecessarily intolerant" (Rorty 1998c: 25) and flummoxing those who think that pragmatism and religion do not mix.

Never mind that, as Alvin Plantinga likes to point out, there are far more Baptists around than believers in Darwin's dangerous idea. Rorty has constructed a rich narrative of cultural history in which philosophy and religion have both suffered roughly similar fates and inherited similar hopes. But it is told from the standpoint of one who has undergone the world-historical shifts described and now occupies the high cultural ground with an external view of religion. What about the perspective of those for whom traditional, supernatural religion is still a matter of intense personal conviction? How might they come to *criticize* those convictions? How does the element of doubt and spirit of fallibilism enter into their set of convictions? What would make it arise? Perhaps here is where Richard Bernstein's detection of a "proto-positivist" strain and a form of "fideism" in Rorty's thinking have some application.

This becomes more evident in the second way in which Rorty treats religion, in terms of understanding the topic of "religious belief" according to a "utilitarian" philosophy of religion that, among other things, regards religious belief as a habit of action, not a representation of anything. In his essay on "Religious Faith, Intellectual Responsibility, and Romance," Rorty (1997) takes up where William James's will-to-believe argument left off. Intellectual responsibility has to do with making religious beliefs coherent with our other beliefs and with the beliefs of our fellow humans, Rorty says. Brilliantly, he sees that James's distinction between issues to be decided by "intellect" and issues to be decided by "passion" only invokes the troublesome positivist dichotomy of the cognitive versus the noncognitive, and so he reformulates it as a distinction between beliefs that will need to be justified to others and beliefs that will not need to be so justified.

Rorty thinks the question of our intellectual responsibility to justify beliefs to others does not arise in religion, any more than in marriage choices. Tolerantly and charitably, he wants religious believers to have a right to their faith without violating any intellectual responsibilities of the stern sort demanded by W. K. Clifford's evidentialist challenge. But the outcome of such a tolerant and charitable spirit toward religious belief is that it is very hard to see what would ever induce criticisms or reformations of religious convictions, especially among believers themselves. Behind the distinction between beliefs-needing-justification-to-others and beliefs-not-needing-justification-to-others is Rorty's overall trope: the distinction between the public sphere and the private sphere. Religious beliefs take up their place in the category of what is "private," along with art and poetry (the usual suspects). Science, though hardly construed according to logical positivism by Rorty (whose hero is T. S. Kuhn, not A. J. Ayer), strides forth (together with democratic politics) into the public sphere of shared discourse. Science can never conflict with or cancel out religion. Of course, if it cannot disconfirm religion, then neither can science confirm it. How then do religious beliefs get judged, and how might they be subjected to criticism *on the part of believers themselves*? Does not this division between science and religion smack of a return to the division of labor that marked the heyday of logical positivism, according to which science deals with matters of fact and religion deals with meaning and values? According to one historian of philosophy: "'Positivism is dead,' so they say. Rightly, too [save] where it touches religion" (Passmore 1957: 125). The long legacy of logical positivism has not yet withered away. One might even suspect that Rorty's earlier vocabulary for banishing what he found "meaningless" and "nonsense" in philosophy betrayed an unintended influence of the spirit of positivism.

How should pragmatist philosophers of religion explain the puzzling persistence of religious belief in the disenchanted postmodern world that pragmatism, as much as anything else, has helped demythologize? Pragmatists are not instrumentalists, as Rorty knows. Neither, I think, should they be functionalists in explaining religion's origin or persistence as a matter of the gratification of human needs. Unfortunately, there are undertones of a functionalist theory of religion behind Rorty's utilitarianism, as when he says: "Beliefs are to be judged solely by their utility in fulfilling these animals' varied needs" (1998c: 21). Although he would not want to be seen as putting forth a theory, the ubiquity of Rorty's references to various human "needs" suggests that he not only yokes pragmatism to ends and utilitarian consequences but also links religion to the fulfillment of various human needs and desires. Once the link is presumed to be a causal and an explanatory one, pragmatism threatens to empty into functionalism, as far as the subject of religion is concerned. And the problem with a functionalist theory of religion is that it rests on the logical fallacy of affirming the consequent.[17] No matter how popular functionalism remains among anthropologists and theologians alike, it is not very "useful," I want to say, to explain the phenomenon of religion in terms of its "useful" functions and supposed ends. Typically, these supposed ends are such things as social solidarity, reduction of anxiety, confidence in the face of the unknown, psychological crutches, and so on. All of these are examples of what we would have to call different ways of "coping." The problem is that the same functions can be and often are performed by different facets of culture other than religion, the same needs fulfilled by other ways of coping than being religious, the same ends reached by different means. Indeed, for any given function attributed to religious belief, we can think of an alarmingly large number of other social or cultural phenomena that could perform the same function. Nothing therefore is explained about religion in this way. Understanding religion by its functions has a lot in common with understanding a sandbar off the coast of Cape Cod by its effects on the Atlantic Ocean; the relation may be real enough, but its specification can never be fine-grained enough to be explanatory. If an account in terms of the gratification of human needs were at all useful in explaining the complex transcultural phenomena of religions, then we might think it would be by pointing to the broad "function" of religion in establishing—or at least asserting—human solidarity. But the hope of human solidarity is not exclusively religious, and pointing to the ideal of community does not clarify what *is* religious. Nor of course does religion always function well as a way of promoting private perfection.

Finally, what of the "fideism" Bernstein detected in Rorty's ethical-political position? In relation to religion, I think that translates into the question of whether Romantic polytheism in any way invites people to *criticize* their own deepest convictions. What is to prevent people's private project of self-creation, or "what they do on their own time," from getting out of hand? Or deteriorating into a license to celebrate sectarian absurdities with a cloud of witnesses, trailing rays of self-authenticating glory, and forming only the most parochial kind of solidarity? When does solidarity become superstition? Or too parochial? Or an incitement to violence in the public sphere? The nearly inviolable line between realms of personal choice and public responsibility makes it hard to see how traditional religious believers could reform or criticize traditional beliefs of exactly the sort that Rorty thinks "pragmatic theists have to get along without: Personal Immortality, Providential Intervention, the efficacy of the sacraments, the Virgin Birth, the Risen Christ, the Covenant with Abraham, the authority of the Koran" (Rorty 1997: 92).

Viewing the privatization of religion in the best light, one could argue that by redirecting religion from public problems to private perfection, we (North Americans) are better able to preserve the wall of separation installed by the First Amendment, better able to forestall the Falwells, and better able to empower our prophets without imperiling the Republic. According to this vision, our social hopes should be focused on a liberal utopia in which a division between private and public life confines projects of self-creation and projects of promoting justice to separate spheres. Far from disastrously dichotomizing important aspects of human life, this is the best way to *combine* private fulfillment, self-realization, with public morality, and a concern for justice. For the belief that the springs of private fulfillment and of human solidarity are the same is a Christian relic we should retire, according to Rorty (Rorty 1989: in passim).

And yet, even from a post-Christian perspective, this may seem too much like a "neat apartheid," as Bernstein suggested (1992: 269).

Let me be clear about the problem I am raising. I do not want to enter into criticisms of Rorty's public/private split per se.[18] Nor do I want to dwell here on the obvious complications of formulating who the "we" is in a society riven by race and class lines. My point is that in connection *with religion* the distinction between the private and public spheres of experience has the potential to leave in place all the ways in which religious beliefs "work" to incite harms, both private and public.

Pragmatist philosophers of religion may also wonder why "private fantasy" should be so unsuited to argumentative challenge or to the self-doubt that leads people to seek better reasons and sometimes to abandon old convictions. The act of demarcating beliefs that one does or does not have to answer for publicly may sound simply like a recommendation for compartmentalizing tools ("I'll keep the screwdrivers right here and put the wrenches over there"). But with equal plausibility *on the part of religious folk*, it could be a recipe for segmenting psyches ("I'll believe the dead don't rise when I go to work at the morgue, and I'll believe Jesus is risen when I go to church").

Perhaps in conclusion I can run together Rorty's two ways of treating religion by asking whether Dewey's "ungrounded social hope" can become the successor to traditional religious faith in the West. It is true that hope is a more subtle virtue than faith, and more resilient, often, than love. Faith and love lean on evidence, however slight, and sometimes seek justifications. Hope surges forth without benefit of foundations, is heedless of counterfactuals, and a little oblivious as to reasons. Hope—utopian—is the hallmark of Rorty's pragmatism, as it was for James. "The essential thing," he has said, "is to dream of a better world. Hope doesn't require justification, cognitive status, foundations, or anything else" (Nystrom and Puckett 1998: 57). Something is missing here, I suggest, that both Davidson and Bernstein would note. "Justification" and "cognitive status" are not on a par with "foundations," or else pragmatism amounts to little more than positivism. Hope is not, for all that, bereft of cognitive content or immune to criticism. Like faith and love, hope, though the greatest of these, is as much a propositional attitude as any belief, as complicated as any desire, as directional as any intention. And like all other propositional attitudes, hope is analyzable according to truth-conditions.[19]

NOTES

1. See "One Step Forward, Two Steps Backward: Rorty on Liberal Democracy and Philosophy" and "Rorty's Liberal Utopia" in Bernstein 1992. For Rorty's reply to "One Step Forward" see Rorty 1987. I interpret Rorty's general thesis that "democracy is prior to philosophy" to mean that liberalism, as an ongoing practice, requires no *philosophical* foundation, not that reasons are unimportant for displaying its strengths or that criticisms of its weaknesses are irrelevant.

2. Bernstein's review was the first major study of *Philosophy and the Mirror of Nature* in print and remains authoritative. See Bernstein 1980 (reprinted in Bernstein 1986: 21–57).

3. From the Left, vigorous critiques have been offered, especially by Laclau 1991; for a realist with leftist politics, see Geras 1995; for an early Habermasian slant, see McCarthy 1990 (also see Rorty's response, Rorty 1990), as well as Habermas himself in Habermas 1998; for a feminist critique, see Fraser 1989; for religious studies, see Bowlin 1997; for a flawed but an absorbing counternarrative tracing the effect of religious and theological ideas in Rorty's pre-1994 work, see Farrell 1994; however, Farrell treats Davidson as a realist and Rorty as an anti-realist in a way that mislabels both and misses the extent of their agreement.

4. The fact that all of his interlocutors in Part I of Rorty 1998a are more or less in the tradition of Anglo-American analytic philosophy indicates Rorty's continued engagement with mainstream professional philosophy, nineteen years after *Philosophy and the Mirror of Nature* (1979) announced the end of capital-P philosophy.

5. "Pragmatism, Pluralism, and Postmodernism" in Rorty 1999 ought to be enough to show that Rorty's conscription into the ranks of postmodernists on the basis of his lighthearted talk about his "postmodern bourgeois liberalism" was a joke. In this volume Rorty brings together various reflections on applied pragmatism, on his political hopes, and on contemporary America that are sophisticated, provocative, and entertaining. See also the Introduction to *Truth and Progress* (1998a) for Rorty's interesting way of framing the essays in Part I on "Truth and Some Philosophers." These essays, he says, may be thought of as "footnotes to Davidson's claim that '[we] should not say that truth is correspondence, coherence, warranted assertibility, ideally justified assertibility, what is accepted in the conversation of the right people, what science will end up maintaining, what explains the convergence on single theories in science, or the success of our ordinary beliefs.' Whether 'pragmatism' is a suitable name for the philosophical outlook that results from accepting Davidson's advice is one of the few issues on which Davidson and I still differ" (Rorty 1998a: 11). For the reference to Davidson, see Davidson 1990a: 309.

6. I appreciate Bernstein's skillful "argumentative retelling" of the metanarrative of pragmatism but wonder whether the divergence he sees between Dewey's liberalism and Rorty's "aestheticized" pragmatism is that great in light of Dewey's *Art as Experience.* One could even draw from aesthetic experience the norms Bernstein thinks Rorty needs for showing that adherence to liberal democratic values is more than personal preference. In brief, the argument would be that aesthetic principles (contrast, harmony, width, and depth) comprise the most general and least restrictive principles of order according to

which things with great differences may be together in some kind of unity. The American ideal of *e pluribus unum* can be interpreted as a conception of the widest possible aesthetic unity. See, for example, Frankenberry 1996.

7. Davidson could describe himself in 1987 as a "pragmatist" about truth, although he has since wobbled (see Davidson 1990b: 134.) In that year he could also depict his views and Rorty's by saying: "Where we differ, if we do, is on whether there remains a question how, given that we cannot 'get outside our beliefs and our language so as to find some test other than coherence,' we nevertheless can have knowledge of, and talk about, an objective public world which is not of our own making. I think this question does remain, while I suspect that Rorty doesn't think so" (Davidson 1990b: 137). Davidson's reluctance to accept the pragmatist label is probably due to the way Rorty has presented "pragmatism" as blurring the difference between truth and justification. Davidson does not think that what is useful is true, and he is uneasy when pragmatism is made to say this. When Rorty seems to want to add truth and justification to the list of things we should "stop distinguishing," Davidson sensibly resists.

8. This makes it especially puzzling that pragmatism can be read so frequently as supporting relativism when what it really has been about, most conspicuously in Rorty's writings, is a deconstruction of all of the distinctions on which relativism relies. Rorty rejects the scheme-content distinction as emphatically as does Davidson. Therefore, his use of the term *incommensurable* should be taken to mean something like "not conducing to agreement," rather than connoting "untranslatable conceptual scheme that differently characterizes an undifferentiated content with no question-begging way to say one scheme is better than another." Although I have not made a study of Rorty's uses of the term *incommensurable* over the years, I suspect that he has given different semantic twists to it that would be interesting to track in light of Bernstein's discussion of incommensurability in Part 2 of his *Beyond Objectivism and Relativism* (1983) and his equally incisive "Incommensurability and Otherness Revisited" in *The New Constellation* (1992).

9. But cf. Davidson's "Reply to Stephen Neale" in which he retracts a portion of this statement when he says: "That was a mistake. I was right about experience and surface irritations, but I gave no argument against saying the world makes some sentences true. After all, this is exactly as harmless as saying a sentence is true because it corresponds to The One Fact, and just as empty. . . . I confess those three little words ('not the world') were seriously misleading" (Davidson 1999b: 668–69).

10. Why cannot a non-belief do the job? Why not appeal to "the facts" or some "state of affairs" or "the way the world is" as justification for our convictions? The reason is in order to do so successfully, we would need a theory that can answer two questions: how do we explain the *relation* between the non-belief (the cause) and the belief that allows the former to justify the latter? And why should we trust it? The major objection to the correspondence theory of truth is that it has not been successful in meeting these two conditions.

11. See especially Davidson 1990a: 325, where he adds, "Given this source, there is no room for a relativized concept of truth."

12. In light of this possibility, the large literature on *akrasia* and the paradox of self-deception is of overlooked relevance to philosophers of religion. For an extensive bibliography on the topic, go to http://www.chass.utoronto.ca/~bsalton/bib.html.

13. This is in response to Charles Taylor's criticism in Taylor 1990 and is reprinted in Rorty 1998a: 92, n. 16). See also Taylor's response in Taylor 1994: 219–22. At footnote 14 of "Taylor on Truth," Rorty also regrets his unhappy tendency in *Philosophy and the Mirror of Nature* "to make existentialist noises, noises which presuppose a usable distinction between *Wille* and *Vorstellung*."

14. Another clarification worth noting is that "the world" is no longer "well lost" for Rorty. In a reply to Frank Farrell, he acknowledged that "The World Well Lost" (1972) went too far in "suggesting that the only alternatives are a radical subjectivism in which the self projects schemes out upon a featureless reality (what Putnam has satirized as 'the cookie cutter view') on the one hand, and an unknowable noumenon on the other" (Rorty 1995: 191). Nevertheless, critics continue to heap scorn on Rorty for that 1972 essay, as though he has staked out an anti-realist position and shaved off one whole corner of Davidson's triangle. Since most of those critics are realists, they should be interested in Rorty's explanation that "'The World Well Lost' was written twenty-three years ago. Lately I have been trying to mark out a position that does not take sides between subject and object, mind and world, but that instead tries to erase the contrast between them. I have, so to speak, been trying to lose *both* us and the world . . . I want to stop using the us-world contrast, and thus to get rid of the realism-antirealism issue" (Rorty 1995: 191). The often-cited essay "The World Well Lost" first appeared in *The Journal of Philosophy* 69 (1972): 649–55; reprinted in Rorty 1982: 3–18.

15. For example, despite their provision of sophisticated typologies or theoretical frameworks or geneologies, the postliberal George Lindbeck returns to a confessional theology, the feminist Mary McClintock Fulkerson simply witnesses to a belief that "ultimate reality is gracious," and the prophetic pragmatist Cornel West owes more to Kierkegaard than to any pragmatist when it comes to justifying Christian convictions. See Lindbeck 1984; Fulkerson 1994; West 1989. Fulkerson explicitly appeals to "non-foundationalism" as an excuse for sheer fideism, as though it is a license that allows Christians to escape the usual obligations of reason giving.

16. I have tried to provide that in a work in progress tentatively titled *Pragmatism and the End of Religion.* [Relevant sources that appeared after this chapter was completed include Brandom 2000 (see especially the essays by Davidson, McDowell, and Ramberg, and Rorty's responses to them); and Rorty, "Cultural Politics and the Question of the Existence of God," Jeffrey Stout, "Radical Interpretation and Pragmatism: Davidson, Rorty, and Brandom on Truth," and Wayne Proudfoot, "Religious Belief and Naturalism," all in Frankenberry 2002.]

17. For a classic critique, too often neglected among scholars of religion and anthropologists, see Hempel 1965. For a critique of functionalism in religious studies, see Penner 1989: 103–28.

18. This has been the target of numerous complaints, not always fairly. Rorty's own recent statement is that "My public/private distinction wasn't an explanation of what every human life is like. I was, instead, urging that there was nothing wrong with letting people divide their lives along the private/public line. We don't have a moral responsibility to bring the two together. It was a negative point, not a positive recommendation about how everybody should behave." Quoted in Nystrom and Puckett 1998: 61.

19. This paper was written for the conference on "The Pragmatic Century: Conversations with Richard Bernstein," sponsored by the Highlands Institute for American Religious and Philosophical Thought in June 2000. I am grateful to Richard Bernstein, Matthew Bagger, Harley Chapman, Sheila Davaney, Terry Godlove, Henry Levinson, Barbara Mesle, Bob Neville, and Wayne Proudfoot for their comments on that occasion.

REFERENCES

Bernstein, Richard. 1980 Philosophy and the conversation of mankind. *The Review of Metaphysics* 33 (June): 745–75.

———. 1983. *Beyond objectivism and relativism: Science, hermeneutics, and praxis.* Philadelphia: University of Pennsylvania Press.

———. 1986. *Philosophical profiles: Essays in a pragmatic mode.* Philadelphia: University of Pennsylvania Press.

———. 1992. *The new constellation: The ethical-political horizons of modernity/postmodernity.* Cambridge: MIT Press.

———. 1995. American pragmatism: The conflict of narratives. In *Rorty and pragmatism: The philosopher responds to his critics,* ed. Herman J. Saatkamp Jr., 54–67. Nashville, TN and London: Vanderbilt University Press.

Bowlin, John R. 1997. Rorty and Aquinas on courage and contingency. *Journal of Religion* 77 (July): 402–20.

Brandom, Robert, ed. 2000. *Rorty and his critics.* Oxford: Blackwell.

Davidson, Donald. 1984. *Inquiries into truth and interpretation.* Oxford: Clarendon.

———. 1986. Empirical content. In *Truth and Interpretation,* ed. Ernest LePore, 320–32. Oxford: Blackwell.

———. 1990a. The structure and content of truth. *Journal of Philosophy* 87 (June): 279–328.

———. 1990b. Afterthoughts, 1987. In *Reading Rorty: Mirror of Nature,* ed. Alan Malachowski, 134–37. Oxford: Blackwell.

———. 1994. Language philosophy, writing, and reading: A conversation with Donald Davidson. In *Philosophy, rhetoric, literary criticism: (Inter)view,* Thomas Kent, interviewer, ed. Gary A. Olsen, 9–28. Carbondale: Southern Illinois University Press.

———. 1999a. Is truth a goal of inquiry? Discussion with Rorty. In *Donald Davidson: Truth, meaning and knowledge,* ed. Urszula M. Zeglen, 17–19. Routledge.

———. 1999b. Reply to Stephen Neale. In *The philosophy of Donald Davidson, the library of living philosophers, vol. XXVII,* ed. Lewis E. Hahn, 667–70. Chicago and LaSalle: Open Court Press.

Farrell, Frank B. 1994. *Subjectivity, realism, and postmodernism: The recovery of the world.* Cambridge: Cambridge University Press.

Frankenberry, Nancy. 1996. The American experience. In *Spirituality and the secular quest*, ed. Peter H. Van Ness, 102–28. New York: Crossroad Publishing.

———, ed. 2002. *Radical interpretation in religion.* Cambridge: Cambridge University Press.

Fraser, Nancy. 1989. Solidarity or singularity? Richard Rorty between romanticism and technology. In *Unruly practices: Power, discourse and gender in contemporary social theory*, 93–110. Minneapolis: University of Minnesota Press.

Fulkerson, Mary McClintock. 1994. *Changing the subject: Women's discourses and feminist theology.* Minneapolis: Fortress Press.

Geras, Norman. 1995. *Solidarity in the conversation of mankind.* London: Verso.

Habermas, Jürgen. 1998. Richard Rorty's pragmatic turn. In *On the pragmatics of communication*, ed. Maeve Cooke, 343–82. Cambridge: MIT Press.

Hempel, Carl. 1965. The logic of functional analysis. In *Aspects of scientific explanation*, 297–330. New York: Free Press.

Laclau, Ernesto. 1991. Community and its paradoxes: Richard Rorty's "liberal utopia." In *Community at loose ends*, ed. The Miami Theory Collective, 83–98. Minneapolis: University of Minnesota Press.

Lindbeck, George A. 1984. *The nature of doctrine: Religion and theology in a postliberal age.* Philadelphia: Westminster Press.

McCarthy, Thomas. 1990. Private irony and public decency: Richard Rorty's new pragmatism. *Critical Inquiry* 16 (Winter): 355–70.

Murphy, John P., ed. 1990. *Pragmatism from Peirce to Davidson.* Boulder, CO: Westview Press.

Nystrom, Derek, and Kent Puckett. 1998. *Against bosses, against oligarchies: A conversation with Richard Rorty.* Prickly Pear Pamphlets, no. 11. Charlottesville, VA: Prickly Pear.

Passmore, John. 1957. Review article: Christianity and positivism. *Australasian Journal of Philosophy* 35: 125–36.

Penner, Hans H. 1988. *Impasse and resolution: A critique of the study of religion.* New York: Peter Lang.

Quine, W. V. O. 1953. Two dogmas of empiricism. In *From a logical point of view*, 20–46. Cambridge, MA: Harvard University Press.

Rorty, Richard. 1979. *Philosophy and the mirror of nature.* Princeton, NJ: Princeton University Press.

———. 1982. *Consequences of pragmatism.* Minneapolis: University of Minnesota Press.

———. 1986. Pragmatism, Davidson and truth. In *Truth and interpretation: Perspectives on the philosophy of Donald Davidson*, ed. Ernest LePore, 333–55. Oxford: Basil Blackwell.

———. 1987. Thugs and theorists. *Political Theory* 15 (November): 564–80.

———. 1989. *Contingency, irony, and solidarity.* Cambridge: Cambridge University Press.

———. 1990. Truth and freedom: A reply to Thomas McCarthy. *Critical Inquiry* 16 (Spring): 633–43.

———. 1993. Trotsky and the wild orchids. In *Wild orchids and Trotsky,* ed. Mark Edmundson, 31–50. New York: Penguin Books.

———. 1994. Taylor on truth. In *Philosophy in an age of pluralism: The philosophy of Charles Taylor in question,* ed. James Tully, 20–33. Cambridge: Cambridge University Press.

———. 1995. Response to Bernstein. Response to Farrell. In *Rorty and pragmatism: The philosopher responds to his critics,* ed. Herman J. Saatkamp Jr., 68–71, 189–96. Nashville, TN and London: Vanderbilt University Press.

———. 1997. Religious faith, intellectual responsibility, and romance. In *The Cambridge companion to William James,* ed. Ruth Anna Putnam, 84–102. Cambridge: Cambridge University Press.

———. 1998a. *Truth and progress: Philosophical papers, volume 3.* Cambridge: Cambridge University Press.

———. 1998b. *Achieving our country: Leftist thought in twentieth-century America.* Cambridge, MA: Harvard University Press.

———. 1998c. Pragmatism as romantic polytheism. In *The revival of pragmatism: New essays on social thought, law, and culture,* ed. Morris Dickstein, 21–36. Durham, NC and London: Duke University Press.

———. 1999. *Philosophy and social hope.* London and New York: Penguin Books.

Sellars, Wilfrid. 1997. *Empiricism and the philosophy of mind.* With an introduction by Richard Rorty and a study guide by Robert Brandom. Cambridge, MA: Harvard University Press.

Stout, Jeffrey. 1988. *Ethics after Babel: The languages of morals and their discontents.* Boston: Beacon Press.

Taylor, Charles. 1990. Rorty in the epistemological tradition. In *Reading Rorty,* ed. Alan Malachowski, 257–75. Oxford: Blackwell.

———. 1994. Reply to Rorty. In *Philosophy in an age of pluralism: The philosophy of Charles Taylor in question,* ed. James Tully, 219–22. Cambridge: Cambridge University Press.

West, Cornel. 1989. *The American evasion of philosophy: A genealogy of pragmatism.* Madison: University of Wisconsin Press.

Richard J. Bernstein's Response to Nancy K. Frankenberry

I have been a friend of Dick Rorty for more than fifty years. We first met at the University of Chicago where I was an undergraduate during the final years of the Hutchins era. Subsequently, Dick Rorty (after getting his MA in philosophy at Chicago) went to Yale. I followed him to Yale in 1953 after spending two years at Columbia. At the time, Yale was one of the few Ivy League graduate philosophy departments that was not being overtaken by the new varieties of analytic philosophy. Dick Rorty went to Yale to study metaphysics with Paul Weiss. Although I was never really a student of Paul Weiss (I did take classes with him), I served as assistant editor of the *Review of Metaphysics*, the journal that Paul Weiss founded and edited. My dissertation, "John Dewey's Metaphysics of Experience," was inspired by John E. Smith and mentored by Charles W. Hendel. Dick Rorty went on to serve in the army and then had his first job at Wellesley College. I stayed at Yale as an assistant professor, and later as an associate professor (without tenure) until 1965. I had the good fortune to be at Yale during the period when Wilfrid Sellars taught at Yale, and as a junior faculty member I attended his classes. It was Sellars who taught me that there was a way to use the techniques honed by analytic philosophers to deal with the major problems of the philosophic tradition. When we were at Yale together, I do not ever recall discussing pragmatism with Rorty. Coming from Chicago, we both were "taught" that pragmatism represented everything that Chicago intellectuals thought was vulgar and decadent. It was only in later years that Rorty and I discovered how much we had in common. Frequently, when I am asked what was the real difference between Rorty and myself, I answer that I *started* my philosophic career accepting Dewey's challenge to the quest for certainty, and his project of reconstructing philosophy. An engaged pluralism and a fallibilistic esprit shaped my early philosophic investigations. But Rorty was much more sympathetic to the viability of systematic philosophy. Even when he "discovered" analytic philosophy, he *initially* seemed to be convinced that this was the right way of "doing" philosophy. Only gradually did his wit and irony become fully manifest and flourish. Ever since Rorty publicly declared his allegiance to pragmatism, we have had many exchanges. When he asked me to read the manuscript *Philosophy and the Mirror of Nature,* it lacked its present introduction. I told him that no one would understand what he was "up to" unless he explained it in an introduction. This is the place where Rorty tells us that Wittgenstein, Heidegger, and Dewey are the three most important philosophers of the twentieth century. There is a story about that book that I have never written about. When Princeton University Press was reviewing the book for publication, the editor received one very positive review and one very negative review. He felt that he needed a third opinion before asking his editorial board to approve its publication. I was asked to write an evaluation. I explained that I was a personal friend of Dick Rorty's, but I felt that I could write a fair evaluation. I explained just why the book would delight some readers and infuriate others. I predicted that it would prove to be one of the most discussed books during the next decade—and told the editor that he would be crazy not to publish it! Naturally, after the book's success, my credibility as a reviewer skyrocketed! Rorty is one of the most challenging and thought-provoking thinkers of our time. I am outraged when I hear those caricatures of him as superficial, flip, and morally callous. Rorty belongs to that great tradition of ironic moralists who are deeply concerned about the abuses of humiliation and the degradation of poverty. These remarks are intended to set the context for my rejoinder to Nancy Frankenberry's perceptive chapter in which she defends Rorty against some of my criticisms.

I have always felt that there are (*at least*) two faces of Dick Rorty. There is the Rorty who delights in being the "bad boy," who mocks the spirit of "seriousness," who enjoys being outrageous and cavalier in his dismissal of philosophers and "traditional" philosophic problems. This is the Rorty who his opponents hate. They accuse him of being sloppy, fuzzy, and intellectually irresponsible. I am still amazed to discover how much venom Rorty brings out in his opponents. There are philosophers—especially "tough-minded" analytic types—who no longer take Rorty seriously, who think he is "playing" to a literary crowd and does not care about "serious" philosophic argumentation. But anyone who reads Rorty carefully knows that there really is another Rorty, someone who is much more reasonable and persuasive—someone who can argue with the best and most acute tough-minded analytic philosophers. This is the Rorty who Frankenberry explicates and defends. I think that her portrait of the *reasonable* Rorty is one of the best that I have read. In this respect, she is certainly right that most of what I criticized in Rorty is based on what he wrote in the period prior to the decade of the 1990s. In the past decade, Rorty's political and philosophical position has been much more forcefully articulated. (I would like to think that some of my earlier criticisms—along with those of other friendly critics—played a role in encouraging him to be more forthright about his political and philosophic commitments.) I also think that when one reads Rorty on Davidson, Putnam, McDowell, Brandom, and Habermas, his argumentative finesse is evident. Frankly, although there are still significant differences between us, I feel intellectually much closer to *this* Rorty. If anything, Frankenberry's case for Rorty is a bit too sane. When she declares "*rational* justifications for preferring one vocabulary over another have to do with their utility," or "justification is simply a matter of being able to give *good reasons* for beliefs," or "*constraints there are*, but these are typically holistic," or "*finding evidence to justify our beliefs* is the goal of inquiry" (emphasis added), she is using a language and a rhetoric that is far more sober and reasonable (and Habermasian) than we find in Rorty's polemical flourishes. What seems to be missing from Frankenberry's Rorty is his wit, insouciance, and irony. Nevertheless, she makes an excellent case for the "reasonable Rorty," and she backs it up with a careful reading of his texts and arguments. Most of my disagreements with *this* portrait of Rorty would turn out to be minor quibbles.

References

Rorty, Richard. 1979. *Philosophy and the mirror of nature.* Princeton, NJ: Princeton University Press.

Being Philosophic and Having a Philosophy

Reflections to Honor Richard Bernstein

Robert C. Neville

How wonderful it is that Dick Bernstein has matured into a famous philosopher so as to provoke this occasion on which I can recur to a discussion begun more than forty years ago at Yale. You understand that Dick then was an extremely young instructor without a single grey hair, and I was a sophomore with some hair. Dick was my favorite classroom teacher and among the other instructors in those days including Dick Rorty, Lewis Ford, and Donald Sherburne. Back then they were a lot older than I, but somehow that has ceased to be the case.

In fact, we, as young philosophers, were responding to three paradigmatic teachers in that place—John Smith, Paul Weiss, and Wilfrid Sellars—each of whom defined a way of doing philosophy and had missionary zeal in promoting it. The topic of the discussion itself was the nature of philosophy or, more generally, human rationality, as Dick Bernstein puts it now. More than any of the rest of us, even Rorty, Dick has kept that topic at the center of his work ever since. His principal contributions to philosophy have been in bringing that old question to maturity and advancing it far beyond its roots in our youthful experience. For this reason, that old Yale context is directly relevant to understanding and appreciating Dick's work.

Let me say first what the terms of that discussion are not. The issue about the nature of philosophy is not between those who do it and those who write about others doing it. That is a real issue, to be sure, and an important one for distinguishing between academic philosophy and intellectual history. But there was no one at Yale in our youth who taught philosophy without discussing historical figures—even the logic teacher taught Whitehead—and the two official historians of philosophy were staunch Platonists and Aristotelians, respectively. Rather, the contested positions in the discussion were epitomized by the three distinguished teachers I mentioned.

To begin with John Smith, it was from him that we all learned our pragmatism, an interpretation original with John in distinguishing pragmatism from the scientistic interpretation prevalent at Columbia in thinkers such as Sidney Hook. Smith related pragmatism positively to the great traditions of Western philosophy that he reinterpreted through Dewey's critique, and he engaged it with both analytic philosophy that he connected to classical British empiricism and Continental philosophy from Hegel, Kierkegaard, and Nietzsche to Heidegger. Although Dick and I have taken pragmatism in somewhat different directions, it was from Smith and the positive, creative ambiance he established for pragmatism that we learned it.

But teaching pragmatism was not Smith's contribution to the discussion about the nature of philosophy, except in that pragmatism offers good solutions. Rather, his contribution was his approach to philosophic issues through commentary on historical figures. Smith is a good historian, but his writing is rarely historical. It is commentarial, and the topic is the philosophic issue at hand as approachable through a critical discussion of the historical position. In addition, Smith taught us to interweave critical analysis of philosophic texts with interpretation of "the situation" of competing views. The idea of "situation" came from Dewey, but Smith focused it as the device for turning historical or logical analysis of philosophic positions into the critical development of his own position on the topic, because the historical situation always connects with our situation. In fact, Smith's way of discussing historical figures was his method for defining our situation and staking out his own trajectory.

Dick Bernstein is surely the best of us in developing Smith's approach to philosophy. Just about every one of his books is an analysis of historical figures or movements in terms of their situation and with an eye to determining what our own situation is. *Beyond Objectivism and Relativism*, a classic of our time, is a classic exercise in Smith's mode of philosophy, carried beyond Smith's usual topics and at book rather than essay length.

Paul Weiss has always criticized Dick for this Smithian mode of philosophy, asking "Where's the System? Where's the beef?" Weiss thinks that philosophy is the development of doctrinal answers to the great questions of philosophy. In the Yale days Weiss identified those with the perennial ones of the Western tradition; now he concentrates on new ways of asking new questions. But for him philosophy is inquiry into the nature of things resulting in a system of answers. Dick once said that when Weiss taught the undergraduate course on the history of philosophy, his introductory lecture was: "Thales was the first philosopher. He said everything is water. What do you think?" When Weiss taught Hegel's *Phenomenology*, the assignments were a quarter of an inch of pages each week, so as to get through the system as a whole.

Dick has decisively not gone Weiss's way of system building, with considerable sadness on Weiss's part because he wanted so much to adopt Dick as his philosophic heir. Dick did succeed Weiss as editor of the *Review of Metaphysics*, though he did not practice metaphysics in Weiss's sense. To my knowledge he has not commented extensively on Weiss, but I suspect his criticism would be that Weiss attempts to do philosophy without regard to a careful analysis of our situation, and hence appears contextless, indeed, clueless, in respect to the state of the philosophic public. I would agree with this criticism but shall argue shortly that Weiss's demand for a system has more merit than Dick (or Smith) credits. Among the strange ironies in this transgenerational philosophic conversation among friends is that Dick has always been associated with Weiss but is far more a philosopher in Smith's mode, whereas I have been closely associated with Smith but have a system even bigger and maybe better than Weiss's (smile).

Wilfrid Sellars took a dim view of both Smith and Weiss, treating the former as a mere historian because he did not solve philosophic problems and dismissing the latter as lacking the method of analysis that seemed so revolutionary to analytic philosophers. Sellars was needlessly critical, I think. He became best known for his critique of what he called "the myth of the given," a critique Smith regularly drew from Peirce and Dewey fifty to seventy-five years earlier; they should have been allies in their antifoundationalism. Sellars once told me that he viewed his work as a restatement of his father, Roy Wood Sellars's, realism in the mode of analytic philosophy. The senior Sellars's realism is very close to Weiss's own systematic position, if not so fulsomely elaborated; if Wilfrid Sellars's and Weiss's doctrinal positions could be compared in some neutral language, I suspect they would be very close on many issues.

Sellars was a committed analytic philosopher who publicly claimed that he wanted to turn the Yale department into a respectable analytic one like Harvard, Princeton, Michigan, Stanford, Berkeley, and so forth. None of us younger people I mentioned became analytic philosophers of that sort, although both Dick Bernstein and Dick Rorty have engaged the analytic tradition as a steady conversation partner. What we all did learn from Sellars, however, is that philosophy needs to have a somewhat conversational form. By this I don't mean the Great Conversation with Plato, Thomas, and Kant, ala Mortimer Adler. Rather, I mean that our own situation needs to be understood as a conversation, with our essays and books being conceived as responses to the recent essays and books of others, seeking to find a way forward. Analytic philosophy sometimes carried that to caricature, with paper titles like "Comment on Jones's response to Smith's critique of Geatch on Wittgenstein." But the point of the conversational mode is that the very topics of philosophy itself are shaped, and in the process of being reshaped, by the contemporary discussion. No essay, book, or even philosopher embodies a philosophic analysis or position as a whole; the whole lies in the public process of conversation, with somewhat arbitrary beginning and ending points.

This mode of philosophy as conversation thus criticizes the big systems for assuming that their positions on a given topic are contextualized by the rest of the system instead of by the lines of conversation external to the system that contribute to the topic's definition. And it criticizes Smith's commentarial mode for attempting to define the current situation rather than being more up front about simply making an interpretive move within that situation. We all learned these points about philosophy as conversation from Sellars. Dick Rorty became famous for the rhetoric of conversation but ruined Sellars's lesson, I think, by interpreting it so closely with his nominalism and idealism, neither of which Sellars would much like.

It was Dick Bernstein who understood this point best and explained it in his long investigation of philosophy as a practice. Although it's an old Platonic and pragmatic point that philosophy is basically practical reason, with theory to be understood in the context of practicing, Dick has interpreted this for our situation, analyzing the philosophical practices going on and showing how philosophic arguments are moves to change practice, better than anyone else, far better. Dick has brought this pragmatic interpretation of what it means to be in philosophic practice to Hegelian heights of self-consciousness.

Now I want to make a case for the missing influence in Dick's philosophic project, Weiss's emphasis on system. Let me say at the outset that

I view a philosophic system as a large complex hypothesis, itself comprising many other hypotheses on various topics, each variously connected with others, variously tested, and all made vulnerable to corrections both internal to the system and external. The nature of system itself is a topic in any system, and I can sell you books spelling out my system's position. Paul Weiss rejects this approach to system unequivocally. He thinks that to call a philosophic position or system a hypothesis is merely to say it is tentative and that one has not thought it through. He believes that when one thinks through a problem thoroughly, one sees, in some kind of intuition, its nature and answer. I believe, by contrast, that both analyses of problems and proposals for answers are fallible hypotheses vulnerable to correction. So I am a journeyman pragmatist regarding philosophical systems, and Dick should have no trouble with this part. Whitehead also, at the beginning of *Process and Reality*, defined his system as a hypothesis.

Furthermore, I agree thoroughly with Smith that an interpretation of the history of philosophy needs to be internal to a philosophy, for two reasons. One is that a dialectical engagement with other philosophers is a powerful argument for one's own position, a point Weiss appreciates. The other is Smith's and Bernstein's point that historical figures need to be understood in terms of their philosophic situation, and that cumulatively this defines one's own situation.

I also agree with Sellars's and Bernstein's point that philosophy is a practice and therefore need to argue that the development of a system itself is a contribution to an ongoing contemporary conversation. The downside of this point is that, on the analogy of a conversation, a philosophic system can be like a person who makes long, boring, monologic speeches. Since I write that kind of book, I shall not develop this point further.

Here is the argument for why systems are important in the philosophic conversation, not necessary for everyone of course, but crucial elements in the conversation. The major premise is that philosophic participation in a conversation should be serious and not trivial; this distinction is contextually defined. The minor premise is that philosophic seriousness requires making oneself vulnerable on all fronts, and vulnerability requires thinking about things from all angles, which is system. Therefore system is required for serious participation in philosophical conversation. Let me gloss the argument.

As to the major premise, a non-serious response is one that does not engage the full potential of philosophical reflection from the resources one should be expected to have. One of the reasons analytic philosophy is treated as trivial, not wrong but trivial, by so many thinkers is that it seems so often to be a set of methodological tools that a student can learn in a couple of years. This too is a caricature when thinking about the learning of analytic philosophers such as Sellars; but he was exceptional. The more a philosophic move is shaped within its practice by a deep understanding of the history of philosophy, and by a grasp of culture, and by ready access to the arts, sciences and other humanities, the more serious it is. The greater the invention and wit in finding new ways to conceive problems and new directions from which to come with suggestions, the more serious. But in addition to erudition and wit, seriousness of response requires making one's response vulnerable to correction. Peirce was right, I think, to say that a philosophic argument is more like a rope with hundreds of interwoven strands than a chain with consecutive links. The weight of truth in one's philosophic move within a conversation lies in the many strands having passed through the fires of correction. If any part of the argument is entrenched against correction, so that if it is wrong that won't be seen, then the argument has a hole in it.

My minor premise is that genuine vulnerability in philosophy requires systematic thinking, ultimately a system all of whose parts and connections have been exposed to criticism. To think about one problem, for instance, personal identity through time, from many angles requires thinking about the relations among the angles, and what stands apart from the problem to establish the angles of analysis themselves. So we would need studies of what identity consists of, the very nature of determinateness, and also studies of what distinguishes the personal from the impersonal, and the nature of time, passing from future to present to past, and enduring through that passing. For the sake of a single argument, a philosopher can just presuppose answers to all of those related issues. But insofar as they are just presupposed, they are not made vulnerable: they are assumed to be not under discussion. The really hard part of systematic philosophic practice is to be able to balance what is called into question in a given part of the conversation with what needs to have been called into question earlier or will be brought up later.

A technical, pragmatic way of defining system in philosophy is this, following Peirce's point that knowledge is the true interpretation of an object by a sign that an interpreter takes to stand for the object in a certain respect. The interpreter with context and purposes, determining the respect in which signs are sought for interpretation of the object, constitutes the angle of analysis, that is, the interpretation in that respect. So a system is interpretation of an object in all (important) respects with a reflection on how the respects differ by different angles of analysis, which in turn requires analysis of the other objects to which the interpretation in its multitude of respects is related. A philosophic system as a whole is a complex sign by which a philosopher hopes to engage all reality in interpretation.

A serious philosophic response in a conversation is one that brings a philosopher's full engagement with reality, resting on a harvest of prior reflection made vulnerable across the board. Mere readiness to make unknown suppositions vulnerable if that should come up is not enough. Any undergraduate can do that. Seriousness requires having risked ideas that might be wrong, having thought them through comprehensively, and sustaining them in such vulnerable form that when something comes up that would correct them, the correction can be taken.

Developing a philosophy with some systematic responsibility is itself a practice that requires perhaps a lifetime, or at least a long time. A truly vulnerable philosophy is never finished. So in one sense, a philosopher of this sort only makes one speech beginning in youth and going on until the end. It's not a monologue, because engagements with others take place within it, constituting part of its correction and part of its contribution to the ongoing public conversation. Perhaps a good philosopher makes only one good, long contribution to a rather leisurely transgenerational discussion. But to the extent that there is force in my argument for system, the things we say at first are not fully said until we have rounded to them again after a tour through all of the ways they might be wrong or miss what is important to say. For my part, I'm still trying to make a serious response in Dick's sophomore philosophy class.

Richard J. Bernstein's Response to Robert C. Neville

Bob Neville recalls the exciting decade that I spent at Yale. I started my graduate studies in 1953, and in the following year I was invited to teach in Yale's undergraduate Directed Studies program. I was able to teach my own course, and many of the undergraduates that I taught in those years have become distinguished professors—including Bob Neville, Ed Casey, David Carr, and Wayne Proudfoot. The graduate philosophy department at Yale attracted some talented philosophers, including Dick and Amelie Rorty (both of whom I had known from Chicago). Because my wife Carol was pursuing her doctorate in English, our circle of close friends included Harold and Jean Bloom (Carol and Jean were roommates who came to Yale from Swarthmore), Geoffrey and Renée Hartman, and Tom and Lilliane Greene. Unlike many graduate students today who are filled with anxieties about getting decent jobs, somehow we did not worry about the "job market." We considered ourselves lucky to participate in the life of the mind. My serious interest in Dewey, Peirce, and pragmatism began at Yale. John E. Smith organized a small group to read Dewey's *Experience and Nature*—and it was a revelation to me. This was a time when philosophic interest in Dewey was at an absolute low point in academic philosophy departments. But I discovered a thinker who was far more original and complex than I had been led to believe—one for whom I felt a deep affinity. Because Paul Weiss was one of the original editors of Peirce's *Collected Papers* (along with Charles Hartshorne), there was lively discussion of Peirce at Yale. Vincent Colapietro (in this volume) presents a succinct account of what I mean by engaged pluralism. But the *practice* of engaged pluralism is something that I learned at Yale. The intellectual ambience at Yale during the years I spent there was one that encouraged encounters with a range of philosophers and philosophic problems (even though there was a hostility to the varieties of analytic philosophy). I discovered Hegel at Yale. I still think the seminar that I took in the *Phenomenology of Spirit* changed the course of my philosophic life. As a young faculty member I had the opportunity to teach (or assist in teaching) a variety of courses: Marxism, Existentialism, American Constitutional Thought. I discovered Wittgenstein (both early and late). Wittgenstein's *Philosophical Investigations* was published when I was a graduate student. My book, *Praxis and Action*, had its origin in a course that I taught at Yale.

There is another aspect of my Yale experience that was vital for my intellectual and personal development. When I initially went to Yale, it was a politically conservative institution. These were the days of McCarthyism. The great hero was a recent graduate, William Buckley. Coming from the streets of New York and Chicago, and identifying myself with Left politics since the time when I was a teenager, I found the dominant ambience of Yale extremely strange—like something out of a Scott Fitzgerald novel. During the years I was at Yale, especially during the early sixties, Yale was undergoing a radical transformation. (There were still no women students as undergraduates and virtually no women faculty members.) But with the coming of the charismatic chaplain, William Sloane Coffin Jr., a more socially conscious group of students and faculty became more active. I was the faculty advisor for the John Dewey Society—a group committed to participatory democracy and opposed to the pernicious influence of McCarthyism. In the summer of 1964, I joined the group of Yale faculty and students who participated in the Mississippi Summer project to help with voter registration and to organize "Freedom Schools."

Bob Neville speaks about my relation with Paul Weiss. Paul was one of the most exciting teachers at Yale. Although I always felt alien to his way of doing systematic philosophy, I learned more from Paul Weiss about what it is to be a philosopher than I have from anyone else. Paul could think and speak faster than anyone I have ever known (with the possible exception of Isaiah Berlin). And in less time than anyone else he could find the weak point in one's argument. Paul would always ask me the toughest questions—even in the last decade of his life. But as Bob

Neville notes, I (along with Dick Rorty) was one of Paul's "failed" students. I was never comfortable with his conception of systematic philosophy—and never persuaded by it. I certainly do not denigrate the importance of systematic philosophy. Who could be more systematic than Hegel? But my deepest proclivities have always been more pluralistic. Typically my philosophic inquiries begin with what Dewey calls a "felt difficulty" or a "problematic situation," although I would like to think that there is an overall coherence to my thinking. I am not convinced that "being systematic" is always a philosophic virtue. Nor am I convinced that dividing philosophers into those who are and those who are not systematic is by itself very illuminating. We sometimes forget just how recently philosophers became preoccupied (obsessed?) with being systematic. The grand "System" is a nineteenth-century invention. Furthermore, it should be evident that "systematic" is an essentially contested concept—for there are many ways of being systematic. I am not convinced that Peirce, James, or Dewey is any less systematic than Neville or Weiss.

References

Bernstein, Richard J. 1971. *Praxis and action.* Philadelphia: University of Pennsylvania Press.

Dewey, John. 1925. *Experience and nature.* Chicago: Open Court.

Peirce, Charles Sanders. 1931–1958. *The collected papers of Charles Sanders Peirce, vols. I–VIII,* ed. Charles Hartshorne and Paul Weiss. Cambridge, MA: The Belknap Press of Harvard University Press.

Wittgenstein, Ludwig. 1953. *Philosophical investigations.* Trans. G. E. M. Anscomb. Oxford: Basil Blackwell.

Festive Jewish Naturalism and Richard Bernstein's Work on Freud and Arendt

Henry S. Levinson

The crux of this chapter is to sketch a view of festive American Jewish naturalism and then to suggest how Richard Bernstein's work, particularly his writings on Sigmund Freud and Hannah Arendt, has helped me clarify and develop it. American Jewish naturalism begins *in medias res* informed by some traditions, two traditions more immediately than others, but in the end, at least reaching out to more. It is a mentality or a practical intellectual orientation to problems of truth, justice, and joy—or, more capaciously, it builds toward one of William James's "visions, modes of feeling the whole push, and seeing the whole drift of life, forced on one by one's total character and experience, and on the whole *preferred*—there is no other truthful word—as one's best working attitude" (James 1996: 20–21).

This is a vision informed decisively by two expanding libraries of books, accompanied by the full-blooded patrons whose lives, like mine, have emerged through transactions of *reading* the literature these libraries hold. One of these is *The Library of America*, or how I imagine it, were I to select its titles rather than, say, Richard Poirier, managing that list. The other of these that I'm imagining is an institution we might call *The Library of the Varieties of Jewish Experience*, for which a good approximation would be the combined textual resources of the various *Hebrew Union College* campuses, the *Jewish Theological Seminary* campuses, the holdings of a World Wide Web of orthodox Yeshiva, and a burgeoning list in Jewish studies available in a host of college and university libraries, secular or not, in the United States and around the world.

In other words, the traditions that have grasped and shaped me, I believe, prior to my grasping them and certainly prior to making any contributions of my own, are constituted as communities of memory, practice, and hope informed first by American literature, Jewish or not, and just as designedly, by Jewish literature, American or not. And, of course, thank goodness, my two core libraries have loaning privileges arranged and in place with all of the other libraries you might think of as relevant. Yes, I have learned to leverage critical distance from one by orienting myself toward it from the other, and vice versa. And yes, I have learned to leverage critical distance from both through lessons of critical comparative appreciation and application in bunches of other traditions or movements in the making. Knowing texts such as Mencius or Aristotle or Kant or de Beauvoir or Sappho or Gadamer or Habermas or Paz or Kundera, not to mention the spurious *Protocols of Zion* and the poisonous *Mein Kampf*, and so on, will help, that is, will contribute to the basically American Jewish figure or temper that is my person, especially intellect, pushed and pulled.

Were I asked to say what my *Library of the Varieties of Jewish Experience* teaches while standing on one foot, I'd say: *TaNaKh* and its commentaries all the way up not only through rabbinic discourse, but further, to Ozick's *Shawl*, Spiegelman's *Maus* cartoons, and Philip Roth's work, maybe especially his American trilogy consisting of *American Pastoral*, *I Married a Communist*, and *The Human Stain*. Given an opportunity to tell more, I'd say: *TaNaKh* and its commentaries leave me informed and motivated and trying to motivate or persuade others by figuring myself and them in a narrative of divine creation, revelation, redemption, and reconstruction. Given even more leeway, I'd hook up these moments of the narrative traditions shaping me with four not exactly traditional, but not entirely idiosyncratic, twists. I mean I'd twist *Torah* or The Way into a library of books about creativity; I'd twist *Nevi'im* or Prophets into a library of books about what Mormons refer to as Revelating; I'd twist *Ketuvim* or Wisdom into a library of books about redeeming; and finally I'd twist rabbinic discourse or *Talmud Torah*, especially, into a library of books given over to the ongoing project of reconstruction, I mean reconstructing Jewish traditions in light of past sagacity interacting with current desires, claims, obligations, and opportunities that stand as live options in an imagined greater Jewish community or, as Schechter put it, in a "Catholic Israel."[1]

Doing this, which of course would take a lot of help from a bevy of research assistants I'll never have, would at least give me the beginnings of a map allowing me to go in Jewish directions, rather than, say, Christian directions set by *TaKhaN,* not *TaNaKh,* and by the New Testament and its commentaries, all the way up through, say, Daly, the Pope, the Patriarchs, the Presbytery, the Conventions, maybe Updike, certainly the Bishops and their current critics: you tell me how far flung I could or should get. But the *TaKhaN* tradition is not exactly informed by *Talmud Torah* and its diversity of descendent literature. Before I could actually go trekking, of course, I'd need to overlay my map of Jewish terrain with my guidebook sketch of American intellectual trail markers and social geodetic surveys, but I'll turn to this superimposition in due time.

But goodness! Think of the world of inquiry in which I've placed us so far. Think of the difference it makes to construe *Torah,* the *Pentateuch,* as a library of books about divine creation, rather than squeezing the creation narratives into the first few pages of Bereshit, or of In the Beginning: a panoply of creativity or creating is going on, from the creating of heaven and earth, to the creating of a procreative and knowing pair of animals among other minerals, plants, and animals—Adam and Hava—to the creating of ethical protocols sufficient for all the world of humankind in the Noahide covenant, to the creating of the covenanted ventures of Abraham, of Isaac, of Jacob, and of Joseph, to the creating of the Mosaic federation, to the creating of its Levitical culture, to the creating of that Levitical culture's domestication of a new and promising land, to the creating of a domesticated Levitical culture in that promising land enjoined by their embrace of a formative and normative word that, quite decidedly, is earthly and earthy, and precisely *not* in heaven. Think of that whole and variegated world—natural, social, political, ethical, and cultural—as the object and subject of reflection of *Torah* understood as the Library of Books of Creation, of Creativity, and/or of Creating. *Torah! Le Chaim!* Creation! Life! Life against Death!

Now go with me through *Nevi'im* construed as the Jewish Library of Revelating[s], contextualized, to be sure, by the Jewish books of creativity that precede them, narratively and conceptually, the books of life against death! Here we see the Jewish tradition configuring revelation as *praxis,* a tradition that shapes up divine knowledge as divine know-how and as divine familiarity, a divine familiarity with living against dying stuck, for better *and* worse, between past and future, a divine know-how about living, not dying, in the present breech or, as Henry David Thoreau would have it, in this nick of time. Revelating is prophetic; prophecy is revelatory, instructing, imploring, demanding the agonistic skills to resist idolatry, to reject oppression, to rebut superstition, to know and make or graciously embrace the conditions of joy and responsibility and gratitude, that make for more divine life, and to know the difference between joyful responsibility or responsible joy over the long haul and the momentary coming of more evanescent if orgiastic pleasures that quickly turn to worm and dust.

Justice, appreciation, would require a textured reading of each of the books of revelatory *Nevi'im*, of the dynamic tradition of conflicting traditions at work in the major and minor prophets from Joshua to Ezekiel and from Amos to Zephaniah. But hopefully, you've caught my drift. The revelation of *TaNaKh* and, more broadly, of a *Talmud Torah*, which includes the likes of Singer's tales for children, Eliach's *There Once Was a World*, Roth's Zuckerman and Rebecca Goldstein's mind-body problems, is practical, not metaphysical, ontological surely in the sense of constituting who and what we [think we] are and are meant to be in the world, but in no more transcendental sense of ontology than that, which carries no more difference that makes a *transcendental* difference than that.

Creation, of us in the world, normatively bent toward life against death; revelation or knowing that if not *praxis* related is not really knowing, because it makes no difference. And ah then the ultimate send-up, redemption. But is Jewish redemption either ultimate or a send-up? Listen to the Hertz ad—"not exactly." Notice what redemption looks like in this *TaNaKh*-based world. Redemption as apocalypse? No. Redemption as Heavenly? Goodness no. If *Torah* is not in heaven, kal-ve-chomer—then how much more so—is *ketuvim* right here on earth—ordinary old earth—no new heaven and no new earth. Isaiah just lost his marbles momentarily; Jeremiah got grandiose; Ezekiel hallucinated; Daniel would too. Redemption salvific? Listen to the Hertz ad again. I mean if this redemption is deliverance, thank God for James Dickey, because it is damned hard paddling. Redemption as transformative? Well, we're getting warmer; it is certainly process more than product. But how transformative? What process? In what sense, no product? The Ta of *TaNaKh* is *Torah*; the *Na* of *TaNaKh* is *Nevi'im*, the Library of Prophets; that leaves *Ketuvim*, which is what? The Library of Wisdom Literature.

Now perform the Jewish superimpositions I have suggested. The Way concerns creation or life enhancement, agonistic life enhancement versus death-dealing life diminishment. The prophets concern revelation or knowledge, the skills including the courage and fortitude to get around in this particular world of life against death in ways that *make life worth living*. And what's the lynchpin in this regard, or better, what is the sense of *TaNaKh*'s ending? What's the *Kh* in *TaNaKh*? Not Easter. Not Golgatha.

Not Calvary, not any of those things, at least as structured by the Christian Bible. *Ketuvim* is the Library that shelves or files sagacity. *Sagacity* is the *Kh* of *TaNaKh.* The Jewish process of redemption—contextualized by a Jewish understanding of creation/creativity/creating as well as by a Jewish understanding of prophetic revelating/revelation, practical knowingness, pragmatic normative or imperative knowing—the Jewish process of redemption *is* the Jewish process of sagacity. Redemption does not lie in a cross; it doesn't address any mystery about empty tombs, it doesn't transform a teacher who virtually had to be a swarthy Palestinian Jew with kinky black hair into the androgynous Aryan whose portrait, long blond hair, flowing dress, scruffy testosteronic beard, and all hangs in our YM—or W—CAs, white or black or multicultural. Redemption lies in sagacity, and *Ketuvim* provides the models, the central texts signifying redemption as sagacity—the Library of books beginning with the Psalter; continuing with a bunch of proverbs; going on *not* with Royce's problem of Job but with Job's problem of God's evil [aspect] and ingratitude; going on with the spiritual and ethical comeuppance of God in Job, a comeuppance that leads to God's practical subsidence—after the Whirlwind, God never has a speaking part in *TaNaKh* again; going on with the celebration of Eros, heterosexual to be sure, in Shir haShirim; going on in the openness to the alien other, indeed, the legitimization of an alien other that traditionally has been reviled and castigated, not to mention the valorization of sisterhood, in Ruth; going on to remind us of the bitter in the midst of prosperity and Shalom in Lamentations; going on to Koheleth and the interface of the Shechkina with Lady Wisdom from Greece, going on in Esther and in Daniel, to put that Hellenistic Jewish wisdom or sagacity into humanly triumphant practice for the Jews, now understanding themselves as one among many people in a vast empire among empires they certainly don't command; going on in the communal maturation of the Jewish people in Ezra and in Nehemiah, accepting the mitzvoth not as a burdensome yoke but in festive joy, the people Israel becoming God's redemptive action incarnate; going on in the rehearsals and recapitulations of Israelite history from the rise of David to the fall of Jerusalem, conceptions of the Jewish saga, in Chronicles I and II, their tails in their mouths in a convocation that closes with an opening imperative: "Any one of you of all His people—may his God be with him, and let him go up!" Go up how, and why and where? To perform an aliyah, to ascend to the bima, to begin again, again [!] to give witness to the word of the Lord, to tell the stories from beginning to end to beginning again, again, to keep the hope of sagacity, to keep sagacious hope alive! Alive in the workaday world, alive among the councils of nations, faith on earth (to steal a title from H. Richard Niebuhr) for earth. And *who* is to do this? Not a priest, not a sovereign, not a prophet, not a card-carrying Pharisee or member of the Rabbinic Assembly or the UAHC, or the Lubavitcher Rebbe, bene Ezra, not a reverend, not an ordinand, not a minister, but *any one of you of all His people*, bene Ezra. Three Deweyan cheers for the democratization of the gracious preaching of just as graceful obedience to normative creativity, that is life enhancement for the faith or trust in *any one of us* to inspire all of us, thousands of years before Luther—who would become viciously anti-Semitic enough to secure eponymous status with John Weiss's historically particular German *Ideology of Death*—thousands of years before, I say, *that* pre-Niebuhrian reformer nailed his ninety-five theses to the door. (I apologize for losing my temper.)

Well, I've gone on and on, but I'm not quite done with my Jewish shtick. Because I must, in some sufficiently pragmatic understanding of that term, go on some more to express my gratitude to the rabbinic movement that emerged in fraternal—or is it sororitorial, or is it panfilial, or is it simply uncivil—struggle with, even perduring opposition to, the nascent Jesus movement that became Imperial Rome's own religion, in a historical move that was almost as fell swoop as it neared full sweep across Carolinian Rome's Eurasian world.

I call attention to the ongoing reconstructive process of rabbinic *Talmud Torah* and its various mutants in postrabbinic literature, mainly literary, but including Jewish philosophy and that oxymoronic geek (I apologize for losing my temper again), Jewish theology. Here I will simply, if—hopefully—not simplistically, reflect on what I'll call the irony of Orthodoxy, the fact that traditional rabbinic discourse is far more conversational, indeed, open-endedly and dialogically conflictual, indeed, inherently controversial, than its liberal competitors, uproariously ironic given Reform's patronage of liberal arts and sciences bent on achieving some sort of Enlightenment inclusiveness, consensus, and a genuine *union* of Jewish sense and sensibility.

In fact, as Moshe Halbertal would have it in his *People of the Book*, rabbinic discourse puts its most distinctive stamp on Jewish culture twice-over. First, it renders that community "text centered," a historically decisive move in itself, having three results: "(1) the scholar rises to become the main authority figure, thereby linking authority to textual expertise; (2) the Torah becomes the object of ongoing reflection and the locus of religious presence and experience; and (3) the boundaries of the community are shaped in relation to a shared canon," which leaves the community able only "to evolve through reinterpretation of the canonical text" (Halbertal 1997: 129). Second, it figures its "text centeredness" in a way that is countercultural, at least to Christendom, perhaps to what Arendt would identify as any ideology. The rabbis engineered a distinctively *Talmudic culture* around a sacred text that, far from settling everything, "canonized controversy" (Halbertal 1997: 50–72). No wonder fathers of the Reformation, especially Luther, urged parishioners to burn Talmud. As rabbis collected their traditions of oral *Torah* for six or seven centuries from, roughly, the destruction of the second Temple into the seventh century, when they committed oral *Torah* to print—you try memorizing all of the Bavli or Yerushalmi, the way top adolescent *Yeshiva Buchers* do—always going out of their way to counter any one opinion given by a sage with a contrary, sometimes even contradictory, set of opinions for adjudicating this or that decidedly practical community-social-political-economic-existential issue given by some other revered sage.

Yes, the rabbis surely read some opinions out of their canonization of controversy. Paul's opinions, for instance, aren't controversial, they're out of the park; okay, the whole Christian New Testament among other witnesses of faith is out of the park. But there's stretching and then there's stretching. And yes, the rabbis established protocols or canons of assessment, indeed, standards of validity, that rendered it possible for a *beit din* or rabbinic court to choose, *usually*, the dicta of one school of sages over others in this or that area of controversy. *Usually, customarily, but not inevitably nor necessarily nor indispensably nor exclusively.* Majority opinions always came with minority opinions, including majority and minority hermeneutic opinions about opinions, and about why and wherefore these opinions carried whatever weight, or lack of it, they did. And opinions at any level were, in principle, open to reconsideration. *That's* the heart and soul of rabbinic *Orthodoxy* and its *Talmud Torah.* Theoretical consensus is just not a high priority. Trying to get things literally right is a *shanda,* a scandal, a sick joke, a slip on the old banana peel. Rendering just and honest decisions bent on keeping peace as graciously and as gratefully as possible was where rabbinic rubber hit the text-centered roads to Jewish community.

TaNaKh: Books of Creativity, of practical prophetic Revelating in society and in solitude, of Redeeming sagacity: a sort of sagacity any one of us could go up with—paradigmatically, Job the gentle gentile—any one of us could go up with to the podium to *make a case*, to make a claim—I, as one of us, commend that x, or perceive a as b—for this or that road to peace. And then a whole other Jewish testament, oral *Torah*, *Talmud*: through which *TaNaKh* gets interpreted, Israel's New Testament, the one churches wanted to humiliate or desecrate in kinky ways before burning it. A text-centered tradition demanding *continual* reconstruction of a tradition of controvertibly conflicting traditions, hoping, sometimes against hope, to do so—to invoke Rabbi James—"with a minimum of jolt and a maximum of continuity."

I, inheritor of something closer to Walter Kaufmann's heretical faith than to the *praxis* of *Yeshiva Buchers*, honor the latter's text-centered community (trying to engage in several of my own). I honor "the canonization of controversy" that the rabbis constructed, not just ludically letting a thousand flowers bloom but argumentively letting opposing traditions enter into what Bernstein refers to as *Spiel*. I honor the narratives and parables and protocols and internal commentaries of *TaNaKh* with its succeeding themes of creativity, pragmatic ethical revelating, redeeming sagacity, and reconstruction in light of the promise and the problems of women and men in our present situations. I honor this tendency of *TaNaKh*, especially seen through the lenses of *Talmud Torah*'s text centeredness and its canonization of controversy.

But I am, frankly, also an Americanist, not just by profession but in terms of James's personal pushes and pulls. I have a striking love for the likes of the Very Reverend Jonathan Edwards, of the very American Scholar Ralph Waldo Emerson, and of the very American Professor William James. I will not labor this love the way I might. But let me admit that I remain captured by William Clebsch's picture of *American Religious Thought* (Clebsch 1973), itself heavily indebted to Perry Miller's seminal works. I profess, perhaps I am even possessed by, its depiction of Edwards's efforts to come to feel at home with divinity, of Emerson's efforts to come to feel at home with nature, and of James's efforts to come to feel at home with humankind, each and all in a way continuous and coherent enough to be labeled for heuristic and argumentative purposes, a tradition of Aesthetic Spirituality in America. As I engage it, at any rate, this is a tradition that does not divinize art but does find a reiterated preoccupation with the notion or sense that beauty is to duty as grace is to law, a vision I believe we see still informing, say, Dewey's *Art as Experience* and even Rorty's *Philosophical Papers*, his "Trotsky and Orchids," maybe even his *Against Bosses and Oligarchies*. We surely see this tension in the works of Poirier, if not Kateb. And it is not just that when I turn to *TaNaKh* I tend to see beauty being to duty what *tszedaqah* is to *mishpat*, that is, what mercy and graciousness and gratitude are to justice. But also that in my own reflections on the syncopated themes of creativity, revelating, redeeming, and reconstruction, I'm as likely to turn to my American shades and *chevrah*, as anywhere or anyone else for critical reflection.

Which brings me to a variety of pragmatisms, presented by readings of Richard Rorty, Cornel West, and Richard Bernstein, respectively. I read all three of these thinkers as mightily and centrally concerned to reflect on ways in which creativity, revelating, redeeming, and critical reconstruction hang together. I do not suggest that they are at one on any of these themes. On the contrary, both the styles and substantial judgments these self-identified pragmatists make are in tension, and to do them any justice, I would want to *Spiel* with their work in much the same way Bernstein, more than once, has played, say, the works of Habermas, Gadamer, and Rorty. I would want to rub them up against one another in ways that would be as likely to cause some sore spots and bruises as it would be to produce any new, vital intellectual offspring.

Rorty, I'd say, is Pragmatism's master of Mardi Gras (or for us Jews in colloquy, he is dressed up like Uncle Mordecai at Purim, or for us Santayanans, he's playing Hermes the Interpreter). This is to characterize him as somewhat more ludic than the other fellows, typically attempting to leave just about any apparent philosophical solution, resolution, or dissolution, of any vexing philosophical problem, *liminal*, that is, *betwixt and between* the appearance of resolution and the reality of yet other intellectual inversions or conversions or dead ends to come. Rorty is the one we can count on to recognize the destructive side of any life-affirming scheme as well as the creative qualities of this or that academic murder, or murderers.

West, in my diorama, is currently Pragmatism's Prophet, the author of prophetic pragmatism. This is to take *The American Evasion of Philosophy* (West 1989) as his key effort to transform his life into a work of art in a way that will trumpet organic socio-politico-intellectual alarm. West is definitely the inheritor of *TaKhaN* traditions rather than of *TaNaKh* ones. His pragmatic essays are more likely to end on a note of *Apocalypse Now* than on any court-jestering gymnastics, a la Rorty the Interpreter, and more with an imperative not simply to remember the wretched of the earth but to encourage us privileged people to link arms with them in revolution, today already, than with any less interventional will to interpret (say, of the sort Arendt expresses when she confides to an interviewer that she doesn't consider herself a doer, but can hardly bear to imagine herself not attempting to understand what has happened or is happening).

Bernstein, I want to say, is the sagacious pragmatist among these three. I'm simply ignorant about any self-conscious identification he may have with any communities of inquiry centered on *TaNaKh* or *Talmud Torah* or subsequent iterations of Jewish text centeredness that end urging people to begin again, again, sagaciously. I find his use of "we" and "us" and "our" near the end of his recent books about Freud's *Moses* and about how Hannah Arendt's "confrontation with the Jewish Question (in its complex and varied aspects) shaped many of the fundamental issues that preoccupied her throughout her life" (Bernstein 1996: 9) at least curious (see also Bernstein 1996: 189; 1998: 116). Bernstein alludes to Scholem characterizing Arendt as "the daughter of our people"; he draws analogies between telling the story of the Exodus "we repeat" annually, as the rabbis have told "us" "we" must do, "as our *own*" story, on the one hand, and Freud's insistence that we had better keep interpreting individual dreams and cultural dreamworks psychoanalytically, and repeatedly, because "in every generation, there is danger of losing our freedom, of falling away from the nobility of our tradition, of succumbing to idolatry and the bondage which our archaic heritage opposes." Whatever. There is a "text centeredness," a careful argumentation, a "canonization of controversy," and, I'd argue, conceptual links between judgment, thought, deliberative pausing, sagacity and (redeeming) *hopefulness* in Bernstein's work that ring true to a *Ketuvim*-inspired, even *Ketuvim*-inebriated American Jewish head like mine.

It is, indeed, to this link between thoughtfulness and hopefulness, especially as it sheds light on "the new Jewry," that I want to devote the rest of this reflection. I do so full well assuming that whatever insight might be accomplished by doing this, such a partial view of Bernstein's work will blind us to important claims he makes, say, about Freud and Arendt, not to mention *praxis* and action, getting beyond objectivism and relativism, working critically at the junctures of social and political theory, interpreting the tensions and overlaps between movements of thought labeled for better and worse, "modernism" and "postmodernism," and finding and making a new constellation or force field in philosophy.

I draw attention first to a view that Freud and Arendt shared with William James and John Dewey, wittingly or not, namely, that both human thinking and human hoping are utterly historical episodes, and that historical episodes are utterly contingent. One fine element of Bernstein's work on Freud is his decimation of the claim that Freud was an orthodox Lamarckian; rather, evidence warrants the claim that Freud continually alluded to Darwin, not Lamarck. Darwin isn't indexed in Bernstein's work on Arendt, but contingency certainly is, as Bernstein underscores Arendt's rejection of *any* belief in historical necessity or historical inevitability. She calls both beliefs dangerous fictions "intertwined with the rise of ideologies that claimed to provide 'the key to history'" (Bernstein 1996: 51). To the contrary, he presents as one of Arendt's most basic convictions "the radical contingency of history." Both Freud and Arendt would have responded positively, in the main, to James's account—in "Great Men and Their Environments"—of the way social history works—such changes occurring by way of interactions between spontaneous social variations and various principles of selection, from ecological to social to political to cultural selective factors. They also would have applauded Dewey's organism-environment transactional account of historical processes of reconstruction, itself dependent on James's biological metaphors (N. B. *not* biologism). For all four, human history carried both the risks and opportunities of an open-textured drama, one enacted by the agents participating diversely in it.

This radically contingent, transactional account of history is an important key to understanding Freud on the problem of tradition, which in turn is central to his *Moses and Monotheism*, where he tries to establish tradition's "real nature" and "special," that is, compulsive, power (Freud 1939: 29). In Freud's own thinking, one large aim of *Moses and Monotheism* was to show that the origin of Judaism was accountable in much the same way he had accounted for Totemism twenty-five years before, an origin that begged for psychoanalytic explanation in terms of a traumatic impression on the part of the Hebrews of having murdered their father figure Moses, the defensive repression of this murder, an extended period of latency, the partial return of the repressed and the ultimate crystallization of Mosaic monotheism "with its harsh disdain for all forms of idolatry, and its emphasis on leading an ethical life of truth and justice that eventually came to prevail" (Freud 1939: 31).

Now this one-liner summing up the Judaism that came to prevail—disdain for all forms of idolatry and dedication to a life of truth and justice, forfeits, let's say at any rate, detail and clarity for simplicity. In fact, and not coincidentally, it does so in a way that fits Freud's twentieth-century—at least his 1930s—yen to identify himself as "a New Jew," or as being Jewish without observing Judaism. This is so because what Freud claims to hang on to, what he virtually identifies with his own Jewish essence, is *Der Fortschritt in der Geistigkeit*, a phrase that, Bernstein notes, is almost impossible to translate but that means something like Strachey's "progress or advance in intellectuality-spirituality." This amounts to the valuable part of Moses's monotheism according to Freud, the part that isn't simply projection and wish fulfillment and compulsion and a psychological evasion and distortion and delusion. It's the part of Jewishness from which, Freud nearly implies, his own psychoanalytic movement descends. It's the part that Freud must think gives himself license to draw a sort of identity between Johanan Ben Zakkai's founding of Yavneh, the first academy of Jewish learning, under Roman occupation and persecution, and his founding of the psychoanalytic movement under Nazi occupation and persecution, when "once again our people are facing difficult times. They call for a mustering of all our strength to preserve unharmed our culture and learning" (Freud 1939: 34).

Here Freud measures the realization of aspiration, of hope, by "the strength to preserve unharmed our culture and tradition." And what is that, according to Freud? A culture and tradition centered on "Literature" and the practical thoughtfulness it expresses. You might recall at this point that James turned to Darwin for an approach to social history, because Darwin had distinguished the causes of origin of species from the causes of their maintenance, in order to avoid "the blunder of clumping," a blunder he believed Lamarck and Spencer to have made. Here Freud has switched his account from the causes of origin of Jewish culture and Judaism in hidden psychic motives and compulsive mechanisms to the causes of preservation of that cultural species, at this point identifying manifest, not sub- or unconscious, "literature," neither neurosis nor psychosis per se, as the vehicle of cultural survival. Again, at best, simplicity beats out either clarity or detail, at this point in Freud's presentation. What literature counts here? *TaNaKh? Talmud Torah?* All that and Maimonides and Spinoza and Shakespeare and Feuerbach too? Range of reference here is a problem that Freud has no particular interest in solving. But we might. At any rate, Freud is pragmatic enough to believe that "essences," as in *his* essence being Jewish and as in *the* essence of civilization *sans phrase* being intellectual and spiritual development, derive from (his and its) interests, not vice versa. And he is Darwinian enough to turn the problem of the one and the many on its head, asking how historical entities, like Jewishness, maintain continuity and coherence in light of all the real changes and variations they undergo. He has abandoned the intellectual world that supposed that things, like Jewishness, maintain numerical identity despite variation and change. Freud may be clumping together Literature as vehicle of Jewish survival and Literature as central to the culture that has survived. But no matter as to linking hopefulness with thoughtfulness. Because Bernstein's work makes it crystal-clear that Freud sees Nazi "Athleticism," or the German (as well as Austrian) embrace of a brutal, humiliating, and deadly might-makes-right ideology, as threatening not just the Jewish community but the West, partly beholden to Jewish culture for its historical embrace of iconoclasm and normative devotion to truth and justice. Those core aspirations—and their being core has of late been problematized—are functions of thoughtfulness, of hearing, of speaking, of listening, of persuading, of sharing thoughts and desires and deciding policies together as a matter of shared intention, of letting intellect not so much suppress emotion—it can't because intellect *is* emotional—as ordering them in ways that would allow for realizing the peaceful and prosperous world we dream about. A redeemed world (for Freud and me, at least, a regulative ideal) is a thoughtful world, a world in which people can, by dint of thoughtfulness, maintain sufficient continuity and coherence, psychologically, ecologically, ethically, socially, politically, and culturally, to continue prizing and permitting social and political idiosyncrasy, differentiated cultures, and private lives the way we people do. Among other things, this hope depends on resisting deep-seated impulses that can make us more like dogs in heat or a gang of murderers than we'd like to admit.

And speaking of gangs of murderers, finally, I promise, I turn to Bernstein on Arendt, especially on evil. Bernstein makes a good case that Gershom Scholem was wrong to challenge Arendt on the grounds that her account of radical evil in *On Totalitarianism* and her account of the banality of evil in *Eichmann in Jerusalem* were contradictory. These two writings seemed to be contradictory to Scholem, because the one appeared to involve ingenuity, while the other amounted to lacking anything like it or conditional for it or on it. But radical evil and the banality of evil are compatible notions, according to Arendt, especially the way Bernstein interprets her work. Totalitarian regimes are radically evil, on Arendt's reading, because they are an organized attempt to render human beings "superfluous." "To make human beings superfluous is to eradicate the very conditions that make humanity possible" (Bernstein 1996: 144). And what are those characteristics? According to Arendt: plurality, spontaneity, natality, and individuality. Destroying these things makes for absolute evil. That's what the camps were organized to do in a laboratory experiment sort of way for the thousand-year Reich. Destroy any difference between one prisoner and another or, as the lingo had it, one stick of timber from another; destroy what Sellars would call any sense of I-as-one-of-us; destroy the possibility of any human expression; destroy any ability to begin again, again, or to initiate anything; destroy the very possibility of being distinct, and so, destroy the possibility of making any difference that made a difference. Bernstein says, "in theological language, it is the audacious attempt to destroy God's creation and to transform human beings into 'perverted animals'" (Bernstein 1996: 149), like Pavlov's dog. Such evil, involving quite a bit of imaginative organization, engineering, and administration at crucial points in the process, seems anything but thoughtlessness, which, according to Arendt, was the characteristic that made Eichmann's evil banal. True, says Bernstein, "the key concept in her earlier analysis of radical evil was *superfluousness.* After she witnessed the Eichmann trial, she turned her attention to *thoughtlessness*" (Bernstein 1996: 152). But these accounts are not contradictory; they are not even accounts of the same things. "Superfluousness" characterizes the *victims* of radical evil, while "thoughtlessness" characterized many *agents* of radical evil, like Eichmann, who banally kept the trains on time when they were running to Auschwitz. Nazi Germany engineered a culture in which banal agents could perpetrate the suffering by victims of absolute evil.

Here then we have two members of the new Jewry, Freud and Arendt, two Jews without Judaism coming to fundamental insight under conditions of Nazi occupation and persecution, when they both were attacked as Jews, retaliating as Jews—true enough, pariah Jews, even pariahs in pariah Jewish culture. Would their insights have been any different had they been members of a New Jewry *with* Judaism, which is the way I'd characterize my own *chevura*: a *chevura* Feuerbachian enough to construe divinity as a predicate, not a subject, a *chevura* seeking not just solace but delight in continuing with a modicum of coherence our archaic tradition one way among many, full well accepting ourselves as continuing to engage in a distinctively human construction?

Freud identified *Der Fortschritt der Geistigkeit* as his essential Jewish character. Hannah Arendt identified the destruction of the conditions of humanity qua human: plurality, spontaneity, natality, and individuality—as the absolute evil, even thoughtless, agents had perpetrated against the Jews, against the West, against humankind. I know it involves a web of inferences I will not now spin out. But surely what Freud found Jewish about himself—the *Geistigkeit* of it all—is what Arendt clarified to us far more clearly and persuasively as the human condition she found Nazi Germany obliterating.

Again, would Freud and Arendt have been better off as Jews with Judaism? I think that's like asking what it's like to be a horse. Or, as the Buddha would say, here we have a question that tends not to edification. Am I better off—is my festive American Jewish naturalism better off—for the works of Freud and Arendt? Assuredly, even if Freud depended on some just-so stories that, I think, are a giggle. Even if Arendt was rhetorically and high-handedly moralizing in her account of *Judenrat* in *Eichmann.* Freud's linkage of hopefulness and thoughtfulness is a baseline against which the Nazi quest for superiority is such an obscenity; it is the standard in terms of which Arendt links hopelessness or despair with thoughtlessness. Would I have had the shock of recognizing what now seems to me so clear, that Freud's celebration and Arendt's distress are two sides of the same normative culture, had it not been for Bernstein? I do not think so.

I have identified my own account of American religious thought with William Clebsch's book by the same name, which celebrates aesthetic spirituality in Edwards, Emerson, and James by pursuing the ratio "beauty is to duty as grace is to law" in the works of those eponymous America thinkers.[2] How do Richard Bernstein's writing projects square up with anything like this interpretive tradition? Is there any sense in which Bernstein's work can be identified as following, or perhaps simply complementing, the aesthetic spirituality in the eponymous American religious thinkers Edwards, Emerson, and James?

On the one hand, I want to say, Bernstein does not identify, much less identify with, the tradition of aesthetic spirituality that Clebsch found in Edwards, Emerson, and James. But, on the other hand, the extent to which he attributes importance to aesthetics in its relation to ethics in the works of Peirce and Dewey, as well as in the writings of Kant, Marcuse, and Gadamer, is telling and deserves more investigation.

Central to Bernstein's interpretations of all of these philosophers, or perhaps to his interpretations of all of them, are links among obligation, desire, spontaneity, freedom, and what Santayana would eventually call aesthetic experience, or the sense of beauty. A book could be written on understanding all of these links in his works. But in concluding this chapter, let me just note, at least, that Bernstein affirms, with Peirce and Dewey, that "all reasoning exists in a logical space of norms" (Bernstein 1971: 191). He recognizes that Peirce thought that the normative sciences could be exhaustively classified into logic, ethics, and aesthetics. But more, he seems favorable to Peirce's placement of practical reasoning within the space of aesthetics quite precisely in the sense that analyzing what one of us ought to do demands analyzing "what it is that one ought to admire *per se* regardless of what it may lead to and regardless of its bearing on human conduct" (Bernstein 1971: 191). Whether he would choose to affirm and/or develop a language of loveliness or beauty to pursue the relevant issues of admiration, much less a language of spirituality, he would have to say.

NOTES

1. For collateral reflections on Soloman Schechter, Mordecai Kaplan, and Louis Ginzberg, see "Festive Naturalism and *The Legends of the Jews*," the William James Lecture on Religious Experience for 2000–01, in *Harvard Divinity Bulletin* 30:2 (Summer/Fall 2001), 5–10.

2. See William A. Clebsch, *American Religious Thought* (Chicago and London: University of Chicago Press, 1973).

REFERENCES

Arendt, Hannah. 1964. *Eichmann in Jerusalem: A report on the banality of evil.* New York: Viking Press.

———. 1968. *The origins of totalitarianism.* New York: Harcourt, Brace & World.

Bernstein, Richard J. 1971. *Praxis and action.* Philadelphia: University of Pennsylvania Press.

———. 1996. *Hannah Arendt and the Jewish question.* Cambridge, UK: Polity Press.

———. 1998. *Freud and the legacy of Moses.* Cambridge, UK: Cambridge University Press.

Clebsch, William. 1973. *American religious thought: A history.* Chicago: University of Chicago Press.

Freud, Sigmund. 1939. *Moses and monotheism.* Trans. Katherine Jones. New York: Knopf.

Halbertal, Moshe. 1997. *People of the book.* Cambridge, MA: Harvard University Press.

James, William. 1880. Great men and their environments. In *Atlantic Monthly,* 46/276 (October): 441–59.

———. 1996. *A pluralistic universe.* Lincoln: University of Nebraska Press.

West, Cornel. 1989. *The American evasion of philosophy: A genealogy of pragmatism.* Madison: University of Wisconsin Press.

Richard J. Bernstein's Response to Henry S. Levinson

The next several chapters deal with various aspects of my views about Judaism, the Jewish tradition, and the Jewish Question. But I feel that a disclaimer is appropriate. I am not a student of Jewish tradition. Indeed, my knowledge of this rich tradition is scanty—and I wish it were much more thorough. Prior to my book on Hannah Arendt, I never explicitly treated any Jewish issues, although I have discovered that many thinkers concerned with religious issues such as Paul Ricoeur, David Tracy, and Robin Lovin have found my writings relevant to their religious and theological interests. Before dealing with the essays that focus on my Jewish concerns, I want to quote a passage that I wrote in 1996 for the preface to *Hannah Arendt and the Jewish Question*:

> Several years ago I was invited to give a series of lectures on a Jewish theme at a major university. At first I thought this invitation was a mistake. Although I have written about a variety of contemporary philosophers and intellectual issues, I had never dealt explicitly with Jewish issues. The individual who had extended the invitation was aware of this, but said that the idea of the series was to provide an occasion for persons who had contributed to other intellectual areas to think about Judaism and Jewishness. Because I was busy preparing *The New Constellation* for publication, I was unable to accept the invitation. But I was also unable to forget a phrase in the letter I received—"to write the one 'Jewish' book

> that you always wanted to write." That phrase struck a deeply resonant chord. I realized that there *was* a 'Jewish' book I wanted to write. I wanted to explore the ways in which several major twentieth-century thinkers who were Jews confronted their Jewishness. In what ways, if any, did such a confrontation affect and shape their own cultural contributions? The idea was to select several twentieth-century thinkers and examine the range of different understanding and responses to a Jewish identity. In the early stages of the project, I thought about writing about Arendt, Freud, Scholem, Benjamin, Derrida, and Levinas. Because writing has always been a personal quest, I thought of this project as a way of exploring my own relation to my Jewish heritage and how it has influenced (or not influenced) my intellectual concerns. (Bernstein 1996: ix–x)

What was supposed to be the first two chapters of single book has turned into two books (*Hannah Arendt and the Jewish Question* and *Freud and the Legacy of Moses*). The last section of my recent book, *Radical Evil: A Philosophical Interrogation*, deals with two other thinkers who were Jewish, Emmanuel Levinas and Hans Jonas (in addition to taking another look at Hannah Arendt). But the journey that I began several years ago is still very much in progress. In reading the chapters by Henry S. Levinson, Gilya Schmidt, Mary Doak, and Rebecca Chopp, I feel more like a student still learning than the author about whom they were writing.

I want to say a word about how I think about (and teach) the American pragmatic tradition. The metaphor that I sometimes use is that of an ongoing conversation. Not quite the civilized conversation that Rorty describes at the conclusion of *Philosophy and the Mirror of Nature*, but more like one of those animated, messy conversations that take place at a New York dinner party that sometimes sound like a cacophony of voices all demanding to be heard at the same time, and where frequently the speakers are talking at cross-purposes. The virtue of such animated conversations—even when there are sharp disagreements—is that they are richer, more varied, complex, and dissonant than polite exchanges. I suggest that this is the way in which we should read and hear the pragmatic thinkers. Anyone who really knows Peirce, James, Dewey, and Mead (as well as the other pragmatic thinkers) realizes how different they are in their temperaments, style, concerns, and emphases. They disagree and even flatly contradict each other. We frequently group them together, but there is plenty of dissonance among them. The same phenomenon is true for more recent thinkers who identify themselves as belonging to the pragmatic style of thinking—for example, Richard Rorty, Cornel West, Hilary Putnam, Louis Menand or Robert Brandom, and myself. Levinson thinks of Rorty as the "ludic" pragmatist, West as the "prophetic" pragmatist, and he classifies me (I consider it a compliment) as the "sagacious" pragmatist. There are tensions, disagreements, and out-and-out contradictions among us. I would like to think that each of us adds something important to a living tradition to which we all contribute. Rorty's wit and irony is a powerful debunking tool. Cornel West is important because the prophetic element in his thinking connects directly with religious concerns. He also makes us painfully aware of the deficiencies of pragmatism in dealing with the problems of racism. Putnam helps bring out the rigor of pragmatism. And Louis Menand has brilliantly set the pragmatic tradition in the context of American intellectual history as a reaction to the horrors of the Civil War. The pragmatic thinkers have never been hostile to religion (although they have been critical of what Dewey calls "supernaturalism"). Rather, they have sought to reveal how the religious dimension of human life is compatible with fallibilism and pluralism and enriches the other aspects of human experience.

Levinson sketches his view of "festive American Jewish naturalism"—a vision that is informed by two expanding libraries—*The Library of America* and *The Library of the Varieties of Jewish Experience.* This vision is a distinctive blend of his American and Jewish experience. In this respect—although I am not nearly as knowledgeable as Levinson about the Jewish tradition and Hebrew texts—I feel that a blending of these traditions has shaped my own vision. The classical pragmatic thinkers were all naturalists—deeply influenced by Darwin. Their robust naturalism can accommodate and even highlight the aesthetic and religious dimensions of human experience. Levinson sees a link in my work between thoughtfulness and hopefulness—a link that is also discerned by Vincent Colapietro. I am gratified also to learn that Levinson appreciates my explications and *critiques* of Freud's and Arendt's reflections on the relation of Jewishness and Judaism. At the end of his chapter, Levinson raises the question of the relation of aesthetic experience or the sense of beauty to the language of spirituality. I have always argued that one cannot appreciate Dewey's philosophic project unless one understands the prominent place he assigns to the aesthetic and consummatory phase of *all* experience. More generally, the classic pragmatic thinkers sought to show how experience—including practical and intellectual inquiries—can (and ought to be) *funded* with a pervasive aesthetic consummatory quality.

REFERENCES

Bernstein, Richard J. 1996. *Hannah Arendt and the Jewish question.* Cambridge, MA: MIT Press.

———. 1998. *Freud and the legacy of Moses.* Cambridge, UK: Cambridge University Press.

———. 2002. *Radical evil: A philosophical interrogation.* Cambridge, UK: Polity Press.

Rorty, Richard. 1979. *Philosophy and the mirror of nature.* Princeton, NJ: Princeton University Press.

Richard Bernstein on the Jewish Question

Gilya G. Schmidt

In the preface to *Hannah Arendt and the Jewish Question* (1996a), Richard Bernstein recounts his bemused reaction to an invitation he received "to give a series of lectures on a Jewish theme." "I thought this invitation was a mistake," he wrote, because "I had never dealt explicitly with Jewish issues " (1996a: ix).

In this chapter I would like to argue that what becomes evident in his recent books on Hannah Arendt and Sigmund Freud's *Moses and Monotheism* (Bernstein 1998) is implicit in most of his writings on what he calls "contemporary philosophers and intellectual issues," from John Dewey to multiculturalism, even though such watchwords as Judaism, Israel, Talmud, and Rabbinics—which many Jews banter about the way we eat chicken soup and lokshen kugel—never find their way into his philosophical conversations. Other Jewish concepts such as hermeneutics, dialogue, community, and obligation are central themes in many of his philosophical and political essays and in his numerous books. Bernstein acknowledges that "writing has always also been a personal quest" (1996a: x), a way of exploring his own relationship to his Jewish heritage and how it has influenced (or not influenced) his intellectual concerns. I would like to suggest that Bernstein *lives* Jewish issues and their implications but in a larger context than that of his birth community, in ever broader concentric circles that criss-cross and interweave (Bernstein 1986a: 11, 16) in the philosophical community, American society, and the world community.

In spite of the very few biographical comments in Bernstein's publications, it is quite clear that his Jewish experience is hugely different from Hannah Arendt's. Since he met her in the early 1970s, Arendt has been one of his favorite subjects to write about.[1] Because of her Jewishness,

Arendt, during the first part of her life, saw herself, and was seen by her society, as a pariah, or an outcast. Bernstein sees her as "a marginal figure" (1997: 157). The pariah concept was an intrinsic aspect of the Jewish Question for German Jews, even after Emancipation in 1871. Under the Nazis, Arendt experienced with a vengeance what it meant to be a Jew in a fascist country that was planning to murder the entire Jewish population of Europe. Soon her status deteriorated to statelessness, as did that of many others. Post-Holocaust, after the scandal that erupted around her book, *Eichmann in Jerusalem* (1963), Arendt, who by now was an American citizen, was marginalized by her own people because of her unpopular views.

By contrast, and in spite of the societal anti-Semitism that existed in the United States during the 1950s, Bernstein gives no indication that he ever felt marginalized because of his ethnicity, or that he had to fight for his rights or was maligned by racial epithets. On the contrary, he was fortunate to receive an Ivy League education at a time when the *numerus clauses* for Jewish students was still a recent memory in the North. In 1958, Bernstein wrote his dissertation on the great American champion of democracy, John Dewey (1859–1952) (Bernstein 1960, 1966, 1986),[2] and went on to an illustrious academic career. Still today he gratefully reflects on the guidance and nurturance that he received at Yale in philosophical plurality and at Haverford in interdisciplinary studies. In fact, one gets the impression that Bernstein chose a sort of intellectual liminality precisely because he could afford to, which doesn't mean that it wasn't without risk.

Two areas of interest arise out of Bernstein's cultural context, with one of them becoming a lifelong vocation: (1) an interest in Israel, and (2) a commitment to democratic values.

First, Bernstein began his college education in 1949, a year after the creation of the state of Israel. While completing his dissertation at Yale in 1957, he spent a year at Hebrew University in Jerusalem as a Fulbright lecturer. The country, in spite of being the Jewish spiritual homeland, was a fledgling state, the only democracy in the Middle East, with a third-world standard of living. Israel had just survived the Sinai campaign in which she was to be strangled and driven into the sea by the Arabs. Instead, she emerged victorious, conquering the Egyptian Sinai Peninsula. Bernstein made two more official visits to Israel, each time to Hebrew University, two years before the Six-Day War, in 1965–1966, and in 1997, as a Fellow at the prestigious Franz Rosenzweig Research Center.

These visits certainly demonstrate a sustained interest in Israel. Until his latest two books, however, only a few outright Jewish publications existed over a forty-year period—a study on education in Israel in Hebrew (Bernstein 1958), two articles on philosophical matters in *Midstream*, a Zionist publication (Bernstein 1973, 1979), and a Hebrew translation of his 1983 essay "What Is the Difference that Makes a Difference? Gadamer, Habermas, Rorty."

Second, the greater body of work has resulted from Bernstein's commitment to democratic values. The 1950s produced some of the worst and some of the best in American history. On the one hand, our nation had to contend with Joseph McCarthy and his witch-hunt for Americans who were or who were suspected of being Communists. This infamous congressional campaign brought out the worst in some Americans who informed on their fellow citizens very much the way Germans did during the Nazi period. It also brought home the fact that Americans could not rest on the laurels of the Constitution and its amendments and had to be forever vigilant for their rights, that at any moment some demagogue in the form of a senator or other elected official might appear and threaten their liberties. And, indeed, many American Jews, whether in Hollywood, the press, politics, academia, or business, became subject to the shameful congressional inquiries that took place.

The second memorable event of the 1950s was Rosa Parks's refusal to give up her seat on a Montgomery bus, thereby initiating one of the great movements for social justice in our century—a political movement that would change the fabric of American society forever. It was Rosa Parks's determination to claim what the Declaration of Independence calls her "inalienable right to life, liberty, and the pursuit of happiness" that rallied the black community around her. Many Jews understood the importance of this struggle by black Americans for *all* Americans. Rabbi Abraham Joshua Heschel, one of the famous teachers in the Jewish tradition, and other rabbis marched arm in arm with Martin Luther King Jr. and other civil rights activists from Selma to Montgomery because they understood the importance of solidarity.[3] Many Jews participated in the civil rights movement. Bernstein joined some of his students during the voter registration drive in Mississippi. In an article in *The Nation*, he reflected that his few days in Mississippi in 1964 were among the most intense, vital, and meaningful in his life (Bernstein 1964: 512). Even though, as he wrote later, he went "more as an observer than as a participant" (Bernstein 1986b), it was nevertheless political action in fulfillment of a philosophical ideal.

"These civil rights workers . . . have forced us to take seriously our own professed ideals about democracy, freedom, and the rights of men" (Bernstein 1964: 515). Bernstein recently noted that there are "rare moments in the modern age when the revolutionary spirit suddenly bursts forth . . . there are those rare moments when plurality becomes a political reality" (Bernstein 1997: 161). The civil rights movement was such a moment, because "their activity is reeducating America, reawakening our social conscience, and most important, pointing the way toward effective social action" (Bernstein 1964: 512).

Bernstein's interests during the 1950s and 1960s reflected the interests of American Jews during this time period—Israel and social justice. The Jewish Question no longer dealt with the European issues of civil rights, integration, and equality for *Jews,* but with justice for *all* Americans. "Justice, justice shall you pursue" (Deut. 16:20). American-born Jews, or Jews who had come to the United States during the immigrant era before the quota system closed the doors in 1924, had a different relationship to life in America than refugees and survivors who came because of Hitler. The latter wanted to keep the heritage alive that they had been forced to abandon. American Jews, whether they were here by birth or had come by choice, wanted to be Americans first. In the 1950s, the cultural melting pot was still very much alive. Despite the fact that we are all hyphenated Americans, in Michael Walzer's words (Brettschneider 1996: 276), from the twenties to the sixties it was expected that one lived on the *American* side of the hyphen, whatever one's ethnicity. Already in nineteenth-century Russia, the wise Jews remembered to "be a man in the street and a Jew in your tent."[4]

It was in this culturally and ethnically assimilationist environment that Bernstein came of age academically. His dissertation on the thought of John Dewey reflected the American anxiety about the fragility of our democratic society and its shortcomings that McCarthyism and a confrontation with the Jim Crow laws revealed. The message was clear—we needed to do a better job of being citizens. We needed to be less apathetic and rethink our civic responsibilities. Bernstein's Dewey project appears to be an All-American undertaking and not at all Jewish. Yet his passionate plea for a fulfillment of Dewey's charge for "a radicalization of democracy, for a reconstruction of local communities, for a revitalization of public life" (Bernstein 1986a: 270)—a plea for which he is still fighting after forty years—is in fact very Jewish. Bernstein came from a cultural milieu where people get involved *as a norm.* Jews as a group are very patriotic and politically engaged—we vote, we form and support special interest groups, and we follow political issues and form opinions on them. In short, Jews make it their business to support and uphold the democratic process. The *Sim Shalom* prayer book of the conservative movement contains three pages of prayers for "America, founded on biblical precepts." Along with passages from the Declaration of Independence, the Bill of Rights, and speeches by Lincoln and Washington, we find such biblical maxims as "Proclaim liberty throughout the land, for all of its inhabitants" (Lev. 25:10), and "How good and how pleasant it is when brethren live in unity" (Psalm 133:1). Every Shabbat congregation says a prayer for the (political) leaders of our country, and the prayer books contain all of the important patriotic songs as well. In fact, the late Rabbi Simon Greenberg compared the signing of the Declaration of Independence to the covenant at Sinai. The Declaration "has become a sacred covenant which the American people, at the beginning of their history, freely and solemnly made not only among themselves but with mankind and the God of history" (Greenberg 1981: 135). Just as Jews today consider themselves having been present at Sinai, so Greenberg expects American Jews to own up to their obligation based on the commitment of their fathers. "Their descendants . . . declare it to be the duty of every American, to the end of time, to identify himself with the historic moment when the Declaration was first announced to the world and to see himself as a veritable signer of it, thus joining the original signers in pledging, as they did, his life, his fortune, and his sacred honor to the implementation of the truths that it proclaims" (Greenberg 1981: 136). Bernstein takes these words seriously.

Although he enjoys critical inquiry for its own sake, Bernstein does philosophy with a purpose. From the beginning, his concern has been with democracy, relationship, and dialogue. What are the problems we are facing, and what can we do to make the world a better place to live?

The task before us is "to fix the world." The notion of *tikkun olam* is one of the obligations with which Jews are charged. We were brought into this world for a purpose, to be God's partner, to do our part in healing or completing the world. By critically exploring aspects of human relationships throughout his career, Bernstein has not ventured very far from the concerns of his ethnic group, yet he deals with these concerns in a larger context. They are not only Jewish problems. In his 1983 book, *Beyond Objectivism and Relativism*, Bernstein reiterated Hans-Georg Gadamer's view that "we belong to a tradition before it belongs to us" (Bernstein

1983: 142). We cannot disassociate ourselves from the prejudices that we bring with us from our tradition. In his 1996 essay, "The Hermeneutics of Cross-Cultural Understanding," Bernstein returns to Gadamer's notion that "as finite human beings we are always shaped by the prejudgments and prejudices [which are] handed down to us and which constitute our being-in-the-world" (Bernstein 1996c: 37) or, as he wrote in *Philosophical Profiles* in 1986, "the historicity of our being" (Bernstein 1986a: ix). Critical inquiry can never take place in a vacuum. It is an engaging process with flesh-and-blood individuals who are themselves already engaged in a social structure—the customs, habits, traditions—of a community. The first American pragmatist, Charles Peirce, already pointed out that "We cannot begin [our philosophical inquiry] with complete doubt. We must begin with all the prejudices which we actually have when we enter upon the study of philosophy" (Bernstein 1986a: ix; 1983: 128). A century later, Bernstein suggests, Gadamer echoed Peirce that "all understanding involves prejudgments and prejudices. They are indeed what enable us to understand anything" (Bernstein 1986a: ix). While it is true that "there is no knowledge and no understanding without prejudices" (Bernstein 1983: 128), we must weed out our prejudices, as not all are conducive to spiritual growth. Bernstein advises, based on Gadamer, that we need to jettison our blind prejudices while retaining our enabling prejudices (Bernstein 1996c: 37; 1992: 301).

Since everyone belongs to a tradition, universal concepts such as "the Rights of Man" or "natural law" have no meaning unless they are applied in a particular political context. In discussing Gadamer, Bernstein explains that "natural law always requires interpretation and specification in concrete, particular situations of *praxis*" (Bernstein 1983: 157). Praxis or doing provides the test for the idea. Both Gadamer and Arendt are useful for Bernstein's construction of a framework within which we can practice democracy. He reminds us through Arendt that, in Greek Antiquity, "men were by nature . . . *not* equal, and needed an artificial institution, the polis, which by virtue of its *nomos* [or law] would make them equal" (Bernstein 1997: 164, emphasis added).[5] This was also the case in the United States. Rabbi Greenberg cites at least two legal rulings in the 1850s[6] that implied, in his view, that "to be an American did *not* commit one . . . to the proposition that all men are created equal" (Greenberg 1981; 124, emphasis added). Our nation began during a time when we perpetrated slavery on a large part of our population and excluded Jews from public office because of their religion. Both disabilities were eventually overcome, because the majority of Americans are committed to our Declaration of Independence.

It is clear from Bernstein's writings that the social and political upheavals of the '60s and '70s influenced him deeply. In 1976 he reflected on the '60s in this way, "I had a profound sense that something new was stirring—something was changing—in patterns, emphases, and concerns of intellectual life" (Bernstein 1976: ix). Ten years later, in *Philosophical Profiles*, Bernstein concluded that these times had echoed what William James had described as "a loosening of old landmarks, a softening of oppositions, a mutual borrowing from one another on the part of systems anciently closed" (James, quoted in Bernstein 1986a: 11). It was a time of flux philosophically, socially, and politically. While previously "philosophers *qua* philosophers" could not contribute anything "to the substantive discussion of normative ethical and political issues" (Bernstein 1986a: 15), a new spirit in the form of "international unrest, protest, and student radical activity" brought "a growing dissatisfaction with the thinness of 'metaethics' and the ideology of value-neutrality" (Bernstein 1986a: 15). The task was to figure out how to transform our thinking—away from the "Cartesian duality" (Bernstein 1986a: 16) that had dominated Europe as well as America for 300 years. In an atmosphere of uneasiness in philosophy—marked by "fragmentation, jaggedness, a deep suspicion about all fixed distinctions" (Bernstein 1986a: 10)—Bernstein sided with the optimists, also a trait he comes by honestly. Rather than taking a negative stance in revolt against the Cartesian framework, he chose to "perceive the present condition as a challenge and opportunity for . . . seeking new ways to make sense of, and gain an overview of, what appears to be so chaotic." Detecting "many signs," such as "coherence and commonness," in the apparent chaos, he suggested that "we are in the process of exorcising the Cartesian anxiety" (Bernstein 1983: 19).[7] In his view, contemporary thinking needs to be based on the radical originality that Bernstein so admires in Arendt and Freud, on the one hand, and in Peirce and Dewey and other Anglo-American pragmatists, on the other.[8]

As a philosopher, it is Bernstein's task to concern himself with theory. As a Jew, Bernstein's tradition, or enabling prejudgments, had likewise instilled in him that study is the highest good. In fact, study is equal to prayer—but so is doing. *Avodah*, the Hebrew word for work or action, also means service or worship. In Judaism, therefore, there is no gap between theory and praxis.[9] Jews study so they have the theoretical knowledge as a "heuristic guide" for doing, for praxis—one of Bernstein's important pillars for life. The individual who "effectively bridged the gap between theory and practice," in Bernstein's mind, is John Dewey (Bernstein 1991a: 55).

Praxis, "the free activity . . . in the 'polis'" (Bernstein 1971: x), requires, in Arendt's words, "'the company of other men' and 'a common public space to meet them'" (Bernstein 1997: 163), two things that we cannot take for granted. While there certainly are human beings and societies everywhere, the conditions for dialogue are often not right. In Gadamer's definition, "A conversation or a dialogue is 'a process of two people understanding each other'" (Bernstein 1983: 161). Dialogue is biblical. God conversed with Adam, with Noah, Abraham, Moses, and other human beings. Yet in Bernstein's conception, for a dialogical relationship to become possible, we have to learn "to listen," not only to talk (Bernstein 1996c: 36). In Judaism, the concept of listening is only second to God's Oneness. Twice a day, Jews recite the prayer known as the Shema, "Hear oh Israel, the Lord our God, the Lord is One" (Deut. 6:4), that admonishes us to listen—to God and to fellow humans. In Gadamer's words, "It is characteristic of every true conversation that each opens himself to the other person" (Gadamer, quoted in Bernstein 1986a: x). This process may make one ill at ease, because this "openness to the other . . . involves recognizing that I myself must accept some things that are against me, even though no one else forces me to do so" (Bernstein 1996c: 36). Proper "openness to the other" results in understanding that goes beyond the individuals who are involved in the conversation. "Understanding a tradition or a culture is like a conversation where 'when we have discovered the other person's standpoint, his ideas become intelligible without our necessarily agreeing with him.'" Martin Buber and Gadamer called this an I-Thou relationship. Bernstein labors to make clear just how important this dialogical relationship is for us today.

Public spaces for discussion are most important. These discussions resemble town hall meetings. According to Arendt, the polis in Greek Antiquity was the place "where 'citizens lived together under conditions of no-rule'" (Bernstein 1997: 164). Based on Arendt, Bernstein evokes the image of the Aristotelian polis as the ideal we need to rediscover. We might, however, just as easily conjure up the marketplace in which, since Antiquity, Jews have met twice a week, on Mondays and Thursdays, to pray and to read Torah, to conduct their business, but above all to talk. And not *just* talk but study the sacred texts, *chevruta* style, one-on-one, creating an argument for the sake of heaven. Some are the actors and some are the spectators, but both are needed. Arendt thought that we show who we are by the way we act and speak—that is, how we make our "appearance in the human world" (Bernstein 1997: 162). We could also say that who we are is evident in the way we engage our surroundings and our fellow human beings. Again, in Arendt's words, "This disclosure of 'who' in contradistinction to 'what' somebody is—his qualities, gifts, talents, and shortcomings, which he may display or hide—is implicit in everything somebody says and does." This "revelatory quality of speech and action" breaks forth between human beings, it is not something that can happen to one single individual, only in dialogue, "in their human togetherness." In a democratic society, the proper way for human beings to relate to each other is by "mutual reciprocal responsibility" (Bernstein 1994: 844). Bernstein observes that "there are [today] times when public spaces are spontaneously created, when the 'lost treasure' of public freedom becomes a tangible world reality" (Bernstein 1997: 162). This is, however, accidental, which is not good enough. Based on Gadamer, it is our obligation to "foster the type of dialogical communities in which *phronesis*[10] becomes a living reality and where citizens can actually assume . . . their 'noblest task'—'decision making' 'according to one's own responsibility—instead of conceding that task to the expert'" (Gadamer, quoted in Bernstein 1983: 159). In an age when everyone seems to be an expert and no one a master, Bernstein's admonition that we create conditions in which we learn to think for ourselves deserves serious consideration.

One reason it is so important for us to be able to think and listen and respond is because at every level in human life there are always new challenges that require a "rethinking of responsibility." A century ago, John Dewey was concerned about the role of technology in American society, because it encourages "passivity and docility among men" (Bernstein 1966: 6). Bernstein admonishes that "although our powers are limited, we can become critical—our intelligence can be nurtured and sharpened so that we do exercise some control over our fate." In a world in which modern technology has radically "transformed the nature of human action" (Bernstein 1994: 836), we experience a new urgency—the need for assurance that there *will even be a future in which human beings can think.* "Traditional moral imperatives are no longer sufficient for the new conditions of human action" (Bernstein 1994: 837), writes Bernstein, because "traditional ethics concerned itself mainly with 'virtue'" (Bernstein 1994: 841) as a concept and did not hold individuals responsible for their actions. With the recent wave of Internet viruses that destroy whole systems, I am sure we understand that there should be personal accountability in the cyberspace age. In an excellent article on Hans Jonas, "Rethinking Responsibility," Bernstein concurs with Jonas that "the long-range effects of modern technology are likely to be disastrous" (Bernstein 1994: 838), a fear that is also realistic given the fragility of the ozone layer, the destructive consequences of acid rain, the El Niño effect, and other atmospheric disturbances that are the consequences of modern technology.[11]

Hence, a new way of evaluating our situation on this planet is needed. According to Bernstein, "the only beings who are capable of assuming responsibility for the future [our future] are human beings" (Bernstein 1994: 847), because we are the only species who are capable of thinking. Or, to put it another way, it is our "primary obligation" as creatures who have been created in the image of the Creator to "assume responsibility for the future" of the world we have been given. Bernstein argues that "there is nothing pejoratively 'anthropocentric' about insisting on the supreme obligation to preserve human life." In fact, Judaism teaches that she or he who saves a life saves an entire universe. What is more, Judaism also teaches that we are to relate responsibly to our environment. Exploitation of nature is not a Jewish option. The imperative of *tikkun olam* obligates all Jews to ensure the preservation and repair of what God has created, and that includes the natural world which is so much at risk as a result of what we call human progress. Bernstein points out that Jonas often used the words "'Versuch' [attempt] and 'search' in the titles of his books" to stress "the ambitiousness and tentativeness of his project" (Bernstein 1994: 851). In 1994, Bernstein in fact argued that "there can be no 'end' to 'rethinking responsibility.' It is a task that always remains before us." Jonas had already expressed the wish for philosophy to "reserve [*sic* = persevere] in this endeavor [of assuming responsibility for our survival], undeterred by all justifiable doubt as to whether it will meet with success." According to Judaism, we are not required to complete the "never-to-be fully realized, but ever-to-be passionately sought" (Greenberg 1981: 136) task, but each and every one of us is obligated to begin—to work at it. Bernstein concurs with Jonas, "if the quintessence of what we are is to be dialogical . . . then whatever the limitations of the practical realization of this ideal, it nevertheless can and should give practical orientation to our lives" (Bernstein 1997: 163). We have now entered the new century and must at least realize with Bernstein "how much more needs to be done to carry out the task he [Jonas] so imaginatively began" (Bernstein 1994:

851) in an effort to avert the final decree of "slow gradual catastrophe" that we ourselves have set in motion.

In the 1970s, there was a gradual shift in American society away from the melting pot ideal and toward cultural pluralism. This meant, in Rabbi Greenberg's words, that people, and especially "black people rose to claim their rights not only as individuals but also as a group having its own distinctive cultural values and historic memories which it wants to preserve, enhance, and transmit" (Greenberg 1981: 163). "Black is beautiful" had its counterpart in the Hispanic claim "We are a people" (Goizueta 1992), a claim that Theodor Herzl had coined for Zionism in 1896. However, cultural pluralism in the seventies was not yet multiculturalism. Political scientist Marla Brettschneider explains in her introduction to *The Narrow Bridge* that while "Pluralism allows for the retention of distinctive characteristics in the private cultural lives of groups, [it] still relies on an assumption of the need for sameness in what it considers to be politics" (Brettschneider 1996: 4). Bernstein repeatedly points out the importance of a plurality of voices in philosophy in order for dialogue to occur. If we are all of the same mind, then no dialogue can or even need to occur. For dialogue to occur, we need to engage in conversation with those who are different, with those with whom we disagree, whether in philosophy or society. In *Praxis and Action* (1971), Bernstein reminds us that "this is really a very old idea in philosophy; giving each man and argument its proper due is central to the Platonic idea of justice" (Bernstein 1971: 8).

Today, multiculturalism in the United States offers an opportunity to establish true dialogue, with the goal of reaching someday the democracy that Dewey dreamed of and that Bernstein pursues. In contrast to pluralism, "multiculturalism does away with the pretense of a separate private sphere to which difference can be relegated" (Brettschneider 1996: 4). Multiculturalism tries to teach us to celebrate our ethnic diversity in public. In fact, Brettschneider asserts that "multiculturalism suggests 'celebrating difference' as a mode of politics itself." Many Americans desire multiculturalism; unfortunately, a true multicultural society has so far not been achieved. In 1996, Bernstein warned that "the most serious social and political problems of the next century [which we have now begun] will continue to focus on the ways in which different cultures cannot only learn to live with each other (without violence and killing), but can live together in ways in which they can genuinely learn from each other" (Bernstein 1996c: 41). One reason this has been so difficult is because, in Bernstein's words, "the mutual respect of cultural, ethnic, and religious differences" (Bernstein 1996c: 32) simply does not (yet) exist. There is no openness between human beings. Ideally, writes Brettschneider, "multiculturalism is developing democratic praxis which, rather than squelching diversity, seeks to welcome difference in the creation of a vibrant and inclusive public sphere (or spheres)" (Brettschneider 1996: 6). In Gadamer's view, "[It is] characteristic of every true conversation that each opens himself to the other person, truly accepts his point of view as worthy of consideration and gets inside the other to the extent that he understands not a particular individual but what he says" (Gadamer, quoted in Bernstein 1986a: x). In the same year in which Brettschneider's book *The Narrow Bridge* came out, Bernstein noted critically that what we are undertaking—"multicultural curricula in our schools and colleges" (Bernstein 1996c: 32)—does not break new ground in thinking. Rather, Bernstein compares these efforts to "those hurried package tours of foreign lands where one rushes from place to place taking snapshots of quaint natives," only to return "safely to the comfort of one's own ethnocentric biases." People who only pay lip service to multiculturalism do not expand their cultural comfort zone but continue to see everything only from their perspective. They do not open themselves to the other, which may be either unfamiliar or threatening to them.[12] Such an attitude is not conducive to dialogue and hence will not produce the transformation in thinking that is needed for a real democracy.

For Hannah Arendt, the highest human task is—"to begin spontaneously something new" (Bernstein 1997: 160–61). "Beginning . . . is the supreme capacity of man," she writes, "politically, it is identical with man's freedom" (Bernstein 1997: 163). Beginning can also be seen as an act of creation. In the beginning, God created. Since in the Jewish conception of things, human beings are created in the Divine image, we are also creators. Arendt calls this beginning, or initiative, "natality" (Bernstein 1997: 162). If carried through to its conclusion, it eventually leads to redemption—for the Israelites, it led from Egypt to the Promised Land; in Bernstein's vision, it will lead to real democracy.

One way we can begin is by learning new methods or techniques of inquiry. About five years ago, Bernstein commented that the debate on multiculturalism had reached a stalemate that needed to be overcome. One method that has been brought into twentieth-century philosophy, and that can be helpful in this task, is hermeneutics, a system of interpreting language and experience that belongs "to the great tradition of practical philosophy which was initiated by Aristotle" (Bernstein 1996c:

35). Actually, that is Gadamer's view. Hermeneutics is also Jewish, which Bernstein readily acknowledges. In 1983, he wrote, "One of the primary traditions that feeds into contemporary hermeneutics has been that of biblical hermeneutics" (Bernstein 1983: 109–10). This he reiterated in 1986. "Traditionally, 'hermeneutics' has been the name of a discipline concerned with the interpretation of sacred and literary texts—certainly a field quite remote from the main interests of analytic philosophy" (Bernstein 1986a: 13) to be sure, but not remote from Bernstein's cultural background. In fact, Rabbinic rules for interpretation of Torah are so important in the Jewish tradition that they are included in the daily morning prayers, lest we forget them. Since, according to Charles Taylor, "the practical and the theoretical are inextricably joined" in the hermeneutical circle, Bernstein sees the possibility of hermeneutics becoming not only a bridge between different types of philosophy, and between disciplines, but most recently also between diverse ethnic groups.

Efforts to bridge the gap are also underway within Judaism today. In the '70s, plurality of expression, *elu v'elu divrei Elohim hayyim*, led to a strengthening of denominational distinctions, to a clarification of identity within each denomination. It also led to the inclusion of women and gays. Dr. David Elcott teaches that "Diversity is and should be real within the Jewish community as it must [be] within all relationships. . . . There is no path to transforming the world that cannot accept diversity at its core" (Elcott 1999). The Jewish Question in the twenty-first century no longer focuses primarily on Israel or civil rights but on self-preservation. With a 50 percent rate of intermarriage, all of the denominations are looking inward to strengthen their appeal to contemporary Jewry and to try to find common ground for dialogue with each other. In the words of Rabbi Abraham Isaak Kook, Ashkenazi chief rabbi of the land of Israel in the 1930s, "The building is constructed from various parts, and the truth of the light of the world will be built from various dimensions, from multiple approaches, for 'all these different views are the living words of God.'" Much good is being achieved in cooperative projects, but even more could be achieved if all of Judaism would be able to speak with one voice and still maintain its denominational distinctions. Bernstein's dialogical guidelines for philosophers and political scientists might also be considered by Jewish community activists.

With his latest books on Hannah Arendt and Sigmund Freud's *Moses and Monotheism*, Bernstein, too, has turned inward, if only momentarily, to articulate his views on issues from the biblical Moses to Zionism and the Holocaust. His strong bond to his people finally demanded expression for its own sake.

One of Bernstein's most admirable achievements has been that he practices what he preaches, and not because it is in vogue. Always a voice in the wilderness, or a gadfly in the philosophical and political system because of his radical views, he is what he so admires in Arendt and Freud—an original thinker who follows through by speech acts.[13] He is, in Martin Buber's words, an activist of the word. Bernstein's definition of "a genuine thinker" is someone who "doesn't instruct, but rather has the gift to infect others with the perplexities that provoke thinking" (Bernstein 1997: 156).

Every year at Passover Jews tell the story of the Exodus, the story of freedom. Telling the story is doing; it is political action. Bernstein has been telling and retelling the story of freedom via the vehicle of philosophy for over forty years. During this time, his joy of storytelling has remained undiminished and his thirst for knowledge unquenched. But the joy of inquiry is always bound up with obligation—an obligation to illuminate, to elucidate the arguments of great thinkers and to lay bare their shortcomings, not to denigrate, for that would be equivalent to public embarrassment, or *lashon harah*, which is forbidden by Jewish law, but to show how far we have progressed and what still needs doing. In "The Rage against Reason," Bernstein wrote, "My narrative is not yet finished because the story I am telling is still unfolding" (Bernstein 1992a: 50). However, over time, Bernstein's initial concern with democracy, relationship, and dialogue from the perspective of philosophy but *in the spirit of Judaism* has become radicalized, or politicized. His message has become more urgent. Dewey pointed out that "'philosophy recovers itself when it . . . becomes a method, cultivated by philosophers, for dealing with the problems of men'" (Dewey, quoted in Bernstein 1986a: 15). Bernstein amends this to mean that "philosophy recovers itself when it . . . becomes a method, cultivated by philosophers, for dealing with the problems of *human beings in their everyday lives*" (Bernstein 1986a: 15, emphasis added).

Bernstein has kept his end of the bargain. Through his many writings, he has provided a heuristic guide for action. It is now up to each of us to begin.[14]

NOTES

1. In addition to Bernstein's *Hannah Arendt and the Jewish Question* (1996a), see especially "Hannah Arendt: The Ambiguities of Theory and Practice" (1977); "Judging—The Actor and the Spectator" (1982); "The 'Banality of Evil' Reconsidered" (1996d);

"Did Hannah Arendt Change Her Mind? From Radical Evil to the Banality of Evil" (1996b); "Provocation and Appropriation: Hannah Arendt's Response to Martin Heidegger" (1997); and *Beyond Objectivism and Relativism* (1983).

2. See Bernstein, ed., *John Dewey: On Experience, Nature, and Freedom* (New York: Liberal Arts Press, 1960); *John Dewey* (New York: Washington Square Press, 1966); "John Dewey: Philosophor of Democracy," *Intellectual History Newsletter* 13 (1991): 48–55; "John Dewey on Democracy: The Task Before Us," in *Philosophical Profiles* (1986a).

3. For another exciting Bernstein example of solidarity, see his cooperation with the Dubrovnik Inter-University Post-Graduate Center, where he, for many years, co-directed the course "Philosophy and Social Science" and co-edited the journal *Praxis International.* For the Bernstein interview by Dunja Melcic, see "Interpretation of Solidarity," *Praxis International* 9:3 (October 1989): 201–19.

4. In the poem, "Awake My People" (1866), Judah Leib Gordon, a nineteenth-century Hebrew poet, wrote, "Be a man abroad and a Jew in your tent." See *The Jew in the Modern World* (1995: 384).

5. In a discussion with my colleague David Dungan, I learned that the Greek term *nomos* in the New Testament as used by Paul does not have the flexibility and elasticity that it had previously. However, in Arendt and, as I would like to argue, in Bernstein, he feels that *nomos* as "law" has the flexibility of "Torah," or *mishpat,* that it had prior to its more narrow use.

6. The reference here is to the 1854 Kansas-Nebraska Bill and the *Dred Scott* decision of 1857.

7. Bernstein writes on Cartesian Anxiety: "*Either* there is some support for our being, a fixed foundation for our knowledge, *or* we cannot escape the forces of darkness that envelop us with madness, with intellectual and moral chaos" (1983: 18)

8. For an insightful article on the problem of the philosophical split, see Bernstein's "Pragmatism, Pluralism, and the Healing of Wounds" (1991: 323–40).

9. For the complicated nature of the relationship between theory and practice, see "Hannah Arendt: The Ambiguities of Theory and Practice," in *Political Theory and Praxis: New Perspectives,* ed. Terrence Ball (Minneapolis: University of Minnesota Press, 1977), 141–58.

10. In *Beyond Objectivism and Relativism* (1983: 157), Bernstein defines *phronesis* as "the shared acceptance and stability of universal principles and laws." In "Reconciliation and Rupture" (1992: 304), *phronesis* is defined as "cultivated practical judgment."

11. While writing this chapter, an article in the University of Tennessee school paper reported that Knoxville is No. 12 in the country in excess ozone. The article explained that "everything that burns fuel at high temperatures, such as cars and power plants [TVA in Oak Ridge], contributes to the problem by putting nitrous oxides in the air. Those nitrous oxides combine with volatile organic compounds, which mainly contain carbon and hydrogen and mainly come from trees such as the pines of the Smokey Mountains to create ozone" (*The Daily Beacon,* Friday, June 2, 2000, front page). Surely we cannot blame the pine trees in the Smokies for causing an unhealthy level of ozone in Knoxville but people who have not learned to interact with our environment in a responsible way.

The brief discussion of ecological and technological crimes here was written more than a year prior to September 11, 2001. The University of Tennessee invited Professor Bernstein for a one-day symposium on radical evil in October, 2001, a topic about which he had written repeatedly over a lifetime, and on which he was working during a research leave in Germany during the period 2000–2001. The conference was scheduled for October 29, 2001. Of course, in the meantime September 11 happened, and it seemed by the time of the conference that Richard Bernstein was nothing short of a prophet with his focus on, even preoccupation with, evil. Accountability, the key idea in his writings on morality, was rendered irrelevant, if not nonexistent, with the idea of suicide bombers and the events of September 11 as well as similar activities in other parts of the world. The philosophy of these terrorists is precisely the opposite of accountability—a rational mental process—namely, a crime of passion or faith that lies beyond the moral realm. In light of September 11, the examples given here that are the most horrendous we could comprehend before terrorism became the top crime against humanity now seem almost benign, even though they continue to plague us and continue to threaten our existence. The crime of September 11 has redefined the map of moral and political philosophy and is forcing us to deal with human thought and action that rejects accountability.

12. See also Bernstein 1992: 295–311; "Incommensurability and Otherness Revisited," in Bernstein 1992a: 57–78.

13. Reena Bernards writes, "Jews are often more willing to talk than to take concrete political action. To many Jews sitting and talking until agreements are hammered out is a natural part of the dialogue process" ("Jews Building Bridges," in Brettschneider 1996).

14. Many thanks to Michael Manning Collier, my 1999–2001 graduate teaching assistant, for collecting the many Bernstein writings for me.

REFERENCES

Bernards, Reena. 1996. Jews building bridges. In *The narrow bridge*, ed. Marla Brettschneider, 136–48. New Brunswick, NJ: Rutgers University Press.

Bernstein, Richard J., ed. 1960. *John Dewey: On experience, nature, and freedom.* New York: Liberal Arts Press.

———. 1958. with M. Eson. *A study of some aspects of education in Israel.* Jerusalem: Ministry of Education Press.

———. 1964. Myths about the Mississippi Summer Project. *The Nation* (December 28): 512–15.

———. 1966. *John Dewey.* New York: Washington Square Press.

———. 1971. *Praxis and action.* Philadelphia: University of Pennsylvania Press.

———. 1976. *The restructuring of social and political theory.* New York and London: Harcourt Brace Jovanovich.

———. 1977. Hannah Arendt: The ambiguities of theory and practice. In the *Political theory and praxis: New perspectives*, ed. Terrence Ball, 141–58. Minneapolis: University of Minnesota Press.

———. 1982. Hanah Arendt: Judging—the actor and the spectator. In *Proceedings of history, ethics, politics: A conference based on the work of Hannah Arendt*, ed. R. Boyers. Saratoga Springs, NY: Empire State College Press.

———. 1983. *Beyond objectivism and relativism.* Philadelphia: University of Pennsylvania Press.

———. 1986a. *Philosophical profiles: Essays in a pragmatic mode.* Cambridge, MA: MIT Press.

———. 1986b. The meaning of public life. In *Religion and American public life*, ed. Robin W. Lovin, 29–52. Mahwah, NJ: Paulist Press.

———. 1991a. John Dewey: Philosophy of democracy. *Intellectual History Newsletter* 13: 48–55.

———. 1992a. Pragmatism, pluralism, and the healing of wounds. In *The new constellation: The ethical-political horizons of modernity/postmodernity.* Cambridge, MA: MIT Press.

———. 1992b. Reconciliation and rupture: The challenge and threat of otherness. In *Discourse and practice*, ed. Frank Reynolds and David Tracy, 295–314. Albany: State University of New York Press.

———. 1994. Hans Jonas: Rethinking responsibility. *Social Research* 61:4 (Winter): 833–52.

———. 1996a. *Hannah Arendt and the Jewish question.* Cambridge, UK: Polity Press.

———. 1996b. Did Hannah Arendt change her mind? From radical evil to the banality of evil. In *Hannah Arendt: 20 years later*, ed. Jerome Kohn and Larry May, 127–46. Cambridge: MIT Press.

———. 1996c. The hermeneutics of cross-cultural understanding. In *Cross-cultural conversations*, ed. Anindita Niyogi Balslev, 29–41. Atlanta: Scholars Press.

———. 1996d. The 'banality of evil' reconsidered. In *Hannah Arendt and the meaning of politics*, ed. Craig Calhoun and John McGowan, 297–322. Minneapolis: University of Minnesota Press.

———. 1997. Provocation and appropriation: Hannah Arendt's response to Martin Heidegger. In *Constellations* 4:2: 153–71.

———. 1998. *Freud and the legacy of Moses.* Cambridge, UK: Cambridge University Press.

Elcott, David. 1999. A Jewish vocabulary for the 21st century. Handout for workshop in Knoxville, TN, June 2000.

Goizueta, Roberto S. 1992. *We are a people.* Minneapolis: Fortress Press.

Gordon, Judah Leib. 1995. Awake my people. In *The Jew in the modern world*, ed. Paul Mendes-Flohr/Jehuda Reinhartz, 312–13. New York, Oxford: Oxford University Press.

Greenberg, Simon. 1981. *A Jewish philosophy and pattern of life.* New York: The Jewish Theological Seminary of America.

Melcic, Dunja. 1988. Interpretation of solidarity. *Praxis International* 9:3 (October): 201–19.

Richard J. Bernstein's Response to Gilya G. Schmidt

Gilya Schmidt is right. I consider myself very lucky, for I never experienced serious anti-Semitism. When I started college many institutions of higher learning still had quotas on the number of Jews admitted. This was also the practice at Yale College when I first started teaching. Paul Weiss was the first outspoken Jew that Yale hired as a full professor. I benefited from the opening up of universities to Jews, which took place in the aftermath of the Second World War. In this respect, I never felt like a pariah, and I certainly never experienced any shame as a Jew. I have always enjoyed and been at ease with my Jewish background. Growing up in an extended second-generation Jewish family was a vital and an integral part of my youth. I agree with Gadamer that we belong to a tradition before it belongs to us. This was certainly my experience. Some of my happiest memories growing up in Brooklyn were participating in Jewish festivities. Friday nights were special events, because it was the one night that the entire family ate together, and my father brought home all sorts of Jewish delicacies. As a teenager, I did rebel against some of the more bourgeoisie aspects of middle-class Jewish life in America. I went to Israel in 1957 as a Fulbright scholar more out of curiosity than commitment. I experienced and enjoyed the daily rhythms of Jewish life—the Sabbath as a day of rest and the holidays as celebrations. Being a secular Jew in Israel (at that time) was common and quite natural. The democratic prospects for the new State of Israel were exciting. I identified with the Israeli Left that was critical of the mistreatment of Israeli Arabs and the refusal of many Israelis to deal with the Palestinian refugees. For a time, I considered *aliyah.* I was invited to join the faculty of the Hebrew University. I would like to think that my concern for social justice was influenced by my Jewish heritage, but I was much more aware of being an American growing up in the aftermath of the Second World War. I was lucky in another respect. I grew up at a time when many of my generation believed that with imagination, energy, and commitment, the world could be a better place. This was the era before the Vietnam War, when political cynicism became so prevalent in the United States. I never lost my utopian faith. At the time, I was not familiar with the Hebrew notion of "*tikkun olam,*" but there is no doubt that this is what I firmly believed. I did and still do believe that we must do *our* part in "healing and completing the world." I learned this from the pragmatic thinkers, but I recognize now how central it has been to the Jewish tradition. Dialogue has always been a central concept in my thinking. I have been concerned with the material conditions that allow for the possibility of genuine reciprocal dialogue. I cannot honestly say that I *consciously* appropriated this theme from the Jewish tradition. I certainly recognize the importance of dialogue (and the different conceptions of dialogue) in Buber and Levinas. I have always been concerned with the theme of responsibility (in all of its aspects)—the responsibility we bear to others, the responsibility to do justice to different and alien points of view, the responsibility to confront critically the problems of human beings, and the responsibility that we bear for preserving the world. And I have come to realize how important this theme is in the Jewish tradition. I would like to think that I live up to Gilya Schmidt's characterization of me as "someone who has been telling and retelling the story of freedom via the vehicle of philosophy." It is certainly true that my joy in storytelling has remained undiminished and my thirst for knowledge unquenched. I would also like to think that what I have always been doing is "in the spirit of Judaism."

Bernstein among the Prophets?

Justice, Public Life, and Fallibilistic Pluralism

Mary Doak

The social criticisms developed by the Hebrew prophets remain for many of us an invaluable resource in the continuing endeavor to achieve a more just society. The rich poetry, utopian images, symbolic actions, and scathing condemnations of these passionate and enigmatic figures continue to inspire us to think again and more deeply about what justice might mean in our own times.[1] Richard Bernstein, of course, is not a biblical prophet but an American philosopher; he is known not for eating scrolls and other symbolic gestures, but for addressing issues of public life through calm and carefully reasoned arguments. Despite his obvious differences from the prophets in style, tone, sources, and context, I believe that Bernstein's focus on praxis and on the public implications of contemporary philosophical debates is not unrelated to a prophetic commitment to greater justice in society. The question I wish to pursue here is, then, does Bernstein's thought make a real contribution to the achievement of a more just American society? In what ways does Bernstein foster our ability to name present unjust structures and practices, and to construct better alternatives?

Bernstein's Theory of Public Life

In his 1983 work *Beyond Objectivism and Relativism*, Bernstein interweaves the insights of Gadamer, Habermas, Arendt, and Rorty in order to construct and to defend his own theory of public life, and he gains much from this astute choice of conversation partners. Bernstein's explicit intention in engaging these four thinkers' ideas is to argue against the specious and unhelpful extremes that hold thought to be either dependent upon objective and ahistorical foundations or to be so relative that there is no basis for public judgment. He attempts to demonstrate instead that a more helpful position is emerging in a consensus that supports a contextual yet nonrelativistic mode of inquiry, "a dialogical model of rationality that stresses the practical, *communal* character of this rationality" (Bernstein 1983: 172).

It is important to note that Bernstein's interest in an alternative that eschews ahistorical foundations without resulting in radical relativism is not motivated primarily by an abstract interest in the problematics of contemporary philosophy but rather by a concern for praxis. "The primary problem today," Bernstein insists, "is to gain some clarity about the critical standards for guiding *praxis* and about how such standards are to be rationally warranted"; the impasse between objectivism and relativism is at heart a practical issue for him (Bernstein 1983: 190). Further, as we will see, the resolution he seeks is not to be found solely in theorizing but in the praxis of developing and strengthening public life. Though he engages the neopragmatism of Richard Rorty, Bernstein's work is thus more consistent with Dewey's pragmatist interest in defending democracy and in the ways that critical thinking might better guide our sociopolitical praxis.

The dialogic theory of public life that Bernstein proposes as a practical resolution to the conundrums of objectivism and relativism draws heavily on Hans-Georg Gadamer's explication of understanding as a process in which one understands another perspective only in and through the particularity of one's own horizon of thought. In Gadamer's account, understanding is ineluctably informed by received traditions as well as by the interests driving the inquiry, thus understanding is an inherently contextual and practical activity. While an ahistorical "objectivism" is ruled out, then, Gadamer's work also provides a basis for rejecting the relativism in which "we are prisoners trapped in closed linguistic frameworks," since, like a visual horizon, the horizon of thought is "*essentially* open" and capable of expansion. To understand another does not require that we escape from our own standpoints, somehow leap out of our own particular horizons of language and tradition, but that we achieve a "fusion of horizons [with the other] . . . whereby our own horizon is enlarged and enriched" (Bernstein 1983: 173, 143).

Bernstein also draws our attention to the insightful critique Gadamer provides of aspects of contemporary society. Gadamer argues that technology and the knowledge of "experts" have come to dominate society based on the erroneous belief that technology and science are (or can be) "objective" and "value free," whereas, in fact, scientific understanding is as informed by historical horizons and practical interests as is all human thought. It is a mistake, then, for ordinary citizens to withdraw from the debate and leave decision making in the hands of such "experts," whose own particular interests will thus dominate public life without the challenge or the broadening that comes through an encounter with other perspectives. Gadamer also criticizes the dangerous and widespread use of techniques to manipulate public opinion, as this prevents the engaged, thoughtful encounters with others through which we develop as "truly dialogic beings—always in conversation, always in the process of understanding." Both trends, the domination of society by technological experts and the manipulation of public opinion, lead to a deformation of public life, since they undermine the "practical and political reason required for citizens to make responsible decisions" (Bernstein 1983: 165, 175).

While he wants us to appreciate that there is much of value in Gadamer's account of the positive role that context, tradition, and practical interest play in producing understanding, Bernstein also agrees with Jürgen Habermas that Gadamer's work needs the corrective of a critical approach. Given the reality of systemic distortion, we need to be able to critique the traditions that inform our own perspectives, the opinions we encounter, and the social structures in which that dialogic encounter occurs. Habermas finds a basis for such critique in the very practice of dialogue, which, he argues, implicitly affirms a willingness to offer warrants that will persuade by no other force than that of the more convincing argument. Dialogue is not only a process through which we come to appreciate other perspectives and expand our horizons, then, it is also the process of testing and rejecting some views based on the quality of the arguments involved.

Further, this communicative process of persuasion presumes the counterfactual standard of an "ideal speech situation" in which all participate equally in a conversation free from the constraints of power, and where all that matters is the force of one's argument. This standard, implicitly assented to in the process of communicative reasoning, provides an admittedly ideal goal of undistorted communication (note that this ideal is described as counterfactual), but this ideal nevertheless serves to critique the social structures that prohibit such undistorted communication. From Habermas, then, Bernstein gains a more adequate account of structural distortions and a "critique that points to the telos [of an ideal speech situation] that should guide our praxis" (Bernstein 1983: 206).

In the work of Hannah Arendt, too, Bernstein finds an affirmation of the possibility of judgment that eschews the extremes of objectivism and relativism. According to Arendt, political judgments are formed within a community, through the process of debate in which opinions are evaluated from various points of view and in light of diverse experiences. Not only are those opinions most worthy that have been tested from a variety of perspectives and interests, but as humans we achieve our distinct individuality only through engagement with diverse individuals and perspectives in public action. Judgment is neither dependent upon recourse to ahistorical standards nor confined to a particular framework but develops through an encounter between various people viewing the same thing from different perspectives. Where many long for a common culture and a more homogeneous society as a solution to the divisions that threaten public life, Arendt insists that plurality, the individual distinctness rooted in "natality" (the capacity to act, to initiate, to begin again), is not a threat to public life but is rather the very basis of it (Bernstein 1983: 215–18, 208).

Bernstein rightly interprets Arendt's corpus as largely devoted to the defense of this plurality. She works to uncover the totalitarian strategies that attempt to prevent political action by supressing the plurality that makes resistance possible. She also strives to defend human plurality against our societal emphasis on the value of the production and consumption of *things* over the public action through which human beings express and develop *themselves.* Every person must be given the opportunity to participate in political decision making, both for the good of the individual who is thus able to share in a common world and for the good of the political process and the judgments formed therein. As Bernstein observes, if Arendt is taken seriously on this point, it follows that all members of society should have access to the material means, the education, and the culture required for meaningful participation in public life (Bernstein 1983: 213–14).

Bernstein believes that the dialogic account of public life that he is developing needs at this stage yet one more voice, that of Richard Rorty, to test its plausibility. Rorty's forceful argument for incommensurability insists that there are no neutral, ahistorical standards to which we can appeal to evaluate the merits of various perspectives. Does Rorty's argument then invalidate the project of dialogue, of reasoning together to determine the better argument in a critical, pluralistic, public life?

Bernstein maintains that it does not, noting that Rorty's powerful criticisms of objectivism do not lead Rorty himself to embrace relativism. Despite his belief that there are no ahistorical, universal grounds on which to defend it, Rorty affirms commitment to the conversation, even if that conversation is "merely our project," as well as commitment to the Socratic virtues (the "willingness to talk, to listen to other people, to weigh the consequences of our actions upon other people") necessary to continue the conversation. Rorty does not consider relativism a serious threat, since he believes that no one, other than the "occasional cooperative freshman," is truly a relativist, affirming that incompatible positions are equally acceptable.[2] What we need, Rorty further argues, is not an ahistorical framework for adjudicating our differences but rather a pragmatic concern with human problems and with the cultivation of our communities and the Socratic virtues, along with resistance to any and every attempt to close off the conversation (whether by seeking an ahistorical truth or by invoking standards of argumentation that limit in advance the moves permissible within the conversation). Although in his later writings Bernstein develops extensive criticisms of Rorty's position, at this point Bernstein affirms that Rorty too participates in and contributes to the emerging consensus that moves us "beyond objectivism and relativism."

The result of Bernstein's interweaving of the insights of these four thinkers is a dialogic, critical, and pluralistic concept of public life in which we converse and argue together not merely to attain our goals but to enrich ourselves and our common life through public debate that tests, validates, and transforms our perspectives. Lacking a neutral framework by which to adjudicate various positions, we must develop the standards of judgment within the conversation itself, arguing over what makes a good argument. Further progress in the revival of such a public conversation "beyond objectivism and relativism," however, depends not solely on a proper theory of public life, Bernstein rightly points out, but also on the practical work of developing the necessary communities of solidarity and dialogue in which such public debate is possible. To the extent that such communities have broken down, we cannot simply "engineer" them anew or (as so many argue) recreate them through retrieval of some putatively common and authoritative tradition. Instead, Bernstein would have us attend to and develop the incipient forms of communal life and solidarity as these emerge around us, and this includes working to change the social structures and power relations that distort our public conversation by excluding or marginalizing some voices while privileging others. Bernstein's position is thus quite the opposite of a recreation of community on the basis of an enforced commonality (Bernstein 1983: 226–31).

THE CONTRIBUTIONS OF BERNSTEIN'S DIALOGIC PUBLIC LIFE

In my judgment, Bernstein's theory of public life is as important and helpful today as when he developed it almost twenty years ago. Certainly his warnings against the deterioration and distortion of public discourse remain valid. In light of the ever-increasing role of money and advertising in political campaigns, it would seem that the manipulation of public opinion has not abated. It is also fairly evident that, despite a sustained economic boom, we have still failed to provide all members of society with the material and educational means that full inclusion in public life requires. Indeed, one might argue that the demands of work now leave even the middle and upper middle classes exhausted, without time or energy for public life, which is then relegated to professional representatives of special interests. In this respect, Bernstein's analyses from the early 1980s seem not outdated but rather prescient.

These problems are not only due to political and economic structures (as significant as these are), but also, I believe, to an ongoing failure to appreciate the value and possibility of public life that Bernstein addresses. Politics is still widely seen as an instrumental power: whether it is viewed as a power over us to be resisted or perhaps as a power we ourselves can use to secure our own interests, politics is more commonly considered a means to our ends rather than a dialogic process through which horizons are broadened, the self is enriched, and we together might attain and enact a fuller vision of justice.[3] If public debate is not valued, understood as important to vital communal and individual lives, then I fear we have little motivation to expend our limited time and energy in public deliberation or to work to change the structures that so distort our political processes. Indeed, when politics is construed as an instrumental value, those who fail to attain their ends politically would seem to have every reason to withdraw and turn to manipulative, unlawful, or even violent methods. It may also be the case that thirty-second sound bites are appropriate if our political process is designed not for mutual engagement and debate but merely for the efficient selection of those who will best represent our ensconced opinions and interests, as theological ethicist Robin Lovin has recently argued (Lovin 1995: 174–75).

Bernstein is thus right to point us "beyond objectivism and relativism," as these extremes are destructive of public life. Most of us have learned well to be wary of the closed-mindedness of "objectivists" who often seem convinced not only that there is an ahistorical truth but also that they possess it; anyone voicing an alternative is considered either purposefully deceitful or sadly mistaken. Such an attitude (in which political opponents can only be intelligent liars or stupid idiots) is certainly not conducive to mutually enriching dialogue, even though objectivists, frustrating as they are, do not deny the possibility of debate and are usually willing to give reasons in defense of their positions.

The danger of a thorough relativism in politics may be less appreciated but is no less seriously detrimental to public life. While Rorty may be right that there are few, if any, relativists who actually hold that contradictory positions are equally valid, there are certainly plenty of people who, while clinging tenaciously to their own preferred views, will invoke relativist rhetoric, proclaiming the ultimate undecidability between alternative traditions in order to avoid defending their views or considering the merits of alternatives. It has been argued that religious fundamentalists, for example, who are probably more commonly thought of as objectivists, are actually "relativists" in public, maintaining a private truth that does not admit of or need public defense (even while some seek public policies in accord with that private truth) (Neuhaus 1984: 36–37). Similarly, thinkers as different as Jean Bethke Elshtain and Cornel West have argued that "identity politics" is destroying public life with its rejection of constructive engagement and persuasion.[4] One's worldview, whether chosen as a matter of taste, developed as a heritage, received through divine grace, or determined biologically, is protected from challenge (by internal "liberalizers" as well as by external critics) if differences cannot be communicatively adjudicated. Such relativism does not lead to Bernstein's mutually enriching, fallibilistic pluralism but rather acknowledges incommensurable differences as a basis for evading any real challenge the "other" might pose. It leaves us with no option for politics other than "strategic campaigns of mass manipulation" that we tend to associate with objectivists (Goldfarb 1998: 3).

As a theologian convinced that religious traditions are rich resources for public life, I am especially concerned about the implications of relativism for the public role of religion. This topic has received considerable attention throughout the 1980s and 1990s from scholars of religion arguing against religion's privatization. David Tracy, for example, has developed a well-known critique of the "mindless pluralism" in which religion is stripped of its public significance and relegated along with art to a "reservation of the spirit" where it is privately available for those who "happen to like that sort of thing." Drawing also on the work of Gadamer (as well as that of Paul Ricoeur), Tracy (1981) too argues for the recovery of methods of interpretation and debate that allow for public assessment of religious claims "beyond objectivism and relativism."[5]

We must not, however, overlook the fact that relativism in public life does not always result in the denial of a public role for religion but also can lead, rather surprisingly, to the assertions of a "public" religion that we more often expect from objectivists. Many presumably well meaning people (by no means all fundamentalists) who are aware of the importance of values in society see no other option than simply to designate an official set of values. Thus it is argued that the Ten Commandments must be displayed on our public school walls, in federal courtrooms, and on city property, not on the grounds that these commandments issue from an objectively true religion, but because they represent a good and rich tradition of values that happens to have wide support in our society and can thus provide the common values we need. After all, if religious beliefs and values cannot enter the public realm as part of the debate, then either religion is banished to private life, leaving a "naked public square" stripped of all that is of ultimate significance, or we must cloak that public square with the mantel of official (even if "minimal") religious beliefs. Without the kind of public debate "beyond objectivism and relativism" that Bernstein defends, religion may be privatized or officially promulgated, but in either case its critique is evaded, and religious freedom is imperiled.[6]

PUBLIC LIFE AND JUSTICE

One might, however, agree with all that has thus far been said about public life and yet be unconvinced that this pluralistic, open public deliberation "really matters" to the pursuit of justice. We may deplore the loss of rousing political and religious debates (especially those of us who "happen to like that sort of thing"), but is not this hand-wringing over the deterioration of public life a far cry from prophetic denouncements of grinding poverty and exploitation? As long as our life, liberty, and pursuit of happiness are protected, as long as we have institutions that place limits on the exploitation of the weak, provide a decent safety net to prevent undue suffering, and guard our freedom to be left alone to pursue whatever religious or secular version of personal fulfillment inspires us, is not public life a nicety, perhaps a sort of luxury, but a concern rather peripheral to the struggle for a more just world?

I am convinced that a vital public life as described by Bernstein is in fact central to the search for greater justice. To be sure, starving people are usually more interested in bread than in conversation, as Arendt maintained. Yet Bernstein has quite rightly noted that Arendt's sharp division between bread and public life cannot be maintained, not only because we must have bread if we are to continue participating in the debate but also because those voices excluded from the debate will not easily have their need for bread recognized (Bernstein 1983: 213).[7] Justice erodes quickly when politics is left to elected representatives and to the political action committees of special interest groups: those voices unable to organize, voice their concerns, and, one must now add, marshal the financial resources to make significant campaign contributions or sponsor their own slick TV commercials are at risk of finding themselves and their interests significantly less protected. As Reinhold Niebuhr argued, democracy is necessary because human beings are inclined to injustice, and their power must be checked.[8]

The idea of public life as envisioned by Bernstein involves, of course, much more than simply ensuring that all have access to the means of influence without which their interests will not long be protected. He is further arguing for a dialogic public life that is not merely an instrumental value but is rather one in which political judgments are formed and tested through encountering alternative perspectives. The relation of this engaged public life to the pursuit of justice may not be immediately obvious, but I believe it becomes evident if we think about what it is we hope for in the pursuit of justice. Both equality and freedom are often thought to be necessary characteristics of a just society; few of us, I suspect, would be satisfied with a society in which goods and services are distributed equally but with few opportunities for the exercise of freedom. The question that Bernstein's work on public life raises, at least implicitly, is: how do we understand freedom? Is a merely negative or individual freedom a freedom *from* interference or freedom to choose consumer products and career options (an urban condominium versus a suburban ranch house), worthy of the name "freedom?" Borrowing Arendt's insights, Bernstein suggests instead that truly free people are those who experience a positive and shared freedom, the freedom *for* self-creativity and self-transcendence in striving with others to conceive of new possibilities and to create the institutions that might make those possibilities into lasting realities. (Bernstein 1983: 207–23)[9]

Robin Lovin has nicely summed up these broader demands of justice: "We cannot," he insists, "render to persons what they are due simply by giving them a full share of their entitlements—though that is important. . . . [We] must resist in the name of this more complete liberty any version of liberty that offers freedom without participation, or any version of equality that offers entitlements without deliberation" (Lovin 1995: 230).

Bernstein's theory of an engaged and a dialogic public life thus remains a valuable and necessary contribution to the struggle for justice. To be sure, greater justice will not follow automatically once we perfect our theories; rather, Bernstein's theory points us to the practical task of fostering the communities of dialogue and solidarity that make it possible for us to meet in the public realm in a spirit of trust and openness. However, we will not have a vital public life in which to transcend our limitations and to work out resolutions to our problems if the possibility of transformative conversations between those with alternative perspectives is inconceivable. Further, as Bernstein has suggested, an open process of public deliberation is not only the means to a deeper understanding of the justice we might pursue and the obstacles we face but is itself an integral part of any true justice. Commitment to civic life would gain much from Bernstein's defense of the intrinsic value as well as the possibility of a pluralistic public life.

THE CHALLENGE OF IRRECONCILABLE DIFFERENCE

Even a sympathetic audience, however, might yet find this account of public life too optimistically harmonious, sensing that it does not adequately recognize the alterity, the differences that result in rupture and that cannot be subsumed into a larger perspective or a broader horizon. Has not Derrida taught us to suspect that any emerging consensus will be built upon yet another systemic exclusion of the Other? Have we not we learned from Foucault that any standards of critique are predicated on a normalizing, disciplining, and finally oppressive rhetoric? These are the challenges that engage Bernstein in his later work, *The New Constellation*, wherein he undertakes to demonstrate that his argument for a dialogic and pluralistic public life does not underestimate the genuine and deeply rooted differences among us (Bernstein 1992: 8–10).

As I read him, Bernstein defends his dialogic hermeneutics primarily with two strategies, the first of which is to show that the critical perspectives developed by Derrida and by Foucault are best understood as warnings of ever-present dangers within the dialogic process rather than as rejections of that process. Derrida, though seeking to reveal "the ways in which we consciously or unconsciously exclude, marginalize, suppress, and repress the otherness and singularity of the Other" (Bernstein 1992: 219), is not best read as maintaining that understanding the Other is impossible, for in that case Derrida would fall into the dichotomous logic he himself deconstructs, affirming difference over identity and alterity over sameness. Instead, Derrida's argument for "both sameness and radical alterity, symmetry and asymmetry, identity and difference" suggests that we should seek harmony while acknowledging that ruptures will remain (Bernstein 1992: 74, 72). Similarly, Bernstein argues that Foucault's work would be self-defeating if all norms for adjudicating differences are to be rejected as inherently oppressive, "normalizing" strategies, for then we would not be able to criticize disciplinary discourses or identify which manifestations of power to resist. A better understanding of Foucault, according to Bernstein, is "as deliberately using hyperbolic rhetorical constructions"; his purpose is to "expose instabilities, points of resistances, places where counter-discourses can arise and effect transgressions and change" (Bernstein 1992: 155, 160). In this more nuanced interpretation of Derrida and Foucault, Bernstein's project of dialogic rationality is not precluded, though it must proceed with awareness of the power and interests involved in all conversations as well as attention to the "hidden dangers of 'false' consensus, dialogue and community" (Bernstein 1992: 52).

The second strategy that Bernstein utilizes in defense of his own approach is to show that Derrida's and Foucault's projects remain incomplete and their liberating intentions unfulfilled, because they fail to account theoretically for the possibility of constructive and critical engagement with the Other. Insofar as Derrida persuasively reveals the pitfalls involved in taking a position but does not explain how we might better exercise judgement in developing positions on political and practical issues that cannot be avoided, the ethico-political interest at the heart of Derrida's project is unredeemed. (It is no wonder, then, that "deconstruction has been almost totally apolitical," as Bernstein observes [Bernstein 1992: 191, 188].) The liberative intentions of Foucault's work are similarly undercut insofar as he analyzes the role of power in all discourse without articulating grounds for "why anyone should favor certain local forms of resistance over others" (Bernstein 1992: 160). A suspicion toward the conversations we engage in and any consensus that may emerge is important but not alone sufficient: we must also be able to find reasons to risk encountering others' views, making judgments, seeking reconciliation, and deciding what actions to take, lest suspicion lead to political paralysis rather than greater justice.

Bernstein also seeks to demonstrate the value of his own hermeneutic approach to public life by again engaging Richard Rorty, this time much more critically. Rorty, too, is unable to provide an adequate basis for public life, Bernstein argues; simply espousing a liberal abhorrence of cruelty as "our tradition" will not do, because this tradition is neither as widely shared nor as politically specific as Rorty seems to believe. To speak of "our tradition" as a historical given glosses over "the breakdown of moral and political consensus, and the conflicts and incompatibility among competing social practices" that have made it impossible for us now to take any tradition for granted (1992: 245). Further, opposition to cruelty, while certainly to be desired, is too abstract to provide specific political guidance. As Bernstein notes, "It doesn't take much imagination to redescribe many . . . political issues in a liberal society as conflicts about cruelty." What we need, and what Rorty cannot provide, is help in deciding between the various traditions, conflicting accounts of cruelty, and alternative solutions to that cruelty (Bernstein 1992: 284).

Rorty's pragmatism is not merely insufficient for public life but, as Bernstein further argues, it may in fact be politically pernicious. Rorty's liberal irony substitutes narrative redescriptions and more attractive "vocabularies" for argument, with the result that not only does it not differ significantly from the relativism that Rorty claims to reject, but it is also very close to a political cynicism that Bernstein warns is "one of the most dangerous and virulent tendencies in liberalism." "The conviction that anything can be made to look good by redescription," he reminds us, "is just the mentality that possessed our political leaders during the Vietnam War and the sordid Watergate affair" (and, we might add, is certainly not unknown in politics today). The similarities between this ruthless cynicism that "corrupts liberal democracy" and a Rortian refusal of argument in favor of enticing redescriptions ought at least to give us pause. Public life requires neither an ahistorical rationality nor an accepted communal tradition in Bernstein's view, but it does depend on the participatory deliberation that proceeds through genuine argument, not merely "redescriptions" (Bernstein 1992: 283).

Having thus argued that the philosophies of Derrida, Foucault, and Rorty all fail to provide satisfactory grounding for public life, and that they need something like the "engaged, fallibilistic pluralism" he advocates, Bernstein's position on public life emerges from these conversations as a more nuanced version of what he originally outlined in *Beyond Objectivism and Relativism.* The commitment to public dialogue remains, even while this later work evinces a deeper appreciation of the inerradicability of difference and of ruptures that can never be reconciled but can be engaged in a way that suggests new possibilities. He now speaks of "new constellations," in which perhaps irresolvably different perspectives together produce a force field of ideas rather than "fusions of horizons" in which differences are overcome in a new perspective. Bernstein still holds out hope for the partial reconciliations and mutual understandings that make public life and the pursuit of a greater justice possible, while emphasizing in this later work that any such understanding will be difficult to achieve and incomplete at best. "The *achievement* of a 'we'—where 'we' are locked in argument with others—is a fragile and temporary achievement," he admits, but it is a real and valuable possibility nonetheless (Bernstein 1992: 336–37).[10]

Before concluding this discussion, I want to interject a note of caution into this otherwise positive reading of Bernstein. We need to beware lest we construct our public lives on too narrow of a concept of rationality, in which all that counts is verbal argumentation and conceptual analysis. A public life envisioned solely as discourse between "talking heads," people without passions or bodies, will not achieve that broader justice we hope for, since we often know more and better than we can articulate. There must therefore be space in public life for considering the genuinely public significance of art and ritual, memory and imagination, bodily knowledge and passions, including, for example, the poetic and symbolic visions of the prophets (whose critiques of injustice are seldom proffered as a rational contribution to civil deliberation).[11]

A broader concept of what is relevant to and admissible in public discourse need not derail the conversation with claims to private and uncriticizable truths. I am not suggesting that we grant instincts, emotions, and traditional practices a veto power in public deliberations, but rather that we recognize the importance of, and think critically together about, insights drawn from the full range of human experiences. That which cannot be formulated as a dispassionate verbal argument ought not to be dismissed from our attention, even if we are limited to verbal argument as a basis for public assessment. As social theorist Eugene Halton has argued, we must develop a "fuller understanding of reasonableness" that combines critical reason with our "spontaneous, passionate, and mythic modes of relation to the wider world" (Halton 1995: 36).[12]

Further attention to the development of this "thicker" concept of reasonableness would only strengthen Bernstein's account of public discourse, an account I have here argued reveals that those aspects of contemporary society that distort or displace public deliberation are destructive of the public life that ought to be of concern to us all. Civility, public discourse, and participatory democracy are far from radically new concepts in our national life, yet they are more countercultural, more resistant to the status quo today, and more central to the pursuit of justice than we may think. Properly understood, they call into question, among other things, the distribution of wealth and quality education, the domination of work in so many of our lives, and the destructive role of money and advertising in distorting political debate and encouraging privatized forms of fulfillment. Fostering communities of solidarity and dialogue may not be the most glamorous of tasks, not as exciting as calls to revolution, strident denunciations, or political broadsides, but what is most glamorous is not always what is most needed. Civil, open, and public deliberation that faces rather than evades our differences is indeed indispensable to the construction of a truly just society, and in helping us see this Bernstein makes an important contribution to the ongoing prophetic task of revealing the demands of justice for our times. Bernstein challenges us not only to hear the cry of the poor but to respond to this cry in a way that attempts not merely to give justice *to* the poor, the marginalized, and the otherwise excluded, but rather to make possible their real inclusion in a shared pursuit of justice and freedom in a life lived with and for others.

NOTES

1. See, for example, Ezekiel 3: 1–3. Although I am here concerned primarily with the prophetic call to a just and an egalitarian society, I do not mean to imply that the role of the Hebrew prophets can be adequately understood only in terms of this one aspect.

2. Richard Rorty, "Pragmatism, Relativism, and Irrationalism," *Proceedings and Addresses of the American Philosophical Association* 53 (1980): 734, 727–28, cited in Bernstein, *Beyond Objectivism and Relativism: Science, Hermeneutics, and Praxis* (Philadelphia: University of Pennsylvania Press, 1983), 198.

3. See Robin W. Lovin, *Reinhold Niebuhr and Christian Realism* (Cambridge: Cambridge University Press, 1995), for an incisive argument on public life that in essentials is very similar to Bernstein's.

4. "If we spurn those institutional forms and matrices that enable us to negotiate our differences and to mediate them in civil and political ways, the result will not be more variety and pluralism but less," Elshtain insightfully observes in her *Democracy on Trial* (New York: Basic Books, 1995), xiii. See also Cornel West, *Race Matters* (New York: Vintage Books, 1993), and "Identity: A Matter of Life and Death," in his *Prophetic Reflections: Notes on Race and Power in America* (Monroe, ME: Common Courage Press, 1993), 163–68.

5. In addition to David Tracy, *The Analogical Imagination: Christian Theology and the Culture of Pluralism* (New York: Crossroad, 1981), especially 99–153, see also Richard J. Neuhaus, *The Naked Public Square* (Grand Rapids, MI: Gerdmann's, 1984), Linell Elizabeth Cady, *Religion, Theology, and American Public Life* (Albany: State University of New York Press, 1993), William Dean, *The Religious Critic in American Culture* (Albany: State University of New York Press, 1994), and Max Stackhouse, *Public Theology and Political Economy* (Grand Rapids, MI: Eerdmann's, 1987) for major contributions to the construction of a public theology.

6. That such debate over religious beliefs is required by a commitment to religious freedom is the point made in Franklin I. Gamwell's *The Meaning of Religious Freedom* (Albany: State University of New York Press, 1995).

7. See also Hannah Arendt, *On Revolution* (New York: Viking Press, 1965).

8. Reinhold Niebuhr, *The Children of Light and the Children of Darkness* (New York: Charles Scribner's Sons, 1944), esp. xiii. It should be noted that Niebuhr wisely realized that well-reasoned arguments alone are never enough to constrain power; institutions that provide for a balance of power will also be necessary, especially to protect the minority from the exploitation of the majority.

9. See also Lovin (1995: 217–48).

10. One is reminded here of John Courtney Murray's similar arguments for a civil society united in reasoned debate as well as his insight that even genuine disagreement is a very difficult thing to achieve. See John Courtney Murray, *We Hold These Truths: Catholic Reflections on the American Proposition* (Kansas City, MO: Sheed and Ward, 1960), especially 5–24.

11. I am indebted to Eugene Halton for much of this critique. See especially his *Bereft of Reason: On the Decline of Social Thought and Prospects for Its Renewal* (Chicago: University of Chicago Press, 1995).

12. Halton's work suggests that the pragmatism of Charles Sanders Peirce provides important resources for this endeavor.

REFERENCES

Arendt, Hannah. 1965. *On revolution.* New York: Viking Press.

Bernstein, Richard J. 1983. *Beyond objectivism and relativism: Science, hermeneutics, and praxis.* Philadelphia: University of Pennsylvania Press.

———. 1992. *The new constellation: The ethical-political horizons of modernity/postmodernity.* Cambridge, MA: MIT Press.

Cady, Linell Elizabeth. 1993. *Religion, theology, and American public life.* Albany: State University of New York Press.

Dean, William. 1994. *The religious critic in American culture.* Albany: State University of New York Press.

Elshtain, Jean Bethke. 1995. *Democracy on trial.* New York: Basic Books.

Gamwell, Franklin I. 1995. *The meaning of religious freedom.* Albany: State University of New York Press.

Goldfarb, Jeffrey C. 1998. *Civility and subversion: The intellectual in democratic society.* Cambridge: Cambridge University Press.

Halton, Eugene. 1995. *Bereft of reason: On the decline of social thought and prospects for its renewal.* Chicago: University of Chicago Press.

Lovin, Robin W. 1995. *Reinhold Niebuhr and Christian realism.* Cambridge: Cambridge University Press.

Murray, John Courtney. 1960. *We hold these truths: Catholic reflections on the American proposition.* Kansas City, MO: Sheed and Ward.

Neuhaus, Richard John. 1984. *The naked public square.* Grand Rapids, MI: Eerdmann's.

Niebuhr, Reinhold. 1944. *The children of light and the children of darkness.* New York: Charles Scribner's Sons.

Rorty, Richard. 1980. Pragmatism, relativism, and irrationalism. *Proceedings and addresses of the American Philosophical Association* 53:719–38.

Stackhouse, Max. 1987. *Public theology and political economy.* Grand Rapids, MI: Eerdmann's.

Tracy, David. 1981. *The analogical imagination: Christian theology and the culture of pluralism.* New York: Crossroad.

West, Cornel. 1993a. Identity: A matter of life and death. In *Prophetic reflections: Notes on race and power in America,* 163–68. Monroe, ME: Common Courage Press.

———. 1993b. *Race matters.* New York: Vintage Books.

Richard J. Bernstein's Response to Mary Doak

The biblical prophetic tradition, according to Mary Doak, involves a practical "commitment to greater justice in society." I am flattered to be placed in this tradition. She does a fine job of showing how—in *Beyond Objectivism and Relativism*—I interweave the insights of Gadamer, Habermas, Arendt, and Rorty in order to construct and defend my own theory of public life. I stressed similarities and overlapping agreements among these conversation partners. At the same time, I clearly acknowledged significant differences among them. But I did this consciously because I felt that many commentators treated them as if their positions were completely incompatible with each other. Doak eloquently sums up my view when she writes: "The result of Bernstein's interweaving of the insights of these four thinkers is a dialogic, critical, and pluralistic concept of public life in which we converse and argue together not merely to attain our goals but in order to enrich ourselves and our common life through public debate that tests, validates, and transforms our perspectives." She is right in noting that I emphasize the "practical work of developing the necessary communities of solidarity and dialogue in which such public debate is possible." When seeking to reconcile what appears to be incompatible, and even incommensurable, there is always a risk that one will be accused of envisioning a public life that is "too optimistically harmonious." This was never my intention. In *The New Constellation*, I confronted the challenge of those who stress—and perhaps overstress—incommensurability, alterity, otherness, rupture, breaks, and cleavages.

Doak gives an excellent account of how I explicate and defend my "dialogic hermeneutics" against those who think that dialogue cannot accommodate alterity and otherness. I reject any suggestion of what Adorno once called a forced or "coerced reconciliation." My commitment to the *practices* of public dialogue is not only compatible with but presupposes an "appreciation of difference and of ruptures that can never be reconciled but can be engaged in a way that suggests new possibilities." In this respect, she echoes the theme developed by Vincent Colapietro, who focuses on how my understanding of engaged pluralism does justice to both sociality and alterity.

Doak expresses some concern that my conception of dialogical public life may be based on too narrow a "concept of rationality, in which all that counts is verbal argumentation and conceptual analysis." Ironically, this concern is at the heart of my criticism of Habermas's understanding of communicative rationality. I thoroughly agree with Doak when she says "There must therefore be a space in public life for considering the genuinely public significance of art and ritual, memory and imagination, bodily knowledge and passions, including for example, the poetic and symbolic visions of the prophets." But this is something that I already learned from John Dewey, who understood the role that the emotions, the body, the passions, art, the aesthetic, and the religious dimension of human experience play for a *vibrant* public life. Dewey preferred to speak about intelligence—especially reflective intelligence—rather than reason and rationality. And he did this because he wanted to emphasize the habits, skills, and emotions involved in imaginative creative intelligence. Furthermore, emotion and passion always inform the robust conception of experience that Dewey defends—and one that I endorse. "The aesthetic" and "the religious" do not designate separate realms or types of experience but rather pervasive qualities that can inform and enrich experience. Like Dewey, I strongly oppose a deracinated understanding of agonistic public life.

REFERENCES

Bernstein, Richard J. 1983. *Beyond objectivism and relativism: Science, hermeneutics and praxis.* Philadelphia: University of Pennsylvania Press.

———. 1992. *The new constellation: The ethical-political horizons of modernity/postmodernity.* Cambridge, MA: MIT Press.

Richard Bernstein on Democracy

Rebecca S. Chopp

The work of Richard Bernstein has much to contribute to American Christian theology. As a theologian who places herself in the American pragmatic tradition, I find Bernstein's work suggestive for how theology might understand its context in the public conversation of democracy, use its rich and varied traditional sources to address contemporary issues, and work with other disciplines to build a flourishing democracy for all. Bernstein represents what one of his favorite authors would call a *via media* between extreme relativism and rigid objectivism, a way of engagement with pluralism that brings together a moral imagination for the future, a dialogue amidst real similarities and differences, and an honest analysis of traditions in the context of engagement of current social, political, and cultural problems. In this chapter, I want to interpret Bernstein's work by foregrounding how he brings together diverse thinkers to address contemporary issues being faced in American democracy. Because as a pragmatist I am interested in how American theology recognizes its own context in the democratic tradition and how it participates in shaping a flourishing democracy for the future, I want to use Bernstein to reflect upon a particular way of understanding and doing theology. But, as in any good conversation, I will also suggest, from my perspective as an American theologian in the pragmatic tradition, some questions to the work of Richard Bernstein.

In an appendix "Pragmatism, Pluralism, and the Healing of Wounds" in *The New Constellation*, Bernstein identifies five themes that characterize the American pragmatic tradition (Bernstein 1992: 323–40). These five themes can rightly be extended to American theologians working in a kind of pragmatic ethos (I am not contending that all are consciously aware that they are working in a pragmatic mode. As one of my teachers said of process theology, at one point everyone became some version of a process theologian—I think we could say for many American theologians in relation to pragmatism!) Let me state the themes Bernstein identifies. Anti-foundationalism is the first theme. Though we should not give all of the credit to Peirce and Dewey per se (many theologians who identify themselves as anti- or post-foundationalists have not even read Peirce or Dewey), to the extent that pragmatism names the notion that there are no fixed foundations that we can or must intuit or unpack, then certainly almost all contemporary theologians are pragmatists.

The second substantive theme for Bernstein is a fallibilism that entails an understanding of inquiry quite different than that of foundationalist attempts to find one pure foundation. Rather, fallibilism means that we begin all inquiry with prejudgments (be it inquiry into culture, situation, interpretations of texts), and that there is no belief or thesis not open to interpretation or question. Philosophy and theology are ongoing interpretations, narrations of the story, contestations of political meanings. And since there is no one foundation upon which all arguments may rest, we must take a more holistic and contextual approach, or, in Peirce's notion, we must replace the metaphor of foundation with that of a cable so that we ought to "trust rather to the multitude and variety of its arguments than to the conclusiveness of any one. Its reasoning should not form a chain which is no stronger than its weakest link, but a cable whose fibers may ever be so slender, provided they are sufficiently numerous and intimately connected" (Peirce 1932–1935: 5.265). Again, fallibilism—and its implications—enjoys almost universal acclaim among theologians today

Fallibilism, as Bernstein points out, brings one to the third theme that is, as he says, "so vital for the pragmatism—the social character of the self and the need to nurture a critical community of inquirers" (Bernstein 1992: 328). This theme is also widely affirmed by contemporary theologians—and, as for the early pragmatists, has many implications. Indeed, reason and thought already imply a community of inquirers. There is no fixed point or logical ruler but ongoing argument and debate—reason is guided by norms and criteria that themselves are open to debate and contestations. There is no prior, individual consciousness—we are our history, our society, and our context. What matters is the back-and-forth ongoing life in community: whether the fixed community of interpreters or the community or publics of church, theology, and society. And the community is the arbitrator of meaning and value, not abstract foundations, sources of origins.

Radical contingency marks the fourth substantive theme of Bernstein's ethos—without foundations, always open to interpretation, nonuniversal in meaning and value: life is filled with contingency and change. On the logical side, contingency and chance introduce novelty and indeterminateness, important themes in twentieth-century theology and philosophy. On the interpretive side, radical contingency underscores the role of some type of hermeneutics: there is no set truth to go back to or down to, and interpretation is an ongoing process brought about by the openness of signs and culture.

The fifth substantive theme that Bernstein mentions is pluralism, and Bernstein's point is important: there is no escape from a plurality (maybe we could say multiplicity) of traditions, perspectives, and philosophical orientations. This is certainly accepted in theology today. As Bernstein helpfully points out in his essay, pluralism can take many different forms and shapes. Fragmenting pluralism leads to little sub-specialties; flabby pluralism leads to glib poaching, polemical pluralism isn't real listening but ideological warfare, and defensive pluralism is a kind of tokenism in which we pay lip service to others but are not attentive to the substance of the other's position. Bernstein goes on to make the claim for engaged fallibilistic pluralism, and by this I believe Bernstein argues for what I will call a rhetorical hermeneutics of and for democracy. I want to contend that one way of reading Bernstein—a way I want theologians to read him—defines or shapes philosophy and theology as practices of rhetorical hermeneutics in the democratic context. While I think the first four themes are embraced by most theologians, I think this one is not. I would like it to be so. In order to make my case, I need to explain at length what Bernstein means by this term, and what I am calling his rhetorical hermeneutics of and for democracy. To get to this contention, I want to reflect a bit on Bernstein's own rhetorical hermeneutics, by which I mean the way in which he himself reads thinkers.

For years I have had my students read Richard Bernstein. Many of my students have well-worn copies of *Beyond Objectivism and Relativism* (Bernstein 1983). This book, as well as much of Bernstein's work, has helped us teach our students and ourselves in two important ways: first, the book provides a clear and sensible framework for the objectivism and relativism debates. And second, in the midst of postliberalism on the one side and deconstruction on the other, the book provides a path in the middle and the progressive front. By the middle I mean that Bernstein has allowed a way of being anti-foundationalist and anti-essentialist while maintaining the importance of rigorous argument, careful reading, and warranted assertability in claims. But perhaps what has motivated me most in adding Bernstein to every reading list of every student is his friendly-critical hermeneutics of reading. I want students to learn how to be able to read a thinker critically and constructively, but to always understand what a thinker is trying to accomplish. I want my students to learn how to ask questions to a thinker that she or he may not ask. And I want students to learn how thinkers can talk back and forth to one another. No one, in my judgment, models these complex practices and virtues better than Richard Bernstein.

While volumes and volumes have been written about the differences that divide Gadamer and Habermas, Rorty and Gadamer, and Arendt and Habermas, let alone the conversation of these four with thinkers such as Derrida, Hegel, Dewey, Peirce, and so on, Bernstein's style of reading is quite distinct. Bernstein describes his style or practice as respecting differences between thinkers but seeking differing approaches that complement one another (Bernstein 1986a: 41). In his essay "What Is the Difference that Makes a Difference," Bernstein explains: "For there is a significant overlap or family resemblance in these respective visions. This, of course, does not diminish the significance of the differences between Rorty, on the one hand, and Gadamer and Habermas, on the other. But once again, these differences now begin to look very different" (Bernstein 1986b: 367). We see Bernstein's particular style in perhaps the clearest fashion in *Beyond Objectivism and Relativism.* I want to point out that this book is dedicated to four friends, Hannah Arendt, Hans-Georg Gadamer, Jürgen Habermas, and Richard Rorty. And I think this particular style of reading is indeed a hermeneutics of friendship (to use a phrase once invoked by Margaret Miles) that is friendly, but never cheap, facile, or touchy-feely!

Bernstein gives this wonderful reading of Gadamer that argues for a practical reading of Gadamer. Bernstein contends that despite the emphasis on praxis, Gadamer is deficient at two important points: first, Gadamer is silent about the complex issues of domination and power; second, he does not clarify the types of discourse necessary for debate about norms. As Bernstein says, "Gadamer realizes—but I do not think he squarely faces the issues that it raises—that we are living in a time when the very conditions required for the exercise of *phronesis*—the shared acceptance and stability of universal principles and laws—are themselves threatened (or do not exist)" (Bernstein 1983: 157). In the next paragraph

Bernstein elaborates this insight into Gadamer, "Furthermore, Gadamer does not adequately clarify the type of discourse that is appropriate when questions about the validity of basic norms (universal) are raised" (Bernstein 1983: 158). Bernstein brings in Habermas, Rorty, and Arendt who, juxtaposed and yet engaged with Gadamer, "show how an underlying common vision emerges" (Bernstein 1983: xv). Bernstein describes his own style:

> In the *Spiel*—the interplay—of contrasting and comparing Gadamer, Habermas, Rorty, and Arendt, I will be employing a notion that runs through all of their work. I want to show how they can be read as different voices in a coherent conversation. After bringing out their strengths and weakness and showing some of the ways in which they complement each other, I want to reflect on the common themes that emerge by speaking more directly in my own voice. (Bernstein 1983: 181)

True to his own five themes of pragmatism, Bernstein is not about a "grand synthesis" but rather finding a way to orchestrate, juxtapose, and complement voices to provide a coherent conversation to engage us in a way, a *via media*, between objectivism and relativism. And he orchestrates, juxtaposes, complements, and finds family resemblances by what I want to call a rhetorical hermeneutics for democracy. That is, Bernstein's hermeneutics, his way of reading, always carries a Dewey-like vision of the task and process of thinking. Bernstein—at least the Bernstein I am pushing theology to engage—is about shaping philosophy and theology to be engaged in the problems of the day. And Bernstein does this both by arguing for this but also by reading thinkers for this task. And through his language shifts and turns along the way, I want to suggest that this Deweyan emphasis almost always guides the way he reads thinkers and casts essays. I use the phrase rhetorical hermeneutics to underscore that the interpretation is always in and about the practical-political realm and that, as in Ciceronian rhetoric, the readings themselves are active, and words are deeds. Bernstein's fundamental vision of philosophy (and one we can borrow for theology) is a practical one, and he connects, complements, and juxtaposes around a common, pressing question. His rhetoric of democracy is deeply interwoven with his understanding of the task and practices of philosophy. I believe Bernstein, in his attempt to reconstruct philosophy as a voice of wisdom for democracy, performs a double rhetorical-hermeneutic maneuver: First, he reads the thinkers for the voice of practical reason. A central way he does this is by seeing multiple positions in one author and focusing on the position that suggests or identifies a view of practical reason. Recall, for instance, in dealing with Habermas, he describes two voices. Or when he describes two sides, a conservative and radical strain, in Gadamer's work. Bernstein always opts for the voice, mood, side that can be described as practical reason. And second, he engages the thinkers around what he considers a quite practical problem: reconstructing philosophy to be engaged in the ongoing building of democracy. To quote Bernstein himself:

> . . . my primary objective is to bring forth the ground that is shared which helps to make sense of the differences among these thinkers. It is this common ground that is most relevant to us and that enables us to grasp what might be called the modern (or post-modern) paradox concerning the prospects of human *praxis*—that the type of solidarity, communicative interaction, dialogue, and judgment required for the concrete realization of praxis already presupposes incipient forms of community life that such *praxis* seeks to foster. Finally, we will see the sense in which the movement beyond objectivism and relativism is itself a practical task. (Bernstein 1983: 175)

I will identify four consistent themes in Bernstein's rhetorical hermeneutics: (1) engagement in the public as defining the task of philosophy; (2) the role for the moral imagination; (3) the resource of traditions and the context of communities; and (4) dialogue as a practice, not just a conversation, an action of words in the public itself. Let me move directly to the first theme in my reading of Bernstein as a philosopher of democracy: philosophy as engagement with contemporary democratic content. Bernstein states many times that philosophy should be engaged with the public. As one reads through his essays in *The New Constellation*, one can be easily convinced that Bernstein—always the masterful hermeneut—could interpret any thinker to be engaged in the political reality of his times! We cannot escape the sense and mood of the times in which we live.

But Bernstein's constructive claim is much stronger than this philosophical expressivism. He wants to fashion the philosopher as very engaged in the times, and, indeed, wants to offer us a definition of philosophy in which engagement with the times and with the open project of democracy is the task of philosophy. I want to offer two avenues of evidence for this claim: first, what Bernstein says directly about the task and practices of philosophy; second, how he himself practices philosophy as an engaged thinker. I also want to contend that Bernstein's early work on Dewey pervades this strand of his thinking. Indeed, when Bernstein speaks in this voice I think we could safely say that he is carrying on Dewey's vision in a more sophisticated or at least timelier fashion than did Dewey.

Bernstein begins his book on Dewey with this statement: "Dewey held that authentic philosophical inquiry arises as a response to the practical conflicts of life, and he proclaimed that philosophy can and ought to be made directly relevant to the 'problems of men.'"[1] As I have already indicated, the rhetorical context for his interpretations of Gadamer, Habermas, Rorty, and Arendt in *Beyond Objectivism and Relativism* is the need to address the practical problem of moving beyond the Cartesian Anxiety. And in the essays in *The New Constellation*, Bernstein interprets every thinker not as achieving a new synthesis but as contributing to the common issue of ethical-political order. Indeed, as Bernstein points out in his book, the question of practical, of the Socratic question "how one should live," inevitably arises even to thinkers such as Derrida, Rorty, Heidegger, and Foucault whose early works do not seem to even consider this fundamental Socratic question. Throughout his work, Bernstein calls us, in various ways, to return to the spirit of Dewey, and again I quote:

> For what is most enduring in Dewey is his sanity and his courage, his refusal to submit to despair. Dewey did emphasize the projective and future-oriented dimension of all thinking, and he was aware of the ways in which history and tradition are always effectively shaping what we are in the process of becoming. But his central focus was with the living present, with facing our present conflicts and problems with honesty and imagination, and with finding the concrete ways in which we can reconstruct experience where free communication, public debate, rational persuasion, and genuine sharing are integrated into our everyday practices. Creative—radical—democracy is still "the task before us." (Bernstein 1986c: 272)

I have already suggested that Bernstein's fundamental context for interpretation is what I call the rhetorical hermeneutics for democracy. The quote identifying the task before us is an apt description of this rhetorical task. Bernstein's rhetorical hermeneutics can also be seen in the particular critiques he makes of thinkers. Take, for instance, his criticism of Gadamer. Bernstein argues, in several places, that Gadamer focuses on questions of *techne* instead of domination, or that the more radical strain of Gadamer—and the one we need—having to do with freedom and dialogue gets hidden among his more conservative emphases on retrieving tradition. Or, again, Bernstein highlights that the issue of addressing power and domination in the common task of addressing the day is the contribution of Habermas as he is put in conversation with Gadamer.

> Iris Murdoch once shrewdly remarked, "it is always a significant question to ask of any philosopher: what is he afraid of?" The answer for Habermas is clear. It is "irrationalism" whatever guise it takes—whether ugly fascist forms, disguised neo-conservative variations, or the playful antics of those who seek to domesticate Nietzsche. In a time when it has become so fashionable to attack, mock, ridicule the claim to Reason, Habermas is not afraid to appear "old-fashioned"—to insist on "the stubbornness with which philosophy clings to the role of the guardian of reason"—a role that "can hardly be dismissed as an idiosyncrasy of self-absorbed intellectuals, especially in a period in which basic irrationalist undercurrents are transmuted once again into a dubious form of politics." (Bernstein 1992: 208)

And because Bernstein understands the danger of the colonial imperialism hidden in the false "we" of common discourse, Derrida sits at the table or workbench as well.

Perhaps one of the strongest proofs on how the rhetoric of democracy provides the context of Bernstein's hermeneutics is his ability to play thinkers back and forth. Indeed, given his insistence on the problem of power and domination, in what he calls a double irony, he uses Gadamer's understanding of hermeneutics to explain what Habermas is saying and cites Habermas as a more plausible interpretation of our historical situation than Gadamer (Bernstein 1983: 196). And Bernstein's rhetorical insistence upon power and domination leads him to be critical of Arendt's distinction of the social and the political (Bernstein 1983: 214). In short, Bernstein's selection of thinkers, the context of his criticism, and where and how he brings in other thinkers is driven by the task of constructing a rhetorical hermeneutics for democracy.

This leads to my second point, which concerns a rhetoric of democracy: the utopian impulse, the moral imagination, the philosopher as artist-ethicist who imagines, shows, and creates spaces for new opportunities. This notion arises, again, quite early in Bernstein's work on Dewey. Bernstein points out that Dewey took Plato quite seriously in the " portrayal of the philosopher whose highest flight of speculative imagination culminates with a social and a practical turn" (Bernstein 1966: 23). Bernstein describes Dewey as one for whom the philosopher is both artist and ethicist. And the role of moral imagination is central to Dewey's very definition of democracy as a moral ideal, or as Bernstein says, "Democracy is a reflective faith in the capacity of all human beings for intelligent judgment, deliberation, and action if the proper conditions are furnished" (Bernstein 1986c: 261).

Likewise, in Bernstein's work on Gadamer, we see the insistence that *phronesis* is about moral imagination, for understanding is always about anticipating a different situation here and now. And in Bernstein's work on Arendt, he constantly cites her notion of natality, Arendt's insistence on the capacity to act, which is the precondition for the exercise of freedom. Natality is the capacity to begin, to initiate, and to morally imagine in new ways. Bernstein observes that Arendt returns to a particular quotation from St. Augustine time and time again: "Beginning, before it becomes a historical event, is the supreme capacity of man; politically, it is identical with man's freedom. *Initium ut esset homo creatus est*—'that a beginning be made man was created,' said Augustine" (Bernstein 1986a: 50). And in Arendt and in Gadamer, the moral imagination is not about providing a blueprint; it is a utopian impulse in the sense of a critique of the present that prepares a space for imagining the future.[2]

Bernstein's explicit focus or theme of moral imagination, or utopian impulse, is not utterly neglected in contemporary theology today. Certainly Gordon Kaufman's work can be interpreted with a strong reliance on the role of the imagination. And liberation theologies ought to be understood precisely as a critique of the present for the future transformation (liberation theology exemplifies Bernstein's insistence on power and domination as the central problem for democracy). But imagination as a theme is rarely examined and explicated in contemporary theology. And until it is, imagination continues to reside in feelings, irrational senses, or individual longings. Indeed, the long practice of theology as a kind of practice of Christian moral imagination is rarely taken seriously in theology today. Perhaps this is deeply related to the ambivalence about moral communities and traditions that is so prevalent in theology today.

The moral imagination, for Bernstein, is bound to the traditions and communities in which it arises and to which it serves. In his work on Dewey, Bernstein underscores the importance of community life and the concern over the unsettling and "unsettlement of local communities." Democracy, for Dewey, is not a form of government but primarily a mode of associated life, what Dewey called "conjoint communicate experience" (Bernstein 1966: 134–35). Bernstein reads the work of Hannah Arendt as calling for public spaces and even the creation of a council system of government, allowing for real debate, engagement, and dialogue. And, of course, Bernstein follows Gadamer to urge the importance of ongoing debate with traditions, the fusing of horizons around particular problems. In Bernstein's vision, one lives in vital, rich, free, and nourishing communities (in which every one has to be given the option to participate in ethical-political debate, and in which the conditions for all persons to engage in debate sustained—a kind of feminist ecclesial vision!). Traditions nourish the community not simply from the back or the source but from the future. That is, Bernstein's temporal relation to traditions comes through the engagement of current issues of the day, and traditions thus become resources in local communities. In my questions to Bernstein and to theology, I want to return to this theme.

Dialogue is the fourth theme of Bernstein's rhetorical hermeneutics of democracy. Certainly theologians will be happy to see the quote at the end of the appendix "Pragmatism, Pluralism, and the Healing of Wounds," by John Courtney Murray:

> Barbarism . . . threatens when men cease to talk together according to reasonable laws. There are laws of argument, the observance of which is imperative if discourse is to be civilized. Argument ceases to be civil when it is dominated by passion and prejudice; when its vocabulary becomes solipsist, premised on the theory that my insight is mine alone and cannot be shared; when dialogue gives way to a series of monologues; when the parties to the conversation cease to listen to one another, or hear only what they want to hear, or see the other's argument only through the screen of their own categories. . . . When things like this happen, men cannot be locked together in argument. Conversation becomes merely quarrelsome or querulous. Civility dies with the death of dialogue.[3]

Dialogue is much more than merely talking; it is the texture of community and the possibility for engagement for change. Dialogue is why hermeneutical philosophy is so important, I think, for Bernstein. According to Bernstein, hermeneutical philosophy provides a way of addressing the problems of humanity that Dewey does not offer. Indeed, in Bernstein's article on cross-cultural understanding, he introduces Gadamer to demonstrate how horizons are ontologically open and how—due to the ontological character of hermeneutics—we can always enlarge our horizons. Dialogue is the role he gives to Habermas, for because of pluralism (a positive value) and distortion (a negative value), dialogue requires not only talking and interpreting but also the ability to challenge norms and to do so as historical contexts change. I think dialogue for Bernstein is hard work. It is not a graduate-level seminar, or an afternoon of talking heads. It is listening to others, learning their categories, comparing differences and similarities, and addressing tough problems and opportunities.

Dialogue is not just a tool or also a possibility but a part of the ontological character of human beings and human traditions. The capacity for dialogue depends upon the openness of human experience and the finiteness, but not closed nature, of traditions. In this theme—as clear as anywhere else—one sees the primacy of the pragmatist incorporated into the fluidity of the hermeneutical philosophy. Or we can quote—again with attentive theological ears—Bernstein as he quotes Edward Schillebeeckx on the topic of dialogue and pluralism:

> Between the Charybdis of insistence upon totality and the Scylla of reverence for what is historically particular and unique there lies only one possible, significant perspective: The imperative need for communication; dialogue instead of totality, and so a ban on any pretension to reduce "the other" to a constituent part of my "total discourse." The place, therefore, where truth may possibly be found is human-being-as-possibility-of-communication.[4]

For Bernstein this ontological possibility is woven into a public practice. Here Bernstein's vision, it seems to me, is close to Dewey's and Arendt's: public spaces where there is genuine, difficult discussion and debate around the crises in the public sphere and how to draw upon tradition and invent new forms, symbols, and practices to continue life together. Like Ciceronian rhetoric, Bernstein thinks it is a good thing that words are a form of action that enable us to shape life together.

Dialogue, communities and tradition, the moral imagination, and engagement with the public combine to form *phronesis*, the practical wisdom of a rhetorical hermeneutics. Bernstein explains the importance of *phronesis*:

> *Phronesis* cannot be reduced to technical know-how. It involves a distinctive mediation of the universal (norms and principles) to particular concrete situations. *Phronesis* is not the subsumption of particulars under pre-determined fixed rules. There is an essential openness and indeterminacy of all principles funded in the life of the community or *polis*. The virtue of *phronesis* requires judgment, deliberation, discernment, friendship, and solidarity. (Bernstein 1986a: 34)

I think that Bernstein hides his light under a bushel a bit, or, to say it differently, that it is not that difficult to ignore that rather strong claim about rhetorical hermeneutics of and for democracy. But I emphasize it because I think it is an extremely important argument for theologians to deal with and, in my vision, to embrace.

Theology obviously has much to learn from the work of Richard Bernstein. As I conclude this chapter, I also want to identify some issues for Richard Bernstein from my perspective as an American pragmatic theologian.

1. Where will communities be found to nurture democracy? In "The Meaning of Public Life," an article published by Bernstein in 1986, Bernstein recognizes that "our primary concern ought to be cultivating those types of public spaces" (Bernstein 1986a: 46). Bernstein talks about the need for vital communities but gives little direction to the formation and endurance of community life in contemporary democracy. While recognizing the problems that plague American religious communities, might religious communities play a role in authentic creating public spaces?

2. Dewey turned to the secular church, the schools, and wrote a great deal about education and its role in promoting democracy. He saw education as the institutional carrier of democracy, the home in which it was nurtured, the laboratory in which new forms were shaped. But Bernstein has not touched upon education as the necessary institution for a democracy. In theology, on the other hand, a great deal of time and energy has been spent on theological education in recent years as the institution that shapes the culture of American Christianity. American theologians might suggest to Bernstein that formation of community and individual in educational institutions is a necessary condition for the flourishing of a tradition.

3. Bernstein emphasizes the importance of the domination, power, and irrationalism in social and cultural forms, yet as the American public loses faith in government and business institutions, it may need to attend to issues of the corporate and of *techne*. Contemporary American theology has a small but nonetheless significant literature on these topics.

In conclusion, I return to the notion that Bernstein's first book on Dewey sets the stage for Bernstein's reading of thinkers in relation to issues that perplex our current democracy. What Bernstein observed once about Dewey applies equally well to Bernstein himself: "Democracy for Dewey was not primarily a set of institutions, formal procedures, or even legal guarantees. It is the culture and practice of democracy in day-to-day life that Dewey stresses. Democracy is a reflective faith in the capacity of all human beings for intelligent judgment, deliberation, and action if the proper conditions are furnished" (Bernstein 1986c: 261). But Dewey and Bernstein do not believe in this in some fundamental and abstract way. Indeed, pragmatism means that one looks at the concrete present, engaging in the issues of the day, forecasting and nudging the future. The philosopher works by engaging not simply in the specific issues of the day but in the cultural conditions, in the view of life, in the virtues and values that are required in a democracy. Bernstein is not convinced by Arendt's distinction of the cultural and the political, nor by Rorty's facile relativism about virtues and values. Arendt fails to understand the blending of the cultural and political and thus fails to interpret the problem adequately, while Rorty fails to engage the real task of philosophy, though he does understand the historical situation. I suppose one can say that Bernstein believes that the task and practices of philosophy have to be "practical," both in the sense of practically engaged in the current situation and also practical in terms of practical wisdom and in shaping, nurturing, and guiding the conditions for democracy. It is this clarity of focus, this voice of rhetorical hermeneutics, that I want to suggest needs to reshape theology today.

Notes

1. Richard J. Bernstein, *John Dewey*, The Great American Thinkers Series (New York: Washington Square Press, 1966), 23.

2. In his essay entitled "Metaphysics, Critique, and Utopia," Bernstein urges us to understand that metaphysics keeps alive the utopian impulse but requires us to uncover

and probe the ideals that are presupposed in the critique. Metaphysics, in my word, is a rhetorical act that allows us to open up the moral imagination for the future. See Richard J. Bernstein, "Metaphysics, Critique, and Utopia," in *The Review of Metaphysics: A Philosophical Quarterly* 62:2 (1988): 272.

3. Appendix," 339. Bernstein is quoting John Courtney Murray, SJ, *We Hold These Truths* (New York: Sheed and Ward, 1960), 14.

4. "Metaphysics, Critique, and Utopia," 271. Bernstein is quoting Edward Schillebeeckx, *Jesus* (New York: Seabury Press, 1979), 614.

REFERENCES

Bernstein, Richard J. 1966. *John Dewey.* The Great American Thinkers Series. New York: Washington Square Press.

———. 1983. *Beyond objectivism and relativism: Science, hermeneutics, and praxis.* Philadelphia: University of Pennsylvania Press.

———. 1986a. The meaning of public life. In *Religion and public life: Interpretations and explorations,* ed. Robin W. Lovin, 29–52. Mahwah, NJ: Paulist Press.

———. 1986b. What is the difference that makes a difference: Gadamer, Habermas, and Rorty. In *Hermeneutics and modern philosophy,* ed. Brice R. Wachterhauser, 343–76. Albany: State University of New York Press.

———. 1986c. John Dewey on democracy: The task before us. In *Philosophical profiles: Essays in a pragmatic mode,* 260–72. Philadelphia: University of Pennsylvania Press.

———. 1992. *The new constellation: The ethical-political horizons of modernity/postmodernity.* Cambridge, MA: MIT Press.

Pierce, Charles Sanders. 1932–1935. *Collected papers of Charles Sanders Peirce,* vol. V: *Pragmatism and pragmaticism,* vol. VI: *Scientific metaphysics,* ed. Charles Hartshorne and Paul Weiss. Cambridge, MA: Harvard University Press.

Richard J. Bernstein's Response to Rebecca S. Chopp

In my opening remarks about William D. Hart's "Theses on Bernstein," I indicated that I was tempted to cross out the references to "Bernstein" in this volume, replace them with the personal pronoun "I," and publish them under my own name. Nowhere has this urge been greater than with Rebecca S. Chopp's extraordinarily perceptive chapter. I learned a great deal about myself from her chapter—or at least the *idealized* self that I would like to be. I dimly perceived, but never grasped so vividly, how the themes I explored in my first book on John Dewey (1966) have pervaded all of my writing since that time. Although the phrase is hers, not mine, I am happy to be identified as arguing for "a rhetorical hermeneutics of and for democracy." By invoking the traditions of rhetoric and hermeneutics, Chopp highlights the ways in which these traditions have been concerned with enlightened *practice.* By speaking of a rhetorical hermeneutics *of and for democracy,* Chopp rightly discerns that my primary concern—following Dewey—has been with furthering our understanding of what democracy means today and what is required to make it a concrete, living reality. Chopp also sees how important the concept (and the reality) of friendship is for my work. We sometimes forget the prominence that friendship once played in understanding ethical and political life—friendship that is not incompatible with, but rather becomes enlivened through, conflict and differences. Chopp subtly explores the five themes in the pragmatic tradition that I identified in "Pragmatism, Pluralism, and the Healing of Wounds": anti-foundationalism, fallibilism, the social character of the self and its relation to the community of inquirers, radical contingency, and pluralism. She thinks that each of these themes has special relevance for contemporary theologians. From her I learned that I perform a "double rhetorical-hermeneutic maneuver"—reading thinkers for the voice of practical reason that emerges in their work, and engaging thinkers around the practical problem of reconstructing philosophy to be engaged in the ongoing building of democracy. I fully accept her characterization of me when she says: "In short, Bernstein's selection of thinkers, the context of his criticism, and where and how he brings in other thinkers is driven by the task of constructing a rhetorical hermeneutics for democracy." Chopp helped me discover something about myself by singling out the following four themes in my "rhetorical hermeneutics for democracy: "(1) engagement in the public as defining the task of philosophy; (2) the role for the moral imagination; (3) the resource of traditions and the context of communities; and (4) dialogue as a practice, not just a conversation, an action of words in the public itself." I want to comment on the way in which she explores two of these themes; that we need to cultivate the moral imagination and also need to preserve a responsible "utopian impulse." These characteristics originally attracted me to Dewey, and later to the project of Habermas. It is the reason I have been drawn to the concept of *phronesis*; the flourishing of *phronesis* requires moral imagination. Cynicism, which is becoming all too fashionable and prevalent, kills moral imagination and utopian hopes. But without utopian aspirations, there is no moral progress. The utopian moment is not about the future but about animating our motivation to change *present* injustices. Chopp is also right in stressing that dialogue is not just talk, but "hard work." It is the "texture of community and the possibility for engagement for change." It is "part of the ontological character of human beings and human traditions." It is an enormous compliment to be read as someone who is carrying on Dewey's vision of furthering the understanding and concrete realization of democratic practices. This is the way in which I have conceived of my philosophical-practical project.

I am, of course, not an American Christian theologian, but it is heartening to learn that Chopp thinks that theologians might learn from my work. In the pluralistic spirit that has always characterized my thinking, I welcome support and encouragement from theologians "in shaping a flourishing democracy for the future." Frankly, I do not know what role American religious communities can and will play in creating authentic public spaces, but with a growing awareness of the dangers of the varieties and appeal of religious fanaticism (Christian, Jewish, and Islamic), they have a role to play in vigorously combating all such tendencies. Recent events—especially the post-September 11, 2001, events—have taught us once again just how fragile democratic practices, pluralism, and an openness to alterity are in the world today. We must—as Dewey taught us—begin at home to nurture the virtues and practices required for democracy as a moral ideal that informs our everyday life, but today more than ever the project of furthering what Dewey called "Creative Democracy" is a global and cosmopolitan project.

Creative Democracy—The Task Still Before Us

Richard J. Bernstein

In the 1950s—almost half a century ago—when I was working on my dissertation on John Dewey, I discovered one of his late essays that has always been one of my favorites. I find myself returning over and over again to this short essay, "Creative Democracy—The Task Before Us." Let me begin by telling you about the occasion for which it was written and the circumstances surrounding it.[1] Dewey wrote it for a conference celebrating his eightieth birthday in 1939. He was still intellectually alert and youthful in spirit. Dewey continued to be active until his death in 1952. He pointed out that his own life had already spanned a period of more than half the life of the country in which events of the utmost significance for the destiny of democracy had occurred. It was characteristic of Dewey to return once again to the theme of democracy, which had always stood at the center of his life and work—and to emphasize that it was still a task before us. Democracy was never simply one topic among others for Dewey. All of his thinking—whether concerning education, experience, aesthetics, philosophy, politics, or inquiry—sprang from and led back to reflections on democracy. His articulation of his vision of democracy in 1939 has a special poignancy, not only because of the ominous threat of the rise of the Nazis and the growing attacks on the very idea of democracy but for another less well known reason.

Two years earlier, Dewey had agreed to serve as chairman of the Commission of Inquiry, which was formed to hear and evaluate the charges made against Trotsky and his son at the infamous Moscow purges. At the time, Trotsky was living in exile in Mexico. When Dewey agreed to chair the commission, Communists and sympathizers with Stalin's regime vilified him. Threats were made against his life, and both friends and family urged him not to go to Mexico. (Trotsky himself was subsequently assassinated in Mexico.) Nevertheless, Dewey made the arduous trip to Mexico City, where the inquiry was held. It was an opportunity to investigate the false charges brought against Trotsky, and to expose the real horrors of Stalinist terror and the scandal of the Moscow purges. Dewey's willingness to set aside his intellectual work—he was working on his *Logic: The Theory of Inquiry* at the time—and to serve as the chairman of the commission was consistent with the way in which he had always lived. He not only wrote about the continuity of thought and action, but he practiced it throughout his life. When Dewey first visited the Soviet Union in 1928, he was enthusiastic about the prospects for freedom and education, but subsequently he expressed his bitter disappointment. Reflecting on what he had learned from the inquiry and his encounter with Trotsky, he wrote "the great lesson for all American radicals and for all sympathizers with the USSR is that they must go back and reconsider the whole question of the means of bringing about social changes and of truly democratic methods of approach to social progress. . . . The dictatorship of the proletariat had led to and, I am convinced, always must lead to a dictatorship over the proletariat and the party. I see no reason to believe that something similar would not happen in every country in which an attempt is made to establish a Communist government" (Dewey 1937). Dewey was remarkably prophetic, especially when we think of the fate of Eastern Europe after World War II. Democracy at the time was threatened not only from the outside by Hitler and Stalin but, as we shall see, Dewey believed that the most serious threat to democracy was an internal one—the erosion, distortion, and manipulation of the very conditions required for the flourishing of democracy. What did Dewey mean by democracy, and what was his vision of a democratic society?

His 1939 essay provides an essential clue, for Dewey focused on democracy as a *moral or ethical ideal*, a way of life to be concretely embodied in everyday practices. Democracy, for Dewey, was not primarily a set of institutions, formal procedures, or legal guarantees. It is not that these are unimportant. They are all-important and deserve serious consideration, but without the continual cultivation of a democratic ethos, they can become empty and dead. It is this ethos that breathes life into them. Democracy involved a *reflective faith* in the capacity of all human beings, no matter how diverse and different their backgrounds, to engage in cooperation, intelligent judgment, deliberation, and collective activity—*if* the proper conditions are furnished. He tells us:

> Democracy as compared with other ways of life is the sole way of living which believes whole heartedly in the process of experience as end and as means; as that which is capable of generating the science which is the sole dependable authority for the direction of further experience and which releases emotions, needs, and desires so as to call into being the things that have not existed in the past. For every way of life that fails in its democracy limits the contacts, the exchanges, the communications, the interactions by which experience is steadied while it is enlarged and enriched. The task of this release and enrichment is one that has to be carried on day by day. Since it is one that can have no end till experience itself comes to an end, the task of democracy is forever that of creation of a freer and more humane experience in which all share and all contribute. (Dewey 1939: 229–30)

This is a rich passage that can be fully grasped only when one understands the linkage between democracy and experimental science, the meaning of experience, the claim about the continuity of means and ends, and the emphasis on communication, interaction, and sharing. But it is worthwhile to pause and reflect on this understanding of democracy. For the truth is that for most of its history, political thinkers, including the founders of the American Republic, have been suspicious and wary about democracy. The rule of the *demos* was frequently taken to mean rule by the mob with its fluctuating, unstable passions. We may speak of government by, for, and of the people, but the "people" did not include all of the people. It excluded slaves, women, and the propertyless. It would be anachronistic to think that this skepticism about the political responsibility of all of the people was the result of sheer hypocrisy. Rather, it was a genuine apprehension that some of the people lacked the temperament, education, stability, and public concern to be responsible citizens. Against this background, it was (and still is) a radical idea to affirm that every individual is capable of the intelligent deliberation required to be a responsible citizen in a democratic community. Dewey admits—indeed, he insists—that this attitude reflects a faith, not a blind faith but rather a reflective faith in the capacities of ordinary people—if the proper social conditions are fulfilled. Robert Westbrook beautifully characterizes Dewey's democratic ideal as one that "calls upon men and women to build communities in which the necessary opportunities and resources are available for every individual to realize fully his or her capacities and powers through participation in political, social, and cultural life" (Westbrook 1991: xiv). When Dewey turned his attention to the religious dimension of human experience (which he distinguished from traditional *religions*), he entitled his book *A Common Faith*. He might have entitled his reflections "A Faith in the Common Man" or, better, "A Faith in Ordinary People." In "Creative Democracy" he tells us:

> Democracy is a way of life controlled by a working faith in the possibilities of human nature. Belief in the Common Man is a familiar article in the democratic creed. That belief is without basis and significance save as it means faith in the potentialities of human nature as that nature is exhibited in every human being irrespective of race, color, sex, birth and family, of material or cultural wealth. This faith may be enacted in statutes, but it is only on paper unless it is put in force in the attitudes which human beings display to one another in all the incidents and relations of daily life. . . . The democratic faith in human equality is belief that every human being, independent of the quantity or range of his personal endowment, has the right to equal opportunity with every other person for the development of whatever gifts he has. The democratic belief in the principle of leadership is a generous one. It is universal. It is belief in the capacity of every person to lead his own life free from coercion and imposition by others provided right conditions are supplied. (Dewey 1939: 226–27)

Dewey recognized the importance of a commitment to ideals—to imaginative projections of a better future. But he never thought of ideals as divorced from reality, just as he challenged the very idea that means could be separated from ends-in-view. An ideal to which we are committed is not just a goal to be attained; it is a significance to be felt, and appreciated. An ideal, like the democratic ideal, arises "when the imagination idealizes existence by laying hold of the possibilities offered to thought and action. . . . The idealizing imagination seizes upon the most precious things found in the climacteric moments of experience and projects them" (Dewey 1934, LW 9.32). Characteristically, Dewey was always skeptical of hard-and-fast philosophic dualisms and dichotomies. Reflective intelligence and a commitment to democracy as a way of life was not simply a matter of reason but involved strong passionate commitment and intelligent action.

During his lifetime, there were those who claimed that Dewey's faith in the capacities of ordinary human beings was naively optimistic. When Reinhold Niebuhr accused Dewey of being "rationalistic," and believing that we can "soothe the savage beast of an imperiled and frantic oligarchy" by sweet reason, when he accused Dewey of failing to appreciate the ineradicable depth of human sinfulness, Dewey responded vigorously. "Intelligence," he affirmed, "has no power per se." It becomes empowering "only as it is integrated into some system of wants, or effective demands."[2] Dewey had a deep appreciation of contingency—and contingency does not mean that things always work out for the best. The primary issue is how to *respond* to unexpected, even tragic, contingencies. Dewey was scornful of those who thought that significant changes could be brought about by calls for moral reform. There is a deep Aristotelian motif in his thinking, with its emphasis on the cultivation of those habits, dispositions, required for virtuous activity and enlightened change. Furthermore, these creative habits can flourish only with the proper social conditions. This is one reason Dewey placed so much emphasis on education—education that begins when a child is born and continues through and beyond formal schooling.

There was another type of objection raised against Dewey's democratic ideal. Throughout the twentieth century there have been those who have been skeptical about mass democracies, the leveling effects of mass culture, and the increasing ability to manipulate public opinion. Dewey was fully aware of these dangers. In his famous exchange with Walter Lippmann, who raised serious questions about the very possibility of the ideal of a well-informed citizen in a mass democracy, Dewey agreed with much of Lippmann's diagnosis of the critical problems facing modern, complex democracies. But he strongly objected to Lippmann's suggested solutions. Lippmann argued that the future of democracy depended on elite experts who could make informed decisions. Dewey responded by arguing that the cure for the ills of democracy was more democracy. He himself argued that there had been an "eclipse of the public" or, more accurately, an eclipse of the plurality of democratic publics in which individuals could confront each other, debate, deliberate, and act together. Let us not forget that Dewey grew up in Vermont at a time when the local town meeting was still a vital democratic institution where ordinary citizens (not experts) could meet together in the activity of self-governing. He never forgot this experience and its importance for the vitality of a democratic society.

> I have been accused more than once and from opposed quarters of an undue, a utopian, faith in the possibilities of intelligence and in education as a correlate of intelligence. At all events, I did not invent this faith. I acquired it from my surroundings as far as those surroundings were animated by the democratic spirit. For what is the faith in democracy in the role of consultation, of conference, of persuasion, of discussion, in the formation of public opinion, which in the long run is self-corrective, except faith in the capacity of the intelligence of the common man to respond with common sense to the free play of facts and ideas which are secured by effective guarantees of free inquiry, free assembly, and free communication? (Dewey 1939: 227)

In an enthusiastic passage from *The Public and Its Problems*, Dewey declares:

> Unless local community life can be restored the public cannot adequately solve its most urgent problem; to find and identify itself. But if it be reestablished, it will manifest a fullness, variety, and freedom of possession and enjoyment of meanings and goods unknown in the contiguous associations of the past. For it will be alive and flexible as well as stable, responsive to the complex world-wide scene in which it is enmeshed. While local, it will not be isolated. (Dewey 1927: 216)

This last point is extremely important. In *The Public and Its Problems*, Dewey spoke of the necessity of transforming the Great Society into the Great Community. By the "Great Community" he meant a community of communities. Dewey might well be characterized as a "rooted cosmopolitan." He did believe that democracy must begin at home. He always emphasized the importance of local communities. He appealed to the patriotism of his fellow citizen to fulfill the promise of effective democracy for all individuals. But he was never parochial. There is clearly a universal thrust to his ideal of democracy. And throughout his life he actively fostered this ideal throughout the world—from China and Japan to Turkey and Russia.

Earlier I indicated that Dewey believed that the greatest threat to democracy was an internal one. The threat is the eclipse of vital publics. Like Hannah Arendt, Dewey believed that the "success" of the American

Revolution was due to the existence of history of effective publics in the colonies where citizens engaged in deliberative collective practices. Jefferson was always one of his heroes, because it was Jefferson who so clearly appreciated the need for local publics to keep the democratic promise alive. This is what Jefferson called wards—little republics. Jefferson had always defended this principle, and late in his own life he wrote to a friend (in a passage that Dewey cites with approval), "As Cato concluded every speech with the words 'Carthago delenda est' so do I every opinion, with the injunction, 'Divide the counties into wards.'"[3] In "Creative Democracy," Dewey emphasizes this task of creating "small republics." What he wrote in 1939 seems even more urgent today. "We now have to re-create by deliberate and determined endeavor the kind of democracy which in its origin one hundred and fifty years ago was largely the product of a fortunate combination of men and circumstances." He goes on to declare:

> If I emphasize that the task can be accomplished only by inventive effort and creative activity, it is in part because the depth of the present crisis is due in considerable part to the fact that for a long period we acted as if our democracy were something that perpetuated itself automatically; as if our ancestors had succeeded in setting up a machine that solved the problem of perpetual motion in politics. We acted as if democracy were something that took place mainly at Washington and Albany—or some other state capital—under the impetus of what happened when men and women went to the polls once a year or so. . . . We can escape from this external way of thinking only as we realize in thought and act that democracy is a personal way of individual life; that it signifies the possession and continual use of certain attitudes, forming personal character and determining desire and purpose in all the relations of life. (Dewey 1939: 225)

I want to probe the significance of Dewey's emphasis on wards, publics, and local communities by appealing to another thinker who shares much in common with Dewey: Hannah Arendt. Arendt, even more than Dewey, takes the creation of public spaces to be the quintessence of political life. Indeed, she closely associates this with the "revolutionary spirit." She believed that individuals under the most diverse historical circumstances could come together and create what she calls "public tangible freedom" in those spaces where they appear to each other, debate, and act together. This is the hidden treasure of the revolutionary spirit—and we are in danger of losing it. Like Dewey, she strongly believed that when individuals cease to act and debate together, then public freedom disappears, and the soul of democratic activity is threatened. And, like Dewey, Arendt thought that there are powerful tendencies in the modern age that undermine and threaten the creation of these public spaces. She spoke of these as "islands of freedom," "oases in the desert," and she saw exemplars of them in the founding of the American Republic, the Paris Commune, and the soviets that spontaneously arose after the Russian Revolution (and were quickly crushed). This revolutionary spirit surfaced once again in the Bupadest uprising of 1956 and in the early civil rights movement. Although Arendt thought that the existence of such public spaces was threatened in modern society, she also believed (like Dewey) that human beings are characterized by their natality, their capacity to initiate, and to begin something new. She too recognized that what she called councils were similar to what Jefferson called wards. We get a sense of the significance of these councils for democratic politics when she writes:

> The councils say: We want to participate, we want to debate, we want to make our voices heard in public, and we want to have a possibility to determine the political course of our country. Since the country is too big for all of us to come together and determine our fate, we need a number of public spaces within it. The booth in which we deposit our ballots is unquestionably too small, for this booth has room for only one. The parties are completely unsuitable; there we are, most of us, nothing but the manipulated electorate. But if only ten of us are sitting around a table, each expressing his opinion, each hearing the opinion of others, then a rational formation of opinion can take place through the exchange of opinions. (Arendt 1972: 233)

Arendt makes an important distinction between liberty and freedom. Liberty, for her, is always liberty *from*—liberty from biological necessity, liberty from poverty, and liberty from tyranny and totalitarianism. But although liberty may be a necessary condition for the manifestation of public freedom, it is never a sufficient condition. Public freedom is something quite different. It requires the active participation of citizens in a public political space. She thinks it is a political disaster to think that once liberty is achieved, then public freedom *must* follow. This is an illusion, and we have to learn this lesson painfully over and over again. The collapse of communism in 1989 illustrates Arendt's point. Many people thought that once liberation from Communist regimes was achieved, then democracy would flourish. But what we have witnessed in the last decade is how much more needs to be done in order for democratic practices to flourish. Like Dewey, Arendt emphasizes the responsibility of citizens debating and acting together.

A standard objection to Arendt and Dewey is that they are nostalgic, romantic, and even utopian. Furthermore, their understanding of "small republics" and the creation of face-to-face local communities is no longer relevant for twentieth and twenty-first century democratic societies. I have two responses to this line of criticism. I find it ironical that Arendt and Dewey are criticized for being naively utopian because they have played such a significant role in inspiring progressive social and political movements. The very language of participatory democracy was appropriated from Dewey in the early civil rights movement and the beginnings of the New Left. Even more dramatic is the importance of Arendt for Eastern European dissidents who initiated those movements that led to the downfall of communism. When Adam Mishnic, a leader of the Solidarity Movement, was in prison, he was reading Hannah Arendt. It is certainly true that Arendt is critical of the growth of bureaucracy, where the "rule of nobody" prevails, and Dewey warned about the antidemocratic consequences when the "business mind" infiltrates all aspects of social and political life. But the intelligent way of reading both of them is to emphasize the ways in which they sought to *invigorate* "really existing," large-scale, complex, "democratic" societies. They focused their attention on the public spaces in civil society. Taking them seriously means that we will frequently find the emergence of these public spaces in places that we do not ordinarily look—at the margins of what we "normally" call politics, in local community organizations, and in insurgent social movements.

Both Dewey and Arendt have complex attitudes toward "classic liberalism." It is not that they are antiliberal—that they denigrate the importance of instituting and protecting the rights of the individual. Both of them appreciate the significance of the eighteenth-century insistence on the universal "Rights of Man" as a turning point in political history. But in the twentieth century, Arendt argued that what is most essential is to guarantee the right to have rights, the right to belong to a polity that protects individual rights. In her study of totalitarianism, she emphatically asserted: "Not the loss of specific rights, then, but the loss of a community willing and able to guarantee any rights whatsoever, has been the calamity which has befallen ever-increasing numbers of people. Man, it turns out, can lose all the so-called Rights of Man without losing his essential quality as man, his human dignity. Only the loss of a polity itself expels him from humanity" (Arendt 1973: 297). And Dewey thought that liberalism, although it was originally a radical doctrine initiating social reform, had become an ideological dogma to defend the status quo and to mask the abuses of laissez-faire capitalism. Classic liberalism is not sufficient to secure a truly democratic society.

> The real fallacy [of classical liberalism] lies in the notion that individuals have such a native or original endowment of rights, powers, and wants that all that is required on the side of institutions and laws is to eliminate the obstructions they offer to the "free equipment of individuals." The removal of obstructions did not have a liberating effect upon individuals as were antecedently possessed of the means, intellectual and economic, to take advantage of the changed social conditions. But it left all others at the mercy of the new social conditions brought about by the freed powers of those advantageously situated. The notion that men are equally free to act if only the same legal arrangements apply equally to all—irrespective of differences in education, in command of capital, and that control of the social environment which is furnished by the institution of property—is a pure absurdity, as facts have demonstrated. Since actual, that is effective, rights and demands are products of interactions, and are not found in the original and isolated constitution of human nature, whether moral or psychological, mere elimination is not enough. The latter merely liberates force and ability as that happens to be distributed by past accidents of history. This "free" action operates disastrously as far as many are concerned. The only possible conclusion, both intellectually and practically, is that the attainment of freedom conceived as power to act in accord with choice depends upon positive and constructive changes in social arrangements. (Dewey 1928: 249–50)

I have been speaking about Dewey's vision of democracy as a way of life embodied in everyday practices, and how it is enriched and supplemented by Arendt's understanding of the public spaces in which freedom becomes tangible. But let me remind you that Dewey speaks of *creative* democracy. What does "creative" add to our understanding of democracy? I think there are two central points that Dewey wants to make. First, that his understanding of democracy both presupposes and fosters creative individuals. Situated creativity is one of the most basic categories in Dewey's thinking. The democratic personality is one that is flexible, fallible, experimental, and imaginative. Here again we see why Dewey placed so much emphasis on education in a democratic society. Without creative imagination and intelligence, individuals lack the resources to deal with novel situations. Ultimately this type of creativity involves a number of virtues: the courage to experiment, to change opinions in the light of experience. It also requires a genuine respect for one's fellow citizens—a respect and an openness that is not simply professed but concretely exemplified in one's practices. These practices do not arise without the careful cultivation of the habits, skills, and dispositions required for creative activity. "Creativity" is not something that is limited to special occasions, nor is it restricted to special aesthetic domains. It can—and indeed ought to—be manifested in all human experience and in our everyday practices.

But there is an even more radical sense in which democracy must be creative. Democracy is forever confronted with the task of creating and recreating *itself*, for democracy can never anticipate the contingencies and the new situations that we confront. A creative democracy is one that always faces new, unexpected challenges. We see this today in what many call "globalization." I sometimes think that "globalization" is what everybody talks about, and nobody quite understands. But there are some noncontroversial features of what we are now living through. We are seeing how all sorts of decisions—economic, social, and political—over which citizens in a given territorial nation have no control, profoundly affect their lives. It is sometimes frightening to realize the electronic speed by which these can occur. Some observers think that we are witnessing the dissolution of the nation-state. The problem we face is how to ensure that new emerging global institutions are genuinely democratic, that they are responsive to the desires and needs of those who are affected by them. Clearly, once one moves beyond the local community or even the nation-state, then one is compelled to think about democratic institutions and decision procedures in new ways. We cannot appeal to the past or to any preconceived blueprints to deal with the new forms of democratic institutions. Frankly, I think we are just beginning this endeavor, and there is a great deal of uncertain groping. But the point I want to emphasize is that a democratic polity can never simply rely on existing institutions and practices. It must strive to recreate itself, to address the issue of what "positive and constructive changes in social arrangements are to be instituted" in these new conditions of risk and uncertainty in order to ensure the transformation and continuation of a democratic ethos. In this sense creative democracy is not and cannot be a fixed, static ideal. It is intrinsic to the very idea of such a democracy that it is always a task before us—a task that demands passionate commitment and reflective, flexible intelligence.

Alan Ryan, who has written a splendid book on John Dewey, concludes his study by telling us:

> Dewey was a visionary. That was his appeal. He was a curious visionary, because he did not speak of a distant goal or city not built with hands. He was a visionary about the here and now, about the potentiality of the modern world, modern society, modern man, and thus, as it happened America and Americans in the twentieth century, and he will remain for the foreseeable future a rich source of intellectual nourishment for anyone not absolutely locked within the anxieties of his or her own heart and not absolutely despondent about the prospects of the modern world. (Ryan 1995: 369)

At the core of Dewey's vision was his moral ideal of a creative democracy—an ideal that becomes living reality only when it becomes a "personal way of individual life" in which we open ourselves to the "fullness of communication." There will always be differences, conflicts, and agonistic confrontations in a pluralistic democratic polity. "To cooperate by giving differences a chance to show themselves because of the belief that the expression of difference is not only a right of the other person but is a means of enriching one's own life-experience is inherent in the democratic personal way of life." Creative democracy is still the task before us!

NOTES

1. The following paragraphs are based on my original article dealing with Dewey's essay "Creative Democracy—The Task Before Us." See "John Dewey on Democracy: The Task Before Us," in Richard J. Bernstein, *Philosophical Profiles* (Philadelphia: University of Pennsylvania Press, 1986), 260–72.

2. For an informative discussion of the exchanges between Dewey and Niebuhr, see Alan Ryan, *John Dewey and the High Tide of American Liberalism* (New York: Norton, 1995).

3. Cited by Dewey, in "Presenting Thomas Jefferson," in *John Dewey, The Later Works*, vol. 14, p. 217.

References

Arendt, Hannah. 1972. *Crises of the republic.* New York: Harcourt, Brace, Jovanivich.

———. 1973. *The origins of totalitarianism.* New York: Harcourt, Brace, Jovanovich.

Dewey, John. 1927. *The public and its problems.* New York: Henry Holt.

———. 1928. Philosophies of freedom. In *Freedom in the modern world*, ed. Horace M. Kallen. New York: Coward-McCann.

———. 1934. A common faith. In *John Dewey, the later works*, vol. 9, ed. Jo Ann Baydston, 32ff. Carbondale: Southern Illinois University Press.

———. 1939. Creative democracy—The task before us. In *John Dewey, the later works,* vol. 14, ed. Jo Ann Boydston, 224–30. Carbondale: Southern Illinois University Press.

Ryan, Alan. 1995. *John Dewey and the high tide of American liberalism.* New York: Norton.

Westbrook, Robert. 1991. *John Dewey and American democracy.* Ithaca, NY: Cornell University Press.

Bernstein Bibliography

Books and Monographs

With M. Eson. *A Study of Some Aspects of Education in Israel.* Jerusalem: Ministry of Education Press, 1958. Published in Hebrew, copy of English translation available.

John Dewey: On Experience, Nature, and Freedom. Edited by R. J. Bernstein. New York: Liberal Arts Press, 1960.
Reprint. New York: Arno Press.

John Dewey, The Great American Thinkers Series. New York: Washington Square Press, 1966.
Reprint. Atascadero, CA: Ridgeview, 1981.

Perspectives on Peirce. Edited by R. J. Bernstein. New Haven, CT: Yale University Press, 1965.
Reprint. Westport, CT: Greenwood Press, 1980.
Japanese translation: Bokutaku Publishing, 1985.

"The Philosophy of Paul Weiss, Twenty-Fifth Year Supplement." Edited by R. J. Bernstein. *Review of Metaphysics* 25 (June 1972).

Praxis and Action. Philadelphia: University of Pennsylvania Press, 1971.
British edition: London: Gerald Duckworth & Co., 1972.
German translation: *Praxis und Handlen* (with new Introduction). Frankfurt: Suhrkamp Verlag, 1975.
Spanish translation: *Praxis y accion.* Madrid: Alianza Editorial, 1979.
University of Pennsylvania Press edition, with a new preface, 1999.

The Restructuring of Social and Political Theory. New York: Harcourt, Brace, Jovanovich, 1976.
Paperback edition: Philadelphia: University of Pennsylvania Press, 1977.
British editions: Oxford: Basil Blackwell, 1976. British paperback: London: Methuen & Co., 1979.
German translation: *Restrukturierung der Gesellschaftstheorie.* Frankfurt: Suhrkamp Verlag, 1979.

Italian translation: *La Ristrutturazione della Teoria Sociale e Politica.* Rome: Armando Armando, 1980.

Spanish translation: *La Reestructuracion de la Theoria Social y Politica.* Fondo de Cultura Economica, 1983.

Beyond Objectivism and Relativism: Science, Hermeneutics, and Praxis. Philadelphia: University of Pennsylvania Press, 1983.

British edition: Oxford: Basil Blackwell, 1983.

Swedish translation: *Bortom Objektivism och Relativism: Vetenskap, hermeneutik och praxis.* Götenberg: Röda Bokförlaget, 1987.

Japanese translation. Translations in Korean, Spanish, and Turkish.

Habermas and Modernity. Edited and with an introduction by R. J. Bernstein. Oxford: Basil Blackwell, 1985.

U.S. edition: Cambridge, MA: MIT Press, 1985.

Spanish translation: *Habermas y la Modernidad.* Catedra: coleccion teorema, 1988.

Philosophical Profiles: Essays in a Pragmatic Mode. Oxford: Basil Blackwell, 1986.

U.S. edition: Philadelphia: University of Pennsylvania Press, 1986. (Papers marked with an asterisk are included in this volume.)

Spanish translation: *Perfiles filosoficus.* Siglo vein tiuno editiones is. a. de c.v., 1991.

The New Constellation: The Ethical-Political Horizons of Modernity/Postmodernity. Cambridge, UK: Polity Press, 1991.

U.S. edition: Cambridge, MA: MIT Press, 1992.

Italian translation: *La nuova costellazione: Gli orizzonti etico-politici del moderno/postmoderno.* Milan: Feltrinelli, 1994.

Bulgarian, Korean, and Japanese translations.

Hannah Arendt and the Jewish Question. Cambridge, UK: Polity Press, 1996.

U.S. edition: Cambridge: MIT Press, 1996.

Freud and the Legacy of Moses. Cambridge: Cambridge University Press, 1998.

(Partial) Hungarian translation included in *Hagyomány és Freudizmus.* Budapest: Új Vilag Liadó, 1998.

Portuguese translation, 2000.

Spanish translation: *Freud Y El Legado de Moisés.* Traduciión de Enrique Mercado. Mexico: Siglo vientiuno editores, 2002.

German translation: *Freud und das Vermächtnis des Moses.* Philo Press, 2003.

Responsibility of the Philosopher. Edited by Obrad Savic. 2000. (Serbian translation of a selection of articles).

Radical Evil: A Philosophical Interrogation. Cambridge, UK: Polity Press, 2002.

ARTICLES, REVIEWS, AND MISCELLANEOUS

1956

"Decision and Indecision in Contemporary Empiricism." *Ideas* 5:4 (1956).

1958

"Education in Israel." *Ha' aretz,* 16 July 1958 (Tel Aviv, Israel).

1959

"Dewey's Naturalism." *Review of Metaphysics* 13:2 (1959): 340–53.

1960

"Knowledge, Value, and Freedom." In *John Dewey and the Experimental Spirit in Philosophy,* edited by Charles Hendel. New York: Liberal Arts Press, 1960.

"Packaged Wisdom." *The Commonweal,* 22 April 1960.

1961

"John Dewey's Metaphysics of Experience." *Journal of Philosophy* 57:1 (1961): 5–14.

"The Thought of Stuart Hampshire." A Discussion of *Thought and Action,* by Stuart Hampshire. *Commentary* 31:3 (March 1961): 262–64.

"Charles Sanders Peirce and the *Nation.*" *Antioch Review* 21:2 (Spring 1961): 15–25.

Reprinted in *The Nation,* 22 March 1965.

Reprinted in *Charles Sanders Peirce: Contributions to the Nation,* Part One 1869–1893. Compiled and edited by K. L. Ketner and J. E. Cook. Lubbock: Graduate Studies of Texas Technical University, 1975.

"Natural Law and a National Consensus." Review of *We Hold These Truths,* by John Courtney Murray. *New Leader,* 22 May 1961.

"A Double-Edged Logic." Review of *The Quest for Being,* by Sidney Hook. *Saturday Review* 22 July 1961.

"Fromm's Concept of Marx." Review of *Marx's Concept of Man,* by Erich Fromm. *New Leader,* 2 October 1961.

"Wittgenstein's Three Languages." *Review of Metaphysics* 15:2 (1961): 278–98.

Reprinted in *Wittgenstein's Tractatus.* Edited by I. Copi and R. Beard. New York: Macmillan, 1966.

1962

Review of *American Pragmatism,* by Edward C. Moore. *Journal of Philosophy* 59:10 (1962): 272–74.

1963

"Undergraduate Education Today: Philosophy." *Yale Alumni Magazine* (January 1963).

Review of *The Predicament of Democratic Man,* by Edmond Cahn. *Yale Law Journal* 72:6 (1963).

"Post-Wittgensteinian Dilemmas." Review of *Reason and Conduct,* by Henry Aiken. *Commentary* 35:6 (June 1963): 547–50.

"The Marxist Revival." *Occasional Stiles* 2 (September 1962): 106–15. (Published by Ezra Stiles College, Yale University).

1964

"Professor Hart on Rules of Obligation." *Mind* 73:292 (October 1964): 563–66.

"Peirce's Theory of Perception." In *Studies in the Philosophy of Charles Sanders Peirce, Second Series.* Edited by E. C. Moore and R. Robin. Amherst: University of Massachusetts Press, 1964.

"Action, Conduct, and Self-Control." In *Perspectives on Peirce* (see list of books).

"Myths about the Mississippi Summer Project." *The Nation,* 28 December 1964: 512–15.

Review of *John Dewey and Self-Realization,* by Robert J. Roth. *International Philosophical Quarterly* 4 (Fall 1964): 485–87.

1966

"Sellars' Vision of Man-in-the-World, Part I." *Review of Metaphysics* 20:1 (1966): 113–43.

"Sellars' Vision of Man-in-the-World, Part II." *Review of Metaphysics* 20:2 (1966): 290–316.

"John Dewey." In *Encyclopedia of Philosophy.* Edited by Paul Edwards. New York: Macmillan and the Free Press, 1966.

"The Challenge of Scientific Materialism" (Hebrew version). *Iyyun* 18:1–2 (1966).

1967

"Buchler's Metaphysics." *Journal of Philosophy* 64:22 (1967): 751–70.

Reprinted in *Nature's Perspectives: Prospects for Ordinal Metaphysics.* Edited by A. Marsoobian, K. Wallace, and R. S. Corrington. Albany: State University of New York Press, 1991.

Review of *Lectures in the Philosophy of Education,* by John Dewey. *The Social Studies* 58:6 (November 1967): 284–86.

1968

"The Challenge of Scientific Materialism" (English version). *International Philosophical Quarterly* 8:2 (1966): 252–75.

Reprinted in *Materialism and the Mind-Body Problem.* Edited by David M. Rosenthal. Englewood Cliffs, NJ: Prentice Hall, 1971.

1969

Review Symposium of *Essays in Sociological Explanation,* by Neil J. Smelser, with a response by Smelser. *Sociological Inquiry* 39:2 (Spring 1969): 201–17.

1970

"In Defense of American Philosophy." In *Contemporary American Philosophy, Second Series.* Edited by J. E. Smith. New York: Humanities Press, 1970: 293–311.

"An Interview by Richard Bernstein: Paul Weiss' Recollections of Editing the Peirce Papers." *Transactions of the Charles S. Peirce Society* 6:3–4 (Summer–Fall 1970).

From 1960 through 1970, numerous short reviews of books published in the *Review of Metaphysics.*

1971

Introduction to paperback edition of William James, *Essays in Radical Empiricism* and *A Pluralistic Universe.* New York: E. P. Dutton & Co., 1971.

"Herbert Marcuse: An Immanent Critique." *Social Theory and Practice* 1:4 (Fall 1971): 97–111.

1972

Critical review of *The Coming Crisis of Western Sociology,* by Alvin Gouldner. *Sociological Inquiry* 42:1 (1972): 65–72.

"Introductory Remarks" to "The Philosophy of Paul Weiss, Twenty-Fifth Year Supplement," ed. R. J. Bernstein. *Review of Metaphysics* 25 (June 1972): 4–7.

1973

"The Frankfurt School." Critical review of *The Dialectical Imagination,* by Martin Jay. *Midstream* (August–September 1973): 55–66.

1974

"Author's Response." Symposium on *Praxis and Action. Philosophy Forum* 14:2 (1974): 171–94.

1975

Review of *Hegel's Theory of the Modern State*, by Shlomo Avineri, and *Hegel*, by Raymond Plant. *Political Theory* 3:3 (August 1975): 344–52.

Review of *The Legacy of Hegel: Proceedings of the Marquette Hegel Symposium*, 1970. *The Owl of Minerva*: Quarterly Publication of the Hegel Society of America (1975).

1977

"Introduction to William James." In *A Pluralistic Universe: The Works of William James*. Edited by Frederick Burkhardt. Cambridge, MA: Harvard University Press, 1977.

"Hannah Arendt: The Ambiguities of Theory and Practice." In *Political Theory and Praxis: New Perspectives*. Edited by Terrence Ball, 141–58. Minneapolis: University of Minnesota Press, 1977.

Review of *The Life of the Mind*, by Hannah Arendt. Sunday Book Review Section, *New York Times*, 28 May 1977.

Review of *The Moon and the Ghetto: An Essay on Public Policy Analysis*, by Richard R. Nelson. *The Chronicle of Higher Education*, 5 July 1977.

"Why Hegel Now?" Critical Study of *Hegel*, by Charles Taylor. *Review of Metaphysics* 31:1 (1977): 29–60.

1979

"Thinking through Critical Theory." Review of *The Critical Theory of Jürgen Habermas*, by Thomas McCarthy. *Review of Politics* 41:2 (1979): 298–301.

"Kant, Hegel, and Ayer vs. Abraham." Review of *Encounters between Judaism and Modern Philosophy*, by Emil Fackenheim. *Midstream* 25:10 (December 1979): 62–64.

1980

"Comment on the Relationship of Habermas's Views to Hegel." In *Hegel's Social and Political Thought*. Edited by D. P. Verene. New York: Humanities Press, 1980.

*"Philosophy and the Conversation of Mankind." Critical Study of *Philosophy and the Mirror of Nature*, by Richard Rorty. *Review of Metaphysics* 33:4 (1980): 745–75.

Reprinted in *Hermeneutics and Praxis*. Edited by Robert Hollinger. Notre Dame: University of Notre Dame Press, 1986.

Review of *Main Currents of Marxism: Its Rise, Growth, and Dissolution*, by L. Kolakowski. *Review of Metaphysics* 33:3 (1980): 635–37.

Review of *Transformation of Philosophy*, by Karl-Otto Apel. *Political Theory* 9:3 (1980): 434–37.

Introduction to English translation of Karl-Otto Apel, *Charles S. Peirce: From Pragmatism to Pragmaticism*. Amherst: University of Massachusetts Press, 1980.

1981

"Towards a More Rational Community." In *Graduate Studies Texas Technical University*. Edited by Kenneth L. Ketner, 115–20. Lubbock: Texas Technical University Press, 1981.

*"Herbert Marcuse—Negativity: Theme and Variations." *Praxis International* 1:1 (1981): 87–100.

1982

*"From Hermeneutics to Praxis." *Review of Metaphysics* 35:4 (June 1982): 823–45.

Reprinted in *Hermeneutics and Modern Philosophy.* Edited by Bruce R. Wachterhauser. Albany: State University of New York Press, 1986: 343–76.

Reprinted in *Hermeneutics and Praxis.* Edited by Robert Hollinger. Notre Dame: University of Notre Dame Press, 1986.

*"Hannah Arendt: Judging—The Actor and the Spectator." In *Proceedings of History, Ethics, Politics: A Conference Based on the Work of Hannah Arendt.* Edited by R. Boyers. Saratoga Springs, NY: Empire State College, 1982.

Reprinted in *The Realm of Humanitas: Responses to the Writings of Hannah Arendt.* New York: Peter Lang, 1990.

"Human Beings: Plurality and Togetherness." Critical Study of *You, I, and the Others*, by Paul Weiss. *Review of Metaphysics* 35:4 (June 1982): 349–66.

Reprinted in *Creativity and Common Sense.* Edited by Thomas Krettek. Albany: State University of New York Press, 1987.

*"What Is the Difference that Makes a Difference? Gadamer, Habermas, Rorty." In *Proceedings of the Philosophy Science Association.* Edited by P. D. Asquith and T. Nickles, vol. 2 (1983): 331–59.

Reprinted in *Hermeneutics and Modern Philosophy.* Edited by Robert Hollinger. Notre Dame: University of Notre Dame Press, 1986.

Hebrew translation: In *Between Theory and Practice.* Edited by Y. Yovel and P. Mendes-Flohr. Jerusalem: Magnus Press, 1984.

1984

*"Nietzsche or Aristotle?" Reflections on *After Virtue*, by Alasdair MacIntyre, with a reply by MacIntyre. *Soundings* 67:1 (1984): 6–20 (MacIntyre's reply: 30–41).

1985

*"Heidegger on Humanism." *Praxis International* 5 (July 1985): 95–114.

Reprinted in *Pragmatism Considers Phenomenology.* Edited by Robert S. Corrington, Carl Hausmann, and Thomas Seebohm. Washington, DC: Center for Advanced Research in Phenomenology and University Press of America, 1987.

*"Dewey, Democracy: The Task Ahead of Us." In *Post-Analytic Philosophy.* Edited by John Rajchman and Cornel West. New York: Columbia University Press, 1985.

1986

"The Question of Moral and Social Development." In *Value Presuppositions in Theories of Human Development.* Edited by L. Cirillo and S. Wapner. Hillside, NJ: Lawrence Erlbaum Associates, 1986.

*"Rethinking the Social and the Political." *Graduate Faculty Philosophy Journal* 11:1 (1986): 111–30.

"Structuration as Critical Theory." *Praxis International* 6:2 (1986): 235–49.

"The Rage against Reason." *Philosophy and Literature* 10:2 (October 1986): 186–210.

Reprinted in *Construction and Constraint.* Edited by Ernan McMullin. Notre Dame: University of Notre Dame Press, 1988.

"The Meaning of Public Life." In *Religion and American Public Life.* Edited by Robin W. Lovin, 29–52. New York: Paulist Press, 1986.

1987

"Philosophy: A Historical Discipline?" In *At the Nexus of Philosophy History.* Edited by Bernard P. Davenhauer. Athens: University of Georgia Press, 1987.

Serbo-Croatian translation: "Filozofija: Istorijska Disciplina?" In *Filozofija i Društvo.* Edited by Mihailu Markovicu. Beograd: Center za filozofiju: drustvenu teoriju, 1987.

"Agnes Heller: Philosophy, Rational Utopia, and Praxis." *Thesis Eleven* 16 (1987): 22–39.

Reprinted in *The Social Philosophy of Agnes Heller.* Edited by John Burnheim. Atlanta: Rodophi Press, 1994.

"Serious Play: The Ethical-Political Horizon of Jacques Derrida." *Journal of Speculative Philosophy* 1:2 (1987): 93–117.

Reprinted in *The New Constellation: The Ethical-Political Horizons of Modernity/Postmodernity.* Cambridge: MIT Press, 1992.

Serbo-Croation translation: "Ozbiljna lgra: Eticko-Politicka Horizont Zak Derrida." *Gledista* 5–6.

"One Step Forward, Two Steps Backward: Rorty on Liberal Democracy and Philosophy." *Political Theory* 15:4 (November 1987): 538–563.

French translation: "Un pas en avant, deux pas en arrvre: la democratie librale wt la philosophie selon Richard Rorty." *Futor antrieur* (1992).

"The Varieties of Pluralism." *American Journal of Education* 95:4 (August 1987): 509–25.

1988

"Interpretation and Its Discontents: The Choreography of Critique"; "Making a Difference: A Plea for Differences—A Reply to Adolf Grunbaum." Both articles in *Hermeneutics and Psychological Theory.* Edited by S. Messer, L. Sass, and R. Woolfolk. New Brunswick, NJ: Rutgers University Press, 1988.

Review of *Whose Justice? Which Rationality?*, by Alasdair MacIntyre. *Commonweal,* 20 May 1988.

"Critical Inquiry, Civic Friendship, and the Pursuit of Community." *Texas Journal* 10 (Spring–Summer 1988).

"Metaphysics, Critique, and Utopia." Presidential Address to the Metaphysical Society of America. *Review of Metaphysics* 42:2 (December 1988): 255–74.

"Fred Dallmayr's Critique of Habermas." *Political Theory* 16:4 (November 1988): 580–93.

"Hermeneutics and Its Anxieties." In *Hermeneutics and the Tradition.* Edited by Daniel O. Dahlstrom, *Proceedings of the American Catholic Philosophical Association* 62 (1988): 58–70.

1989

"Radical Plurality, Fearful Ambiguity, and Engaged Hope." Review of *Plurality and Ambiguity,* by David Tracy. *The Journal of Religion* 69 (January 1989): 85–91.

"Foucault: Critique as a Philosophic Ethos." In *Zwischenbetrachtungen Im Prozess der Aufklärung.* Edited by A. Honneth, T. McCarthy, C. Offe, and A. Wellmer. Frankfurt: Suhrkamp Verlag, 1989.

Reprinted in *Philosophical Interventions in the Unfinished Project of Enlightenment.* Ed. Axel Honneth. Cambridge: MIT Press, 1992.

Reprinted in *Critique and Power*. Ed. Michael Kelly. Cambridge: MIT Press, 1994.

"Pragmatism, Pluralism, and the Healing of Wounds," Presidential Address, A.P.A. Eastern Division. *Proceedings and Addresses of the American Philosophical Association* 63:3 (1989): 5–18.

Reprinted in *The New Constellation: The Ethical-Political Horizons of Modernity/Postmodernity.* Cambridge, UK: Polity Press, 1991.

"Interpretation and Solidarity: An Interview with Richard Bernstein by Dunja Melcic." *Praxis International* 9 (October 1989): 201–19.

1990

"Social Theory as Critique." In *Social Theory of Modern Societies: Anthony Giddens and His Critics.* Edited by D. Held and J. B. Thompson. Cambridge: Cambridge University Press, 1990.

"Rorty's Liberal Utopia." *Social Research* 57 (Spring 1990): 31–72.

Reprinted in *The New Constellation: The Ethical-Political Horizons of Modernity/Postmodernity.* Cambridge, UK: Polity Press, 1991.

1991

"The Lure of the Ideal." In *Peirce and Law.* Edited by Roberta Kavelson. New York: Peter Lang, 1991.

Portuguese translation: "A seducdo ideal." *Revista de Semitica e Communico* 3:2: 195–206.

"Does Philosophy Matter?" *The New School Commentator* 2:6 (March 1991): 1–4.

Reprinted in *Thinking: A Journal of Philosophy of Children* 9:4 (1991).

"Una revis'on de las conexiones entre incommensurabilidad y ortredad." *Isegor'a, Revista de Filosof'a Moral y Politica* 3 (April 1991): 5–25. (Spanish translation of "Incommensurability and Otherness Revisited.")

"John Dewey: Philosopher of Democracy." Critical study of *John Dewey and American Democracy,* by Robert Westbrook. *Intellectual History Newsletter* 13 (September 1991): 48–55.

1992

"Reconciliation and Rupture: The Challenge and Threat of Otherness." In *Discourse and Practice.* Edited by Frank Reynolds and David Tracy, 295–314. Albany: State University of New York Press, 1992.

Reprinted in *The New Constellation: The Ethical-Political Horizons of Modernity/Postmodernity.* Cambridge, UK: Polity Press, 1991.

"The Resurgence of American Pragmatism." *Social Research* 59 (Winter 1992): 813–40.

Spanish translation: "El Resurgir del Pragmatismo." In *El Giro Posmoderno,* edicion a cargo de José Rubio Carracedo. Malagra: Philosophica Malacitena, 1993.

Review of *The Critique of Power,* by Axel Honneth. *Political Theory* 20 (August 1992): 523–27.

1993

"An Allegory of Modernity/Postmodernity: Habermas and Derrida." Reprinted in *Working through Derrida.* Edited by Gary B. Madison. Evanston: Northwestern University Press, 1993.

Reprinted in *The New Constellation: The Ethical-Political Horizons of Modernity/Postmodernity.* Cambridge, UK: Polity Press, 1991.

"The 'Modern/Postmodern' Debate." In *Development and Modernity.* Edited by Lars Gule and Oddver Storebø. Bergen, Norway: Ariadne, 1993.

"Postmodernism, Dialogue, and Democracy: Questions to Richard J. Bernstein." In *Postmodern Contentions: Epochs, Politics, Space.* Edited by J. P. Jones, W. Walter, and T. Schatzki. New York: Guilford, 1992.

1994

"Hans Jonas: Rethinking Responsibility." *Social Research* 61:4 (Winter 1994): 833–52.
Reprinted in the *Hastings Journal.*

"Linguistischer Idealismus bei Fraser und Gordon." In *Auf der Suche nach der Gerecten Gesellschaft,* Herausgegeben von Gunter Frankenberg. Frankfurt: Fischer Taschenbuch Verlag, 1994.

1995

"American Pragmatism: The Conflict of Narratives." In *Rorty and Pragmatism.* Edited by Herman J. Saatkamp Jr. Nashville, TN: Vanderbilt University Press, 1995: 54–67.

"Whatever Happened to Naturalism?" *Proceedings and Addresses of the American Philosophical Association* 69:2 (November 1995): 57–76.

"Are We Beyond the Enlightenment Horizon?" In *Knowledge and Belief in America.* Edited by William M. Shea and Peter A. Huff. New York: Cambridge University Press (Woodrow Wilson Center), 1995.

"Rethinking Responsibility." *Hastings Center Report* 25:7 (1995): 13–20.

1996

"The 'Banality of Evil' Reconsidered." In *Hannah Arendt and the Meaning of Politics.* Edited by Craig Calhoun and John McGowan, 297–322. Minneapolis: University of Minnesota Press, 1996.

"Did Hannah Arendt Change Her Mind? From Radical Evil to the Banality of Evil." In *Hannah Arendt: 20 Years Later.* Edited by Jerome Kohn and Larry May, 127–46. Cambridge, MA: MIT Press, 1996.

"The Retrieval of the Democratic Ethos." *Cardoza Law Review* 17:4–5 (March 1996): 1127–46.

Reprinted in *Review of Japanese Culture and Society* 7 (December 1995) 1–12.

Reprinted in *Habermas on Law and Democracy: Critical Exchanges.* Edited by Michel Rosenfeld and Andrew Arato. California: University of California Press, 1998.

"The Hermeneutics of Cross-Cultural Understanding." In *Cross-Cultural Conversation (Initiation).* Edited by Anindita Niyoga Balslev, 29–41. Atlanta, GA: Scholars Press, 1996.

1997

"Hans Jonas's *Mortality and Morality.*" *Graduate Faculty Philosophy Journal* 19:20 (2/1) (1997): 315–21.

"Provocation and Appropriation: Hannah Arendt's Response to Martin Heidegger." *Constellations* 4:2 (October 1997): 153–71.

"Demokratie als moralische Lebenweise." *Frankfurter Rundschau,* April 1, 1997.

1998

"Community in the Pragmatic Tradition." In *The Revival of Pragmatism: New Essays on Social Thought, Law, and Culture.* Edited by Morris Dickstein, 141–56. North Carolina: Duke University Press, 1998.

"Faire la part de ce qui sépare Rorty et Habermas et se situer dans l'entre-deux." In *De Rorty à Jürgen Habermas: La Modernité en Question.* Edited by Françoise Gaillard, Jacques Poulain, and Richard Schusterman. France: Centre culturel international de Cerisy-la-Salle, 1998.

1999

"Responsibility, Judging, and Evil." *Revue Internationale de Philosophie* 53:208 (1999): 155–72.

"Faith and Reason: Response to Pope John Paul II's Encyclical Letter, *Fides et Ratio.*" *Books and Culture: A Christian Review* (July–August).

"Provocazione e appropriazone: la reposta a Martin Heidegger." Italian translation of "Provocation and Appropriation: Hannah Arendt's Response to Martin Heidegger." In *Hannah Arendt: Intoduzione e cura di Simona Forti.* Milano: Edizion, Bruno Mondadori.

Review of "Alexander Nehamas, *The Art of Living.*" *Bryn Mawr Review of Comparative Literature* 1:1, http://www.brynmawr.edu/bmrcl, accessed January 21, 2006.

"Jan Assmann's *Moses the Egyptian*: The Memory of Egypt in Western Monotheism." *Graduate Faculty Philosophy Journal* 21:2 (1999): 233–53.

New Preface for 1999 edition of *Praxis and Action.* Philadelphia: University of Pennsylvania Press, 1999.

2000

Gadamer. "Tiefe Affinität zum Pragmatismus." *Frankfurter Rundschau* (February 2000).

"Arendt on Thinking." In *The Cambridge Companion to Hannah Arendt.* Edited by Dana Villa. Cambridge, MA: Cambridge University Press, 2000.

"La identidad hispano/latino." *Revista Internacional de Filosofia Politica* 16 (December 2000): 181–83.

"Creative Democracy—The Task Still Before Us." *American Journal of Theology and Philosophy* 21:3 (September 2000): 215–28.

"Verantwortlichkeit, Urteilen und das Böse." In *Hannah Arendt Revisited: "Eichmann in Jerusalem" und die Folgen.* Edited by Gary Smith. Frankfurt: Suhrkamp, 2000.

2001

"Comment on Hispanic/Latino Identity." *Philosophy and Social Criticism* 27:2 (2001): 44–50.

"Religion and Public Life: Engaged Pluralism." *The Modern Schoolman* 78 (2–3) (January–March 2001): 189–98.

"Arendt's Zionism." In *Arendt in Jerusalem.* Edited by Steven Ascheim, 194–203. Berkeley: University of California Press, 2001.

"Kant at War with Himself." In *Rethinking Evil.* Edited by Maria Pia Lara, 55–85. Berkeley: University of California Press, 2001.

2002

"Reflections on Radical Evil: Arendt and Kant." In *Culture and Enlightenment: Essays for György Markus.* Edited by John Grumley et al. Burlington, VT: Ashgate, 2002.

"Reflessioni sul male radicale: Arendt e Kant." *La Società Degli Individui* 5:13 (2002).

"Putnams Stellung in der pragmatistischen Tradition." In *Hilary Putnam und die Tradition des Pragmatismus.* Edited by Marie-Luise Raters und Marcus Willaschek. Frankfurt: Suhrkamp, 2002.

"The Constellation of Hermeneutics, Critical Theory, and Deconstruction." In *The Cambridge Companion to Gadamer*. Edited by Robert J. Dostal, 267–82. Cambridge: Cambridge University Press, 2002.

Forward to *Richard Rorty: An Annotated Bibliography of Secondary Literature* by Richard Ruma. A Volume in Studies in Pragmatism and Values SPV. Edited by John R. Shook. New York: Rodopi Press, 2002.

"Evil and the Temptation of Theodicy." In *The Cambridge Companion to Levinas*. Edited by Simon Critchley and Robert Bernasconi, 252–367. Cambridge: Cambridge University Press, 2002.

"McDowell's Domesticated Hegelianism." In *Reading McDowell on Mind and World*. Edited by Nicholas H. Smith, 9–24. London: Routledge, 2002.

"The Origins of Totalitarianism: Not History but Politics." *Social Research* 69:2 (Summer 2002): 381–401.

2003

"Hegel in America. La tradizione del pragmatismo." In *Hegel Contemporaneo*. Edited by Luigi Ruggiu and Italo Testa. Milano: Angelo Guerini e Associati SpA.

"Rorty's Inspirational Liberalism." In *Richard Rorty*. Edited by C. Guignon and D. Hiley, 124–38. Cambridge: Cambridge University Press, 2003.

"Pragmatism's Common Faith." In *Pragmatism and Religion*. Edited by Stuart Rosenbaum, 129–41. Urbana: University of Illinois Press, 2003.

Forthcoming

Pragmatic Reflections on Tolerance.

About the Contributors

Richard J. Bernstein is Vera List professor of philosophy at the New School University. His books include *The Abuse of Evil: The Corruption of Politics and Religion Since 9/11; Radical Evil; The New Constellation: The Ethical-Political Horizons of Modernity/Postmodernity; Beyond Objectivism and Relativism: Science, Hermeneutics, and Praxis;* and *Praxis and Action.*

Rebecca S. Chopp is president of Colgate University. She earned her PhD at the University of Chicago and has written numerous books and articles in the areas of women's studies, Christian theology, and the role of religion in American public life, including *The Power to Speak: Feminism, Language, God* and *Feminist Practices of Theological Education.*

Vincent Colapietro is professor of philosophy at Pennsylvania State University. His main area of historical research is American thought, and his systematic interests include aesthetics, semiotics, psychoanalysis, political philosophy, and literary theory. His most recent book is *Fateful Shapes of Human Freedom,* and his current projects include a study of Peirce, and a project which explores the connections between psychoanalysis and pragmatism.

Sheila Greeve Davaney is Harvey H. Potthoff professor of Christian theology at Iliff School of Theology. She holds a ThD and an MTS from Harvard University. She is the author of *Historicism: The Once and Future Challenge for Theology* and *Pragmatic Historicism* as well as the editor, with Kathryn Tanner and Delwin Brown, of *Converging on Culture.* Her current research projects continue her interest in historicism, pragmatism, and religious naturalism.

Mary Doak received her PhD in theology from the University of Chicago in 1999. She is an assistant professor of theology at the University of Notre Dame. Her research has focused on narrative and public theology, and she is currently working on issues in feminism and politics.

Nancy K. Frankenberry is the John Phillips Professor of Religion at Dartmouth College. She is the author of *Religion and Radical Empiricism*, the editor of *Radical Interpretation in Religion*, and the co-editor of *Language, Truth, and Religious Belief* and *Interpreting Neville.*

Warren G. Frisina is associate professor of philosophy and religion and chair of the Department of Religion at Hofstra University. He is the author of *The Unity of Knowledge and Action: Toward a Nonrepresentational Theory of Knowledge.* He earned his PhD at the University of Chicago (1987). His continuing research interests include American pragmatism and neo-Confucian thought.

William D. Hart, is associate professor of religious studies at the University of North Carolina, Greensboro. He received his PhD from Princeton in 1994. He is the author of *Edward Said and the Religious Effects of Culture* and is currently writing the book *Dark Passages: Malcolm X, Black Religion, and Me.*

Henry S. Levinson is professor of religious studies at the University of North Carolina-Greensboro and is the author of *Science, Metaphysics, and the Chance of Salvation: An Interpretation of the Thought of William James* and *Santayana, Pragmatism, and the Spiritual Life.* He received his PhD from Princeton University in 1976.

Robert C. Neville is professor of philosophy, religion, and theology at Boston University, where he is also dean of Marsh Chapel and chaplain of the university. A student from Bernstein's youth, he writes about philosophical theology. His latest book is *Religion in Late Modernity.*

Gilya G. Schmidt is professor and head of the Department of Religious Studies, as well as chair of the Fern and Manfred Steinfeld Program in Judaic Studies at the University of Tennessee at Knoxville. She received her PhD from the University of Pittsburgh. Her primary academic research is in German and European Jewry, Zionism and Israel, and the Holocaust.

Index